WE
WANT
FISH
STICKS

WE WANT FISH STICKS

THE BIZARRE AND INFAMOUS
REBRANDING OF THE NEW YORK ISLANDERS

NICHOLAS HIRSHON | Foreword by Éric Fichaud

University of Nebraska Press | Lincoln and London

Library of Congress
Cataloging-in-Publication Data
Names: Hirshon, Nicholas author.
Title: We want fish sticks: the bizarre and
infamous rebranding of the New York
Islanders / Nicholas Hirshon;
foreword by Éric Fichaud.
Description: Lincoln: University of
Nebraska Press, [2018] | Includes
bibliographical references and index.
Identifiers: LCCN 2018006595
ISBN 9781496206534 (cloth: alk. paper)
ISBN 9781496212559 (epub)
ISBN 9781496212566 (mobi)
ISBN 9781496212573 (pdf)
Subjects: LCSH: New York Islanders (Hockey
team)—History. | Stanley Cup (Hockey)—
History—20th century. | National Hockey
League—History—20th century.
Classification: LCC GV848.N4 H57
2018 | DDC 796.962/64097471—dc23 LC
record available at
https://lccn.loc.gov/2018006595

Set in Lyon Text by E. Cuddy.
Designed by L. Auten.

For the players of the New York Islanders from 1995 to 1997

CONTENTS

ILLUSTRATIONS

FOREWORD

Éric Fichaud

Those of us who wore the fisherman jersey with the New York Islanders played through one of the weirdest chapters in sports history. Today, after six seasons as a National Hockey League goalie and a decade as a hockey analyst on television, I know how teams are usually run and realize what happened on Long Island back then was so bizarre. But at the time I was a rookie, and that was all I knew.

My first memory is playing in the minor leagues in Worcester, Massachusetts, in January 1996 and receiving a call from the Islanders' goaltending coach, Bob Froese, on Super Bowl Sunday. He told me to report to Nassau Coliseum the next morning at eleven o'clock for practice. The ensuing hours were wild. Of course, I called my parents to let them know I was heading to New York to play in the NHL. A friend from Montreal had come to visit me for the week, so we changed his flight so he could return home the next day instead. I tried to pick up my gear by calling the equipment manager in Worcester, but he was out at a Super Bowl party and did not have a cell phone, so I had to go to the rink unannounced, explain what happened, and pack up my stuff. Then I took a map and drew the way to the Long Island Marriott. Cars didn't have GPS yet, and I was scared of getting lost on the four-hour drive. I must have gotten there around one in the morning. I didn't sleep much. When I showed up for practice, I found out I would be in goal the next night against Buffalo. It happened so fast. I think the original plan was to leave me in the minors for a while, and that would have been better. The Islanders had lost five games in a row, and you never want a young goalie to debut during a bad stretch for a team. No organization would make that mistake now. But the Islanders felt pressure to win right away, and the media expected me to be the next big thing.

I was really nervous in my first NHL game. I've always loved video games and played a lot of hockey on Sega Genesis, so I couldn't help but look at the lineups for the Islanders and Sabres and think, That guy was good on NHL 94! I also grew up idolizing Pat LaFontaine, as far back as when he played in juniors for Verdun in Montreal, and now I was playing against him. I was jittery for the first seven or eight minutes until a few saves calmed me down. We went up 4–3 in the third, and I was just five seconds from my first NHL win when, sure enough, who tied the game for Buffalo? Pat LaFontaine. It was like a movie script. I grabbed my head with both of my hands, and I almost cried. Thankfully, Mathieu Schneider picked me up by scoring in overtime for a dramatic 5–4 victory. Because the Islanders had lost so many games that season, we celebrated on the ice as if we had won the Stanley Cup. It was so cool to think that I had beaten Dominik Hašek, the best goalie in the league.

One of my favorite memories from my first season was when Mike Milbury, our coach and general manager, told me that I should move out of the Long Island Marriott and find a place to live. Ask any young player in the NHL, and they will tell you that is a big step, because it means you're going to stay in the league for a while. I felt much more stable. I moved in with Bryan McCabe and Dan Plante for the rest of the season, and the next year I lived with McCabe and Bryan Berard, the top pick in the 1995 draft. We were a funny mix: I'm French Canadian, Caber grew up in Calgary, and Berard is from Rhode Island. McCabe and I listened to Pearl Jam and Nirvana, while Berard played Tupac and Biggie. But the three of us got along so well. Most people our age don't even know what they want to do for a living, but playing in the NHL is a different world. You're making a ton of money. You're playing against guys like Wayne Gretzky. You're eating, traveling, and spending almost all your free time with your teammates. We tried to be normal kids. We went to a lot of movies, we bought CDs at Nobody Beats the Wiz, and, thanks to a dead-on recommendation from Pierre Turgeon, we ate all the time at Vincent's Clam Bar in Carle Place. But the players' lifestyle is hard to explain. You have to live it.

For some reason the fans on Long Island embraced me immediately. Girls ran up to me outside Nassau Coliseum and shouted, "Can you hug me? I just want to touch your hair!" I even had a bodyguard escorting me to my car. You feel like you're a rock star. It was surreal. Sometimes I'd skate around in warm-ups and look into the stands, and I'd see a lot of fans wearing Žiggy Pálffy and Darius Kasparaitis jerseys. I expected that because they were the most popular players on the Islanders. But after a while I started to see fans wearing my own name and number, and that was so much fun. It brought back memories of wearing the jerseys of my childhood favorites, and I started to feel like I was becoming a real NHL player. One time I went to the city with my roommates to see a taping of the *Late Show with David Letterman* and somebody screamed, "Fichaud!" I thought that was pretty awesome. I wasn't even on Long Island, and somebody recognized me.

Even though my English wasn't great at the time, I was comfortable on camera. I remember winning a game early in my career, quickly taking off some of my gear in the dressing room, and heading to a studio interview with Stan Fischler without my T-shirt. I don't think players today get away with bearing their chests in an interview, but this was one of my first times on SportsChannel and I didn't know any better. I probably weighed about 165 pounds back then, and my arms didn't have much muscle. My teammates were watching, and Scott Lachance crashed the interview with a two-pound dumbbell, the type the players used for rehab. He said, "Fitch, we're looking at you on TV, and we think you might need this." That was on live television. Scott handed me the dumbbell, and I started posing like I was bodybuilding. Stan told me it was one of the most fun interviews he had ever done.

The Islanders had a lot of young players with talent and chemistry, and we hoped that we could develop into a good team together. But as we kept losing, many of us were traded away. In my last season on Long Island, Bryan McCabe was sent to Vancouver in February 1998. My teammates were close to tears when we said good-bye. Then I was traded twice in a four-month span, to Edmonton in June and then to Nashville in October. The next January Bryan Berard went to Toronto. We were so far away from each other, and we realized the good times we had together were coming to an end. It was like losing your brothers.

I know we didn't play well, and I understand if people remember us as a terrible team engulfed in chaos. But from my perspective as a player, it wasn't all bad. When I look at the fisherman jersey today, I think about the start of my NHL career and my relationships with teammates, trainers, and fans. As players we wanted to win for each other and for Long Island. I am sorry we never could, but I am glad our story is being told.

This project relies on insights from many people associated with one of the most colorful periods in sports, the rebranding of the New York Islanders from 1995 to 1997. I am indebted to the fifty-three hockey insiders who agreed to be interviewed for the book. By sharing memories of the rebranding process, they allowed me to depict its complexities and peculiarities, although I alone decided how to construct the narrative.

Several men who engineered the rebranding were generous with their time. Fred Scalera, the former vice president of licensing for NHL Enterprises, offered a nuanced explanation of the league's branding strategies, while former Islanders executives Tim Beach and Pat Calabria provided important perspectives from within the organization. Ed O'Hara, whose firm designed the Islanders' fisherman jerseys, and the late Pat McDarby, who sketched the mascot, were also helpful. Given the widespread mockery of the logo over the years, I am grateful that they trusted me to tell this story responsibly.

I contacted former Islanders players with the assistance of Danielle Bernstein of the San Antonio Rampage, Mark Caswell Jr. of the Utica Comets, Brian Cobb of the Spokane Chiefs, Rob Crean of the Rochester Americans, Jeff Moeller of the Los Angeles Kings, Radim Prusenovsky of the Czech Ice Hockey Association, Todd Sharrock of the Columbus Blue Jackets, Dylan Wade of the NHL Alumni Association, and Jonathan Weatherdon of the National Hockey League Players' Association. Thanks to Éric Fichaud, an Islanders goaltender in the fisherman era and a hockey analyst for TVA Sports in Canada, for sharing his experiences in the foreword.

Special gratitude goes to Rolando Pujol, director of digital strategy at WPIX Channel 11, who indulged my request to view period newscasts. I am also appreciative that Ricky Abarno and Michael Matteo Jr. loaned Islanders game programs and that Art Feeney provided copies of a fan newsletter he edited. Arnold Leo, secretary of the East Hampton Baymen's Association, and Andrea Meyer, archivist at the East Hampton Library, steered me to valuable documents.

This manuscript began as my doctoral dissertation at the E. W. Scripps School of Journalism at Ohio University, where I benefited from the counsel of my committee members, Catherine Axinn, Roger Cooper, Marilyn S. Greenwald, and Michael S. Sweeney. As committee director, Greenwald was a continuous source of encouragement. Several colleagues in my program were also supportive, including Carol Hector-Harris, Lu Sirui, Pamela Walck, and Xinying Wang, as was my friend Will Mari.

Rob Taylor, my editor at the University of Nebraska Press, had a terrific vision for this book, and I appreciate his enthusiasm and guidance. A grant from the William Paterson University Center for Creative Activity and Research made possible the inclusion of period photographs from the Associated Press. I am also grateful to author Douglass K. Daniel for his keen and thorough comments on the manuscript.

Finally, I thank my parents, who passed away between the completion of this manuscript and its publication, for nourishing the two obsessions of my youth, history and hockey, through trips to countless Islanders games and destinations such as the Hockey Hall of Fame and the NHL All-Star Game. I love you both.

John Tavares, the all-star captain of the New York Islanders, had to expect some tough questions from the media on February 3, 2015. Only two months before the Stanley Cup playoffs, his team sat in first place. The season so far had been exhilarating. The Islanders, playing their final year in the only arena they had ever known, were off to one of the best starts in franchise history and attracted electric sellout crowds almost every night. But the home stretch was unforgiving. The Islanders had thirty-three games in the next sixty-eight days. Their top right wing, Kyle Okposo, was out with a detached retina. If they did not win that night, in Tavares's four-hundredth NHL game, their losing streak would stretch to a momentum-killing three games.

But at morning practice on Long Island, Tavares faced a reporter who did not ask how the Islanders would make up for Okposo's team-high thirty assists, or fix their league-worst penalty kill, or approach the game versus the young, playoff-hungry Florida Panthers.[1]

In fact, the question had nothing to do with the games ahead. Instead, the reporter wanted to know: Had Tavares seen the Islanders' warm-up jerseys?

"Yeah, obviously I've seen them."[2]

On most days the Islanders would warm up in the same jerseys they planned to wear in the game. But on this night the players would skate out and stretch in uniforms bearing perhaps the most infamous logo in sports history. The crest—a bearded, grimacing fisherman gripping a hockey stick—was created twenty years earlier, when the Islanders created a new brand identity in 1995. The effort flopped. Players complained. Fans protested. The logo was declared among the all-time worst by a wide range of media outlets, from Bleacher Report to CBS, from *Sports Illustrated* to Yahoo! For two decades the Islanders had tried to whitewash the embarrassment of the fisherman era, removing signage with the logo from the arena and taking merchandise off the shelves at team stores. But in 2015 the team was playing its last season at Nassau Veterans Memorial Coliseum, its arena of forty-three years, before relocating to a new venue in Brooklyn. The Islanders decided to bring back the logo for one final hurrah, no doubt in a ploy to sell tickets and garner media attention.[3]

Tavares was diplomatic when asked about the logo. "You know, it was a different time. It was a part of history here. Whether it was good or bad, I think, you know, certainly, I think we're proud to be Islanders."[4]

Social media was less forgiving. On Twitter, fans called the jerseys dumb and hideous. They made sneering comments like "Ahoy, captain!" and "Yarr!" One person tweeted, "They're a disgrace." Another wrote, "MY EYES." The negativity toward the logo was summed up in a single post: "People are treating the 'Fisherman' logo like it's a swastika."[5] Clearly, the passage of two decades had done little to soften hatred among the fan base.

In three seasons from 1995 to 1997, the Islanders won only 66 games and lost 119. In defeat and disarray they ditched their original logo, the most salient symbol of their brand for a quarter century, in favor of a new look. But they did more than just change jerseys. The Islanders created a new mascot, altered the arena experience, hired a larger-than-life coach, and transformed the player roster through a combination of high draft picks and blockbuster trades. It was a last-gasp attempt to rejuvenate a small-market team on the brink of collapse, and it failed due to poor planning, penny-pinching, miscommunication, and misfortune.

By rebranding around a new logo the Islanders hoped to enhance the public perception of a franchise that had been in decline for the previous decade. Every professional sports team is a brand that tries to trigger loyalty among its fans in order to draw media coverage, attract lucrative sponsorships, and increase attendance, ratings, and merchandise sales.[6] Through monikers, slogans, signs, symbols, and designs, sports brands identify teams and engender an emotional connection with the public.[7] Marketing consultant David A. Aaker described a brand as a company's "most important asset—the basis of competitive advantage and of future earnings streams."[8] Of course, winning can elevate the brand of a sports franchise, but building a competitive team can be costly and unpredictable. To insulate teams from the potentially detrimental financial effects of a losing record, marketers emphasize more consistent attributes of a team's brand, including logos, mascots, players, and coaches.[9] Establishing a positive brand is crucial to attracting and retaining fans.[10] Jay Gladden pointed out in *Leveraging Brands in Sport Business* that a strong brand protects a team against intense competition for fans' leisure dollars.[11] In mid-1990s New York the Islanders were fighting for fans' time and money against not only the two other NHL teams in the market, the New York Rangers and the New Jersey Devils, but also professional and collegiate teams in other sports, concert halls, movie theaters, shopping malls, amusement parks, bowling alleys, and other forms of recreation. Switching the Islanders brand made their product stand out.

The fisherman logo was a product of the birth of the modern sports-branding industry. At the time sports branding was transforming from an afterthought into a sophisticated business. In the early 1990s the annual sales of all products bearing sports logos surpassed $11.1 billion, and professional and college teams realized that developing new uniforms could send their revenues soaring even higher.[12] A book published in 1995, the year the fisherman logo was unveiled, was titled *Sports Marketing: It's Not Just a Game Anymore*, indicating the mounting seriousness with which teams were approaching their branding strategies. However, most sports executives still did not realize the full significance of logos. *Sports Marketing* mentioned logos only in passing, focusing instead on sales of throwback jerseys and acquisitions of superstar players.[13] In 1995 a leading journal, *Sports Marketing Quarterly*, did not contain a single study on logos. Instead, the journal discussed subjects such as the importance of word of mouth, newspaper and radio advertising, fielding a winning team, and violence in hockey.[14] Teams knew there was money to be made from clever branding, but they had no time-tested models to follow. By rebranding and failing, the Islanders became a cautionary tale for the next generation of sports marketers, providing a list of dos and don'ts that continues to influence the industry today.

The fisherman logo has received little attention despite its universal designation as one of the worst logos in sports history. In 2002 two Islanders beat reporters published a book named *Fish Sticks*, recalling a chant that fans of opposing teams used to taunt the Islanders. Although the title might suggest a focus on the two seasons when the jersey was worn, the book looked more broadly at the Islanders' roller-coaster history, from winning four Stanley Cups in the early 1980s to crashing in the 1990s to returning to glory in a dramatic playoff series in 2002. The fisherman logo has also appeared on the small screen, but again the treatment was cursory. In 2013 ESPN aired a documentary named *Big Shot* in its *30 for 30* series that chronicled the failed sale of the Islanders in the 1996–97 season, the last year of the fisherman jerseys. As in *Fish Sticks* the documentary paid only passing attention to the rebrand, reducing its coverage of the logo to a brief montage of game footage and interviews played to the sort of mischievous music that laces together scenes in a Hollywood comedy. The presentation suggested that the logo was only a trivial precursor to the sale.[15]

For this book oral history interviews were conducted with twenty-three players on the Islanders' roster at some point between 1995 and 1997; participants in planning meetings for the fisherman mascot and logo, including six Islanders executives, one NHL executive, and two logo designers; four broadcasters; three fishermen who appeared at the press conference to unveil the logo; two members of Islanders ownership groups; two coaches; two fans who founded an organization that protested the logo; two men who played the Islanders' mascot; a woman who won a contest to name the mascot; the attorney who filed the paperwork to trademark the logo; the team photographer; the team statistician; the assistant general manager of the Islanders' arena; and a radio host critical of the team. The designer of the Islanders' fisherman mascot, Pat McDarby, died only a year after being interviewed. His premature passing at the age of fifty-seven illustrates the race against time in preserving memories through oral history.[16] A complete transcript of the interview with McDarby is included as an appendix.

When today's fans and media snicker about the fisherman logo, they are largely unaware of the conditions that brought it about. The rebranding of the Islanders is worth a more deliberate investigation. In order to understand the thought process behind one of the worst rebranding efforts in sports history, the narrative must be traced several years earlier, to the greatest hockey player ever.

1

BIRTH OF A BRAND

The room was buzzing when Bruce McNall, the owner of the NHL's Los Angeles Kings, stood before dozens of reporters, photographers, and camera crews in the Sheraton La Reina on August 9, 1988. "We'd like now to go to the reason you all came—to introduce our new team colors," McNall said, drawing laughter from the media contingent. "Let's see. I think we have a model here somewhere for the new colors. I'm not sure."

Eyes turned to a black curtain beside the dais. Out stepped the greatest player in hockey, Wayne Gretzky, a seven-time scoring champion, eight-time most valuable player, and the NHL's all-time assists leader, still in his prime at age twenty-seven. With cameras rapidly flashing, Gretzky pulled on a jersey. Gone was Los Angeles's old purple and gold uniform. Gretzky's Kings would wear silver and black.[1]

The Kings anticipated the largest turnout at a press conference in their history. As news spread that Gretzky had been traded from the small-market Edmonton Oilers to Los Angeles, there was an expectation that the sport's brightest star would awaken interest in ice hockey across the United States. The Kings made a calculated decision to unveil their new superstar in a new jersey.

"You had the biggest name in the sport coming into the second-largest market in the U.S.," said Fred Scalera, then the vice president of licensing for NHL Enterprises. "It was just too big an opportunity to pass up. Said another way, if they didn't do it, they may have gotten criticism like, 'Well, here's your opportunity for a coming-out party, and you guys didn't even bother to get dressed up for it.'"[2]

At the time the NHL's revenue stream was driven largely by ticket sales. Scalera, who had spent a decade working for the clothing company Warnaco, was hired shortly before the Gretzky trade in an effort to centralize merchandise sales through the league office. He had experience as a design and product sourcer and advertising strong brands such as Hathaway, Jack Nicklaus, and Christian Dior, but he faced skepticism from NHL teams that viewed uniform sales as merely a game-day pursuit for fans wanting to take home a souvenir from the arena. Scalera tried convincing the clubs that selling licensed products would expose their brands to customers who might never attend a hockey game. But teams that competed against each other on the ice did not embrace working together as a league.

Then the Kings, who had not advanced to the Stanley Cup Final in their first twenty-one seasons, traded for Gretzky, who had steered the Oilers to four of the past five titles. The NHL's uniform manufacturer, CCM, scrambled to stitch a number-99 jersey in time for the press conference in Los Angeles. All the rushing paid dividends. A month into the season *Sports Illustrated* called Gretzky's jersey the "hottest piece of merchandise around."[3] Sales of number-99 jerseys sustained a Kings team store near the Los Angeles airport.[4] Even in Edmonton, where many fans viewed Gretzky as a traitor and vilified the Kings, a single store sold sixty-five Kings jerseys with Gretzky nameplates in just two days.[5] Los Angeles, which had been last in NHL merchandise sales before the trade, soared to first.[6]

As teams in other professional sports leagues had already figured out, NHL clubs learned that people would buy jerseys from out-of-market teams to be fashionable. "I'll almost call it a revolution," Scalera said.[7]

Not every team could acquire Wayne Gretzky to sell more jerseys. But the Kings' dramatic and successful change from purple and gold to silver and black inspired other clubs to start experimenting. In 1991 the NHL expanded with a second California team, the San Jose Sharks, whose jerseys blended silver, black, and teal and featured a cartoon logo of a shark snapping a hockey stick in its mouth. The Sharks rode their jerseys to an NHL-best $125 million in merchandise sales in 1992.[8] A year later California welcomed its third team, the Disney-owned Mighty Ducks of Anaheim, named after the company's popular kids movie about a peewee hockey club. The Mighty Ducks unveiled jerseys with the dubious color combination of eggplant and jade, plus a cartoon logo of a *Friday the 13th*–like goalie mask shaped to fit a duck's face. Media critics yukked at a hockey team wearing a less than intimidating logo, but Disney had the last quack. Before the Ducks played a single game, merchandise with the goalie-mask logo had overtaken off-season sales of NHL products.[9] Soon the Ducks became one of the NHL's most profitable teams, landing a mammoth five-year, $600 million television contract, even though the expansion roster had little hope of winning a championship.[10]

Three teams in the unlikeliest market for ice hockey, perpetually sunny California, had redefined NHL branding. Scalera's office began identifying teams in crowded sports markets that could stand out by updating their look. "Once we were able to show success stories with the Kings and the Sharks and some of the other things, then we started getting more and more believers," Scalera said.[11] Even outside the NHL, clubs dreamed of the potential windfall from new jerseys. Between January 1995 and August 1997 twenty-five professional sports franchises introduced new logos, uniforms, or both.[12] Many of the new looks were forward thinking and successful. But one change was derided in the press box and the stands, roused fans to sign petitions and march in protest, and came to symbolize the most bizarre and humiliating chapter in the history of a storied hockey franchise. Even today, nearly a quarter century later, the jersey appears on lists of the all-time worst sports designs.[13]

By the mid-1990s the New York Islanders had one of the most recognizable brands in the NHL. Born through expansion in 1972, the team adopted a moniker that honored its home on Long Island, an amalgam of beaches, farmland, and suburban homes east of New York City. To distinguish the team from its instant rival, the big-city New York Rangers in Manhattan, the Islanders developed a blue-and-orange scheme to match the official colors of Nassau County, one of the highest-income areas in the country and home to the team's state-of-the-art arena, Nassau Veterans Memorial Coliseum, built on a former air force base in the hamlet of Uniondale. As another homage to the region, John Alogna, who ran an advertising agency in the county seat of Garden City, hastily created the Islanders logo on three days' notice—a basic map of Long Island topped by the letters NY, with part of the Y made to look like a hockey stick.[14]

The Islanders experienced the typical growing pains of an expansion team, winning only twelve of seventy-eight games in their inaugural season, but graduated faster than most. Within several years the Islanders parlayed high draft picks into one of the strongest rosters in the sport, including future Hall of Famers Mike Bossy, Clark Gillies, Denis Potvin, Bryan Trottier, and Billy Smith. In an extraordinary display of dominance in the early 1980s, the Islanders won a record nineteen consecutive playoff series and four straight Stanley Cups, even defeating Gretzky's Edmonton Oilers for their last championship, in 1983. A decade later Long Island's only major professional sports team shocked the hockey world in the 1993 playoffs by knocking out Mario Lemieux and the two-time defending champion Pittsburgh Penguins to reach the conference finals.[15] Meanwhile, the Rangers, who entered the NHL in 1926, had only three Stanley Cups to the Islanders' four. At Nassau Coliseum, Islanders fans tormented the Rangers with singsong chants of "Nineteen-forty," referring to the last year that the hockey team from supposedly superior New York City had won a championship.

Then the power shifted. In 1994 the Islanders squeaked into the first round of the playoffs to meet the Rangers, who had finished with the NHL's best record. The Islanders had some hope heading into the series after going 2-1-2 against the Rangers in the regular season with Al Arbour, their Stanley Cup dynasty coach, still behind the bench. But their dynasty players were all gone, and they were a heavy underdog against the Rangers, who seemed destined to capture their first Cup in fifty-four years. Rangers games aired on the world's first all-sports radio station, WFAN 660 AM, whose thousands of listeners often heard host Steve Somers dismiss the Islanders as the "Icelanders" and their arena as "Nassau Mausoleum."[16] Somers sensed the hockey tide turning and gloated on air. "In every single phase of the game you see as an Icelander fan, it's hard for you to admit that the New York

Rangers are better than your Icelander team. They used to be a strong rivalry, but no more."[17] True to Somers's assessment, the Rangers shut out the Islanders 6–0 in each of the first two games of the series at Madison Square Garden and finished the four-game sweep on Long Island.[18] The Islanders were outscored 22–3 versus the Rangers, with final scores of 6–0, 6–0, 5–1, and 5–2. "They called it the tennis series," said Islanders television broadcaster Stan Fischler. "Disgraceful."[19]

Inside Nassau Coliseum, triumphant Rangers fans celebrated the sweep by raising the brooms that they had schlepped to Long Island. "That last home game was, as a game operations guy, a nightmare," said Tim Beach, the Islanders' director of game events. "It literally was a Rangers home game that day."[20]

While the Islanders headed home, the Rangers continued their fairy-tale season. By June they were Stanley Cup champions and toast of the town. One and a half million people lined the route of the ticker-tape parade through the Canyon of Heroes, the section of lower Broadway where New York City celebrates its championship teams. Long Island had always come a distant second to New York in the worlds of entertainment and finance and politics and seemingly everything else that mattered—except for hockey. For a decade and a half the Islanders proved that Long Island was better at something than its big brother. To be crushed so decisively by the team of Wall Street and Times Square, of taxis and subways, of greed and grime, pummeled the psyche.

"We couldn't so much rally around our own superiority anymore—far from it," said Brett Pickett, the son of Islanders owner John Pickett, who oversaw the Islanders' dynasty era and still owned the team in 1994. "The last thing we had to cling to was our recent Stanley Cup championships and the Rangers not having won since 1940. You remember 'Nineteen-forty' being the chant that it was in the Coliseum all those years. It's what gave Islander fans their identity vis-à-vis Ranger fans. The Rangers winning the Stanley Cup in 1994, speaking as an Islander fan, was a crusher. It was a crusher in terms of the superiority that we felt over the Rangers and therefore the identity that we felt as Long Islanders."[21]

Before the season there had been reason to believe the Islanders would follow up on their 1993 playoff run with an exciting drive for a fifth championship. Afterward, they were not even the top team in their own market. "It was absolutely devastating," said Eric Mirlis, the Islanders' assistant director of media relations. "To go from a team that everyone was viewing on the upswing, not just in New York but around the league, to be getting your asses kicked like that in the playoffs by that team, it's going to have an effect mentally on an organization. The organization, certainly at that point, always had that redheaded-stepchild mentality. The Rangers were always gonna be king."[22]

The Islanders were desperate to move past the humiliation of the Rangers series at a time when the NHL was selling its teams on jump-starting their brands with new jerseys. As Beach put it, "Things got weird in Islander Land after that."[23]

In the spring of 1994, the Islanders began to reevaluate their brand. Pickett, the team's majority owner, had moved to Florida and cut a deal that ceded day-to-day operations to four Long Island businessmen with minority stakes in the team, Paul Greenwood, Ralph Palleschi, Robert Rosenthal, and Stephen Walsh. They became known as the Gang of Four. Nassau Coliseum was obsolete, and the Islanders' season-ticket base had dwindled from a peak of about fourteen thousand to just five thousand, suggesting that older fans who supported the team in the 1970s and 1980s had moved away, lost interest, or both.[24] Speculation mounted that Arbour, the last high-profile link to the championship teams, would resign.[25] The Gang of Four was concerned that hockey fans might associate the Islanders logo with the team's recent futility, punctuated by the humiliating sweep by the Rangers, more than the increasingly distant Stanley Cup run.

"They wanted to refresh the brand, and understandably so, because while there was a great tradition, there were quite a few years of under-achievement," said Pat Calabria, the Islanders' vice president of communications. "Aside from that '93 jolt, the team was underperforming, the building was in poor shape, season tickets were down, and the franchise needed a refreshing. The brand needed a refreshing."[26]

Others did not see the need for an overhaul. Although the Rangers series was demoralizing, the Islanders could find some solace in making the playoffs for a second straight season and falling to a worthy opponent that was steamrolling the rest of the league. Besides, the Islanders were only a season removed from their magical playoff run in 1993, when they improbably defeated the Washington Capitals, who had nine twenty-goal scorers, and Lemieux's Penguins, who had an NHL-record seventeen-game winning streak in the regular season. "That memory was so fresh in the minds of Islander fans," said Islanders radio broadcaster Chris King. "It was certainly a disappointing '93-'94 season coming off that great run to the conference final the year before. But to say that four straight Stanley Cups in the early eighties and nineteen straight playoff series wins and all those Hall of Famers who wore that crest proudly would cast it aside based on one tough playoff loss, no, I would not agree with that at all."[27]

Like King, Howie Rose, the Rangers' play-by-play television broadcaster in 1994, watched every cringe-worthy moment of the playoff series versus the Islanders. He saw Islanders defensemen Darius Kasparaitis and Uwe Krupp on the ice for four even-strength goals in Game One; saw Ron Hextall allow goals on the first two shots he faced in Game Three; saw the top line of Pierre Turgeon, Steve Thomas, and Derek King stymied by the Rangers' checkers; and saw the power-play unit go one for seventeen.[28] Still, in Rose's mind, none of the ineptitude justified abandoning the Islanders logo. "I think that's about the dumbest thing I've ever heard in my life. No, Islander fans have always associated that crest with the very best days in the franchise's history. That's sheer lunacy to suggest that even one fan would think that a logo that stood for so much was essentially desecrated by having lost a playoff series to their main rival. That's just idiotic, moronic."[29]

But the opinions that mattered most were in the executive offices. Although the Islanders occupied a seemingly lucrative spot within the New York media market, they were in effect a small-market team because of the hour-long distance between Nassau Coliseum and Manhattan, with a paucity of major media outlets in Nassau County, a weak drawing potential for prospective fans, and a consistently low payroll that ranked them among franchises in the least populated NHL locales.[30] They were unable to turn around their fortunes quickly by throwing money at superstar players or arena renovations, so they looked elsewhere to revitalize their flagging brand. Sales of licensed products for sports teams and major colleges had eclipsed $9 billion in the early 1990s, with sales of licensed NHL products projected to jump from $600 million to $800 million in a year's time.[31] The Sharks and the Ducks proved that a flashy logo could generate more merchandising money than even a winning season. "They were in the top five of the league's numbers 'cause, heck, people were buying these jerseys and their gear, not because they were Sharks fans or Ducks fans, but they were buying 'cause they thought that they looked cool," Beach said. "The Kings switched over to black and silver. It wasn't necessarily fans. At the time the NHL was certainly starting to push other teams to say, 'Hey, you know what? You can enjoy this type of success as well if you're willing to take the leap to design a new jersey.'"[32]

The NHL approached rebranding on a case-by-case basis. The Sharks and the Ducks were expansion teams forging new identities, and the Kings had little to show in their twenty-year history besides a bunch of losing seasons and first-round playoff exits. Other teams had stronger brands. "There were certain franchises that we always felt you never messed with," Scalera said. "We were never gonna say to the Montreal Canadiens or the Detroit Red Wings or the Toronto Maple Leafs or the Chicago Blackhawks or the Boston Bruins or the New York Rangers, your Original Six, 'You guys should change.' They were the Original Six. They were so steeped in tradition that it would have almost been sacrilegious to change those things."[33] The Islanders posed an interesting case: they were not a member of the Original Six, the teams that made up the NHL for twenty-five seasons between 1942 and 1967, but they had won four Stanley Cups, more than three-quarters of the league, and were the only NHL team in the United States to win four in a row. Nevertheless, the league did not place the Islanders in the do-not-touch category. Scalera doesn't remember whether the Islanders approached him or he pitched them first, but both sides were receptive.

Time became a factor, too. If the Islanders set the rebranding process into motion in 1994, the team could be wearing new jerseys, and reaping the financial benefits, by the 1995–96 season. If they waited, they would have to either unveil the new jerseys in the twenty-fifth anniversary season in 1996–97, making for an awkward departure from tradition at a time when most teams celebrated their past, or postpone the rebrand and the monetary rewards till 1997–98, hoping that rebranding would not be passé by then. "The thinking was that, as the marketing consultant for the franchise at the time said, the franchise needed a rocket up its ass," Calabria said. "Attendance was declining, the building was in poor shape, the team wasn't performing, and something needed to be done, and they thought this would be a fresh coat of paint."[34]

More than anything the Islanders feared anonymity. The Rangers were reigning champions in 1994, and the third team in the market, the New Jersey Devils, had made the postseason for a fourth straight year and pushed the Rangers to the brink in the seven-game conference final. Both had franchise goaltenders, Mike Richter in New York and Martin Brodeur in New Jersey. And then there were the Islanders, first-round flops, with shaky goaltending, raw rookies, and aging veterans. "They weren't drawing a lot of the next generation of fans," Scalera said. "Those new owners came and said, 'We'd like to have a new look.'"[35]

The first step was finding a designer. Scalera pointed the Islanders to a Manhattan firm named Sean Michael Edwards Design, Inc., or SME, run by partners Ed O'Hara and Tom Duane. SME had developed uniforms and logos in all four major sports leagues in North America, for the NHL's Florida Panthers, the National Basketball Association's Denver Nuggets and Toronto Raptors, the National Football League's Carolina Panthers and Philadelphia Eagles, and Major League Baseball's California Angels, Cincinnati Reds, New York Mets, and Seattle Mariners.[36] Like the Sharks and the Mighty Ducks, the Panthers were an expansion team entering a nontraditional warm-weather market, seeking a snazzy look to compensate for what figured to be a lean inaugural season. SME designed the original Florida jerseys with a primary logo that featured a pouncing panther extending its claws and a shoulder patch that showed a hockey stick crossed with a palm tree against a sunset, tying hockey to the Sunshine State.[37] The jersey was a hit and cemented SME as the NHL's go-to design firm. "We were at the forefront of it," O'Hara said. "There was a whole set of criteria that we had helped, with our clients, develop and we were following. We wrote the book on it. It could have been an interesting book. *How to Design Sports Logos for Dummies* didn't exist."[38]

Better yet from the Islanders' perspective, SME understood Long Island. O'Hara had lived most of his life in Huntington, a twenty-minute drive from Nassau Coliseum, and watched the Islanders' Stanley Cup dynasty unfold in the early 1980s. When he played hockey, he wore Bryan Trottier's number 19 on his back. He admired Mike Bossy, calling him "the Rolls-Royce of that team." O'Hara didn't need to learn about the Islanders' history, as other prospective designers might have. He had experienced the glory days firsthand. "I remember believing it would never end," he told a reporter. "We didn't know how lucky we had it. But times change, teams change, markets change."[39] SME also had experience working on a brand identity for another sports concern on Long Island, Stony Brook University athletics, as their moniker changed from the Patriots to the Seawolves.

Although O'Hara appeared to be the right man for the job, he was skeptical when he heard the Islanders wanted to rebrand. "Hey, when I first went into this, I had mixed feelings," he told Long Island's daily newspaper, *Newsday*, at the time. "As a fan, I was a little leery." The departure from tradition was not the only element of the rebrand that worried O'Hara. After a wave of new looks from teams like the Kings, Sharks, Mighty Ducks, and Panthers, the novelty of unconventional color combinations and cartoonish logos was wearing off. "The party was ending," O'Hara said. "The notion of all these teams that had rebranded—there were dozens of them that did this. By the time the Islanders got to it, it wasn't as much the rage anymore."[40] Nevertheless, SME signed on. The rebranding of the Islanders had begun.

As the NHL's point person for rebranding, Scalera organized meetings between O'Hara and a contingent of Islanders executives at Nassau Coliseum and the league's Manhattan offices. According to several people with knowledge of the meetings, including participants, the Islanders were usually represented by Stephen Walsh, one of the four minority stakeholders running the team; Arthur McCarthy, the chief financial officer; Pat Calabria, the vice president of communications; and Don Maloney, the general manager. At times the group also expanded to include other minority owners and former Islanders player Bob Nystrom, then the director of amateur hockey development and alumni relations.[41] An original Islander who spent his entire fourteen-season career with the franchise, Nystrom was best known for scoring the overtime goal that clinched the Islanders' first Stanley Cup, in 1980. By virtue of his on-ice achievements and involvement with Long Island charities, Nystrom was nicknamed "Mr. Islander."

It made sense for Mr. Islander to help the group tackle a simple yet confounding question: What, exactly, is an Islander? The answer would not only influence the Islanders' new jerseys. Branding meant accentuating the associations that both fans and nonfans already had with the Islanders and Long Island through logos, a mascot, game presentation, and events that would collectively sell tickets, garner media attention, and generate radio and television ratings. Scalera encouraged the Islanders to think about their brand holistically. "We tried to stress to them and say, 'Look, there's two places you have to fit. Yes, you want to fit within the greater hockey context, but don't forget that there's a bigger world out there.' And then we would stress to them that it's a branding identity, not just a logo that goes on your uniform."[42]

The Long Island identity proved hard to pin down. Known by Native Americans as "Paumanok," or "island that pays tribute," Long Island consists of four counties, including two boroughs of New York City, Brooklyn and Queens. But Long Island is much more commonly associated with its two easternmost counties, Nassau and Suffolk, which are more affluent and less racially diverse than New York City. Earning power and ethnicity were only two factors that separated Long Island from New York City. In Nassau and Suffolk the subways do not run, few buildings scrape the sky, and geese are more common than pigeons. The Islanders played in Nassau County, whose 285 square miles include the most frequented beach on the East Coast, Jones Beach, and one of the nation's busiest malls, Roosevelt Field. To the east of Nassau is Suffolk County, at 2,373 square miles, most of it water, best known for the lavish homes of the Hamptons.

Long Island had other claims to fame: it was the birthplace of Walt Whitman, the father of free-verse poetry; the longtime home of President Theodore Roosevelt, whose residence is a national landmark; and the site of the gold-coast mansions that inspired *The Great Gatsby*. What made branding difficult, though, was Long Island's reputation as an assortment of impressive pieces that did not make a cohesive puzzle. Other sports markets were synonymous with particular scenery or world-famous attractions. As the *New York Times* wrote, "Miami: you think palm trees. San Francisco: the Golden Gate Bridge. Philadelphia: the Liberty Bell. But what universally recognized symbol could Long Island possibly boast? A traffic jam? A shopping mall?" Calabria jokingly proposed the Islanders build their brand around a woman with a Bloomingdale's bag stepping into a Lexus.[43]

Joking aside, the group reflected on the imagery associated with islands. "One of the first ones we talked about, when you think of an Islander, most people go tropical," Scalera said. "An Islander is tropical, somebody who lives on an island, and there's water and beaches and boats and sunsets and sunrises and all this kind of stuff. But we all said, 'That's not Long Island.' If it was a team from Jamaica or Bermuda, yes, we've got something." Besides, sunrises and sunsets were hardly unique to Long Island and would be difficult to convey in a mascot. Recognizing SME's success in developing the logo for the NBA's Raptors, the group also entertained the dubious argument that dinosaurs were native to Long Island millions of years ago.[44] That, too, was quickly dismissed.

The best candidate for the mascot was also the riskiest. Before the Islanders were formed in 1972, Long Island rallied around a semipro hockey team named the Long Island Ducks, who played from 1959 to 1973 in a rough-and-tumble league that inspired the movie *Slap Shot*. By adopting a duck mascot, the Islanders would be honoring their hockey forebears, a beloved team that attracted four thousand people to the Long Island Arena in Commack, a half hour from Nassau

Coliseum, for its lone championship celebration in 1965.[45] The choice made sense to the Islanders' radio broadcaster, Barry Landers, who had done play-by-play for the Ducks. "I don't think they ever really paid any kind of public tribute to the Long Island Ducks, which gave many Long Islanders their real first taste of hockey, especially people who lived further away from the city out in Suffolk County, where the Ducks played."[46]

The duck mascot would also evoke a unique roadside attraction, the Big Duck, a twenty-foot-tall, thirty-foot-long souvenir shop built in the shape of an American Pekin duck in Flanders, an hour east of Uniondale. The Big Duck symbolized the duck farms that put Long Island on the menu, if not the map. "Long Island is known nationally in terms of food for the duck itself," Landers said.[47] One of the most famous sports figures living on Long Island, former shortstop Bud Harrelson of the 1969 world champion New York Mets, liked to describe how he ordered the Long Island duck on his first big-league road trip in Chicago and became a fan for life.[48] The Islanders wanted to appeal to East Enders who would not travel into the city to see the Rangers, so honoring a former hockey team and a prominent landmark in Suffolk County seemed perfect. The problem was the very team responsible for the NHL rebranding craze. A duck mascot could create brand confusion with the Mighty Ducks. "We would have had an issue because rightfully the Ducks would have complained, 'Why are you letting another team do something that is our main entity?'" Scalera said.[49]

The Islanders moved on. They tossed around more maritime images to typify Long Island, from ships and lighthouses to lobsters and seagulls. Then they began talking about Billy Joel, the singer-songwriter who grew up in Hicksville, only six miles from Uniondale. Joel personified local boy makes good. Unlike other celebrities who eschewed their roots and moved away, Joel embraced them. As the *New York Times* wrote, "There are Long Islanders who have become famous, and there are the famous who have become Long Islanders. Mr. Joel is one of the few Long Islanders who became famous and remained a Long Islander." Even with fame and fortune, Joel never left Long Island, living in Cold Spring Harbor, Cove Neck, Dix Hills,

East Marion, Hampton Bays, and Oyster Bay. He raised a family with his then wife, model Christie Brinkley, in East Hampton. He owned a twenty-eight-foot lobster boat built on Shelter Island. His band members hailed from Long Beach, Oceanside, and Seaford. By the time the Islanders were rebranding in 1995, Joel had performed eighteen concerts over two decades at Nassau Coliseum, drawing sellout crowds for every tour. "I've been all around the world," he once said. "There is no place like Long Island."[50]

The Islanders were drawn to Joel's status as the quintessential Long Islander. After dropping out of Hicksville High School to pursue a singing career, he had worked on an oyster boat in Oyster Bay and clammed in Bayville, engaging in a rite of passage familiar to many young men from the region. Then a string of hits made him a household name—"Piano Man" in 1973, "Just the Way You Are" and "Only the Good Die Young" in 1977, "My Life" in 1978, and "It's Still Rock and Roll to Me" in 1980. Joel's empathy for the fishermen on the East End of Long Island did not wane with time and money. In the late 1980s he was touched by the book *Men's Lives*, which somberly portrayed the decline of Long Island's formerly mighty seafaring industry, illustrated with a mix of historical and contemporary photographs. The author, Peter Matthiessen, described how sportsmen's organizations were seeking to limit the commercial harvest of striped bass, a species that represented "the difference between bare survival and a decent living" for the baymen. Despite mounting obstacles, the prideful baymen refused to pull up their nets and leave Long Island. "They are tough, resourceful, self-respecting, and also (some say) hidebound and cranky, too independent to organize for their own survival," Matthiessen wrote. "Yet even their critics must acknowledge a gritty spirit that was once more highly valued in this country than it is today."[51]

The baymen's tenacity appealed to Joel. They were fading hallmarks of the Long Island where he grew up, a Long Island he wanted to preserve for his daughter. In 1989 Joel released his eleventh album, *Storm Front*, including the song "Downeaster *Alexa*," which conveyed the baymen's plight. The single, which rose to number 57 on the Billboard Hot 100 chart, was sung from the perspective of a struggling bayman faced with depleted fish stocks and burdensome environmental regulations on a boat bearing the same name as Joel's daughter. The concluding line referenced the dying breed of "Islander."

For a hockey team seeking to brand itself around Long Island, the song struck a chord. Joel, who drew the sorts of crowds and media attention to Nassau Coliseum that the Islanders longed for, was singing passionately about tangible figures in the region's heritage.[52] Mirroring the images in *Men's Lives*, the music video for "Downeaster *Alexa*" depicted older, gruff, bearded fishermen in rain slickers navigating choppy waters off Long Island, providing a masculine tone befitting a hockey team. According to O'Hara, Islanders executives cited the song as a model for the new brand. "They definitely led us towards the maritime," he said. "They had an idea. Billy Joel's song 'Downeaster *Alexa*' really personified the Long Island coastal experience. And that was told to us. It was a direction that we pursued."[53]

Branding around a cause championed by Billy Joel presented a tempting scenario of pairing sports with celebrity. Spike Lee was a regular at New York Knicks games. Jack Nicholson sat courtside to cheer the Los Angeles Lakers. Perhaps Long Island's best-known singer would show his appreciation for the Islanders' homage to the baymen by attending their games and elevating their brand. According to Tim Beach, the Islanders' director of game events, the team had tried to capitalize on Joel's popularity before. "I think the Islanders invited Billy Joel to every event for twenty years. If he was invited to one event [every year] for twenty years, the Islanders went zero for twenty with Billy Joel." But circumstances had changed, and now the team had a reason for Joel to listen. A year after "Downeaster *Alexa*" was released, Joel organized benefit concerts that raised hundreds of thousands of dollars for the baymen and environmental groups dedicated to preserving the bay. He even lobbied New York governor Mario Cuomo to ease the state regulations that threatened the baymen's way of life.[54] Honoring the baymen seemed to be the Islanders' way to the heart of Long Island's favorite son. "When you mention Billy Joel, his association with Long Island is very strong," Scalera said. "He's a natural kind of guy for the team to reach out to. And if he's willing, if he's an Islanders fan, he's a great guy to build awareness of it and publicity for it."[55]

Of course, the Islanders knew they could not bank on Joel's support. "I don't think you would put your eggs in that basket and say, 'We should do this hoping that Billy Joel shows up at the event,'" Calabria said. But even if Joel never set foot at a hockey game, branding around the baymen would mesh with the depiction of the Long Island identity that his music had circulated across the country. Designers often try to match and build on a region's self-image to appeal not only to local fans but also to customers in other markets. O'Hara imagined visitors to Long Island wanting a souvenir related to the baymen. "I still think if you come to the airport from another city and you see something regional, you're going to want it," O'Hara said. "It's kind of an 'I was there' versus some generic thing that's trying to please everybody."[56]

Besides, the Islanders were desperate to stand out in the New York hockey scene, and they couldn't afford costly arena upgrades or player acquisitions to energize the fan base. Maybe departing from the only logo they had ever known would encourage fans to move on from the failures of recent seasons. As other NHL teams had proved, a new brand meant new merchandise that would probably fly off the shelves even if the team kept struggling. "They wanted to broaden what they could market from," O'Hara said. "They can't guarantee winning, but a platform like maritime or a platform like the bayman is expandable, and there's things you can do when you're not winning to keep fans entertained." He added, "Only one team in a league is going to be a champion. What do the other teams do in their markets to stay relevant?"[57]

With the baymen as inspiration, O'Hara and the Islanders spent the rest of the summer of 1994 determining how to integrate Long Island's seafaring heritage into the brand. At the crux of any team's brand is the logo on its uniforms. Designers began imagining a new symbol for the Islanders, but the lengthy process for NHL approval of new jerseys would not be resolved in time for the looming 1994–95 season. The Islanders did not want to wait a year to roll out their new image. "They wanted to be able to personify it on their mascot,"

O'Hara said. "They wanted to appeal to kids. A lot of these teams, the culture of the time was, Let's appeal to children. So everything became animated with teeth and mouths and these in-your-face looks. That's kind of what drove it." According to Beach, Islanders ownership specifically suggested that SME model the dimensions of the costume on the big-headed mascot for George Washington University, which had just played at Nassau Coliseum in the regionals for the 1994 NCAA men's basketball tournament.[58]

To create the mascot O'Hara relied on a freelance designer named Pat McDarby. A graduate of Manhattan's High School of Art and Design, McDarby had spent a decade working for advertising agencies and supplying designs to magazines such as *Fortune*, *Life*, and *Sports Illustrated*. McDarby, who grew up in the Bronx rooting for the Rangers, was summoned to rejuvenate the brand of their rivals.[59] He never hesitated. "I have a lot of pride in what I do, and I think everybody at SME did too," he said.[60] McDarby scribbled sketches during his long railroad trips from his home in Connecticut to meet clients in New York City. O'Hara thought the early designs for the mascot looked either "too Disneyesque" or too complex, with crabs tangled in his beard or fish at the end of his hockey stick.[61]

Eventually, McDarby sketched a figure that resembled a caricature of the gruff fishermen in *Men's Lives* and the "Downeaster *Alexa*" music video. The seven-foot mascot, brought to life by a costume designer in Jersey City, had a fifteen-pound head, bushy eyebrows, a bulbous nose, and a full beard that often covered the logo on his Islanders jersey. He wore suspenders and hockey gloves, and a red light atop his white helmet flashed when the Islanders scored a goal. The jersey, gloves, and helmet gave the fisherman a hockey element that had been toned down or absent in McDarby's initial sketches. "Before he meant a little bit more to the region," O'Hara said at the time. "Now he means more to the Islanders. I think that's okay." O'Hara believed the cartoonish mascot would resonate with the next generation of Islanders fans, citing studies showing that children directly or indirectly represented $160 billion in buying power in the United States. "I think marketers now have an understanding of the importance of children," he said.[62]

Beach and Calabria interviewed candidates to become the Islanders' new mascot. The most impressive was Rob Di Fiore, a twenty-nine-year-old graduate of St. John's University in Queens, where he spent three years playing the school's mascot, Johnny the Beast, at basketball games. It was not easy work: St. John's fans were resistant to Johnny the Beast, a replacement for the Red Man, the longtime mascot who was shelved due to perceived racism toward Native Americans. Di Fiore had endured the worst of New York sports fans, spitting, punching, and throwing beer at Johnny the Beast as if no one was inside the costume. It was the type of daunting experience that could be considered good preparation for the job navigating Nassau Coliseum as the Islanders' new mascot.[63]

Thanks to Di Fiore's hyper and hilarious antics, St. John's fans eventually accepted Johnny the Beast. Then Di Fiore graduated and began searching for full-time mascot jobs. He applied to become one of the most recognizable mascots in sports, the Phillie Phanatic, the furry green mascot for Major League Baseball's Philadelphia Phillies, but he didn't get the gig. Instead, he went to work for Barneys, the high-end fashion store in New York. He still longed to suit up again, so he sent his mascoting résumé to all the sports teams in the area. When the Islanders summoned him to Uniondale, they showed him artwork for the unnamed fisherman mascot. It did not strike Di Fiore as the sort of figure that children would run up to and hug. "Usually when I think of mascots, I think of a warm and fuzzy character like the Phillie Phanatic," Di Fiore said. "It's really not like a real animal. I see it's this fisherman costume and I'm like, Okay."[64]

Despite the problems with the costume, Di Fiore was enamored with a dream job as a mascot for a professional sports team. Still, he lacked a skill he feared was crucial to being hired. "Even though I was a jock and played sports," he said, "I never really learned how to ice-skate really well." He tried to convince the Islanders that hockey mascots didn't spend much time on the ice anyway, since the Zamboni came out between periods. The Islanders agreed: they wanted their new mascot interacting with fans in the stands and on the concourse. Charisma was required. Skating ability was secondary. Di Fiore was hired in September at the rate of seventy-five dollars per game.[65]

The Islanders had the first component of their new brand. What they didn't know, because Di Fiore had not told them, was that the man hired to represent the brand was recovering from alcoholism, cocaine addiction, and depression. What they did know, and had little power to prevent, was that the 1994–95 NHL season, which they hoped would be a test run for the Islanders' new identity, might never happen.

While the Islanders were shaping their new brand over the summer of 1994, the National Hockey League had been negotiating with its seven hundred players on a new collective bargaining agreement. A major sticking point was a proposal by the owners of the twenty-six NHL teams for a wage structure based on team revenues. Players viewed it as an onerous salary cap that would reduce their earning potential. Owners wanted to eliminate salary arbitration and cut insurance benefits, pension funds, expense money, and roster sizes. Players accused the league of negotiating in bad faith. Although the regular season was scheduled to start on October 1, tough rhetoric from both camps gave the impression that a lengthy lockout could ensue.[66]

The prospect of a work stoppage threatened the Islanders' plans to rebrand. Work stoppages in professional sports leagues tend to anger fans who view the process as selfish bickering between billionaire owners and millionaire players. In August 1994 wealthy Major League Baseball players initiated a strike that canceled the rest of the season and alienated middle-class fans. Smatterings of discontent were also apparent at NHL exhibition games. Crowds booed when the unionized players from their home teams shook hands with opponents at center ice as a show of solidarity. Fans also didn't buy the cries of poverty coming from owners who raked in revenues of $700 million in the 1993–94 season and had just struck a $155 million television deal with Fox. As weeks passed without an agreement, the lockout had begun souring fans and making them less receptive to NHL hockey, let alone new jerseys and mascots.[67]

The postponement was especially painful for the Islanders, eager to refresh their brand after the humiliating playoff sweep by the Rangers six months earlier. Every day without new games left fans with the memory of the last one that counted, with the Rangers clinching their first Stanley Cup in fifty-four years. The arrival of October brought confirmation: the NHL would postpone the season pending a collective bargaining deal. Months passed without an agreement. On January 11 the owners narrowly rejected a deal for a shortened season that had been ratified by the players. "There was absolute disbelief that they turned down our proposal," Islanders captain Pat Flatley said. "It's beginning to look like they didn't want a deal."[68] The next day, on the 103rd day of the lockout, the league and the players settled. The chance for a full eighty-four-game season had been lost. In its place would be a truncated forty-eight-game schedule starting in late January.[69]

Islanders fans were torn. They were happy their team would return to action, but they were also angry the owners and players let the lockout drag on for more than three months, canceling half the season. One fan told *Newsday*, "I think it's ridiculous for both the players and the owners to get into this situation." Another wrote an angry letter to the editor: "As far as the players and owners go, we must be sure to welcome them back with what they truly deserve. For the owners: BOOOOOO! For the players: BOOOOOO!"[70]

Despite widespread reports of fan unrest, the Islanders chose to move ahead with the rebrand. The team took out ads in *Newsday* that put a positive spin on the shortened season. "With half as many games," the ads pointed out, "each one counts twice as much."[71]

2

A FROZEN-DINNER FRANCHISE

As soon as the pact between the NHL owners and players was announced, ending the lockout, hundreds of Islanders fans began calling the ticket office at Nassau Coliseum. The team would begin the shortened season, and take their first public step toward rebranding, at home against the Florida Panthers on January 21, 1995. If anything, the absence of hockey seemed to make fans grow fonder for the Islanders, and the Islanders grow fonder for playing again.

"It's such a plus in our lives," raved one fan. "We went crazy without hockey," said another.[1] There was reason for optimism. Behind the bench Al Arbour was replaced by his assistant Lorne Henning, a player on the Islanders' first Stanley Cup team and a coach on the three others, providing continuity from the championship years. But the new brand would become most associated with the players, and the Islanders had a pair of exciting rookies to usher in the era of the fisherman mascot: right wing Brett Lindros, the Islanders' first-round draft pick in 1994 and the brother of Philadelphia Flyers captain Eric Lindros, and left wing Žiggy Pálffy, a highly touted prospect from Slovakia who scored twenty-five goals for the Islanders' minor league affiliate the previous year. Neither Lindros nor Pálffy had laced up in the disastrous 1994 postseason, so they did not bear the stain of the humiliating Rangers series. With the lockout over, the Islanders were upbeat. "Now we're fighting for what we really like, jobs and a playoff spot," said right wing Brad Dalgarno.[2] Center Pierre Turgeon, a hero of the 1993 postseason run, suggested the Islanders could regain the momentum that took them to the conference finals: "There is a good feeling on this team. And down the line, it doesn't matter what we have done in the past. Last year, the Rangers won the Stanley Cup and the year before, they didn't make the playoffs."[3]

More than any other player, Lindros was put forth as the center-piece of the team's new brand. By most reports the nineteen-year-old Lindros was not the same player as his older brother Eric, who had exceeded forty goals in each of his first two seasons with the Flyers. In fact, the younger Lindros did not skate well enough to make the Canadian world junior team.[4] Nevertheless, the Islanders sold him as the second coming. General manager Don Maloney raised expectations by trading respected defenseman Uwe Krupp for the right to draft Lindros ninth overall in 1994 and signing him to a five-year, $7.5 million deal that guaranteed a long-term presence on Long Island. Teammate Ray Ferraro said that Lindros could "dominate" play. A newspaper columnist drew a generous comparison between Lindros and a mainstay of the Islanders' Stanley Cup dynasty, calling him "the new Clark Gillies." The *Blade*, the Islanders' official program and magazine, said he was the team's most heralded prospect since Pat LaFontaine, a five-time all-star who twice scored more than fifty goals in a season.[5] To some, Lindros even had the good looks to be the face of the franchise. "He can be the heartthrob of a generation of girls growing into women wearing his name across their shirts," *Newsday* raved. "He is the great hope of a new generation of Islanders hoping to grow into their history. He is tall, dark, and handsome, and single." The Islanders plastered Lindros's image across full-page ads beneath the quote "I've waited eighteen years to play professional hockey. I'm through waiting."[6]

The positivity boded well for rolling out the mascot at the home opener versus the Panthers. On a night the Islanders were crafting their new brand, they would very literally be fighting their past: the Panthers were built by Bill Torrey, the former Islanders general manager who assembled the players on the Stanley Cup teams, and their goaltender was Mark Fitzpatrick, who had played parts of five seasons on Long Island, including the 1993 playoff run. The Panthers had beaten the Islanders in all five meetings the previous season, almost costing the Islanders the final playoff spot. But this was the new postlockout era in Uniondale. Lindros, about to make his NHL debut, wolfed down his traditional pregame dinner of grilled chicken and linguini. A message board on Hempstead Turnpike exulted, "Welcome Back, Islander Fans!" An excited crowd of 14,106 filed into Nassau Coliseum and picked up free Pierre Turgeon cards at the turnstiles. Some fans had Islanders logos painted on their cheeks. Energy pulsed through an arena that had not seen hockey for the past nine months.[7]

At about seven o'clock Rob Di Fiore came onto the ice in the mascot outfit to rev up the fans. He was as nervous as the players, momentarily getting tangled up on the back of the net during his first skate around the rink but escaping unscathed. Then the public address system blared AC/DC's hard-rock "For Those About to Rock," starting a ten-minute display of lasers and fireworks to accompany player introductions. Out came the 1994–95 New York Islanders, led by their new coach. The last players on the ice, by virtue of the numbers on their backs, were Lindros, number 75, and Turgeon, number 77.[8]

The Islanders controlled play from the start. Fifteen seconds into the game Lindros roused the large crowd with a hit behind the Panthers net. The Islanders fired nine shots on Fitzpatrick through the first ten minutes. Florida struck with a goal at 10:06 of the opening period, but the Islanders kept hitting, getting scoring chances, and generally playing strong defense. When the second period ended the Islanders were down only 1–0.[9]

Between periods Di Fiore had a chance to overcome his pregame gaffe. Three young fans were picked from the crowd to dance with the mascot, allowing Di Fiore to showcase the friendly personality that he constructed for the mascot.[10] "Some mascots are obnoxious," Di Fiore said. "I just said, 'You know what?' One, I just wanted to be liked. I want them to like me and warm up. I just tried to be personable, and that was the difference between me and so many other mascots."[11]

The third period was Pálffy's. At 9:42 he scored a backhanded goal to tie the game. Two minutes later he rocketed a slap shot from the slot past Fitzpatrick to put the Islanders up 2–1. The score held.

"All I know is, I like it right now," Pálffy said. Lindros, though kept off the score sheet, made an impact, too. "I didn't have my greatest game, but I thought I played well," Lindros said, giving Islanders fans hope for more to come. "It was a special feeling. It made me feel at home."[12]

Opening night had been a mixed bag for the Islanders' new brand. Fans booed the mascot, which *Newsday* labeled "a cross between a fire hydrant and Grizzly Adams," the bearded California mountain man.[13] However, the mascot's facial hair mattered less than the red light atop his head, which flashed for the Islanders' two goals. If the fans embraced the 1995 team, the mascot might benefit from association. And the come-from-behind win made for a memorable home opener. The Islanders outshot Florida 39–18. Lindros backed up the hype. Pálffy had the crowd chanting, "Žiggy!" The rebrand was rocking.

The night after the raucous home opener the Islanders were back in action against the Ottawa Senators, with a chance to win the first two games of a season for the first time since 1987. They didn't make history, but they left with a 3–3 tie punctuated by a feel-good goal from Ray Ferraro, whose father had died several weeks earlier from congestive heart failure. Their young goaltender, Jamie McLennan, had his second straight solid start. The Islanders had fired an impressive thirty-nine shots on goal for the second straight night. They had faced two hot goalies and come away with three out of a possible four points. Things were looking up.[14]

The next game would be crucial. It was one of those dates that fans circle on their calendars, that produces headlines long before the puck is dropped. In their third game in four nights Brett Lindros and the Islanders would face Eric Lindros and the Flyers, the first time the brothers would meet in an organized hockey game. There was little debate about which Lindros was better. Eric was in the starting lineup in the 1994 NHL All-Star Game; Brett wasn't even in the league back then. Eric centered the Flyers' top line; Brett was on the Islanders' second. Eric already had an assist in the young season, giving him 173 NHL points; Brett was still waiting for his first. But the Islanders were selling Brett as the face of the rebrand, and his team had one win and one tie, while Eric's Flyers had dropped both of their first two games.

Brett downplayed the sibling rivalry, telling reporters, "You guys will make more of it than there really is."[15]

Eric, who already knew how brightly the sports media spotlight could shine, was concerned about the impact on his younger brother. "The less pressure on him, the better he'll play," he said. "He doesn't need advice. Leave the guy alone."[16]

Lacking much star power, the Islanders were desperate to market Brett Lindros, perhaps to the detriment of his development. While Brett was bound to be judged against Eric to a certain degree, Don Maloney encouraged the comparison by claiming that the Islanders had drafted "the better Lindros." Salivating over his marquee last name, the organization treated Brett as if he were an established star. Less than a month into his first NHL season he was appearing in newspaper ads, dispatched to sign autographs at Sunrise Mall, and splashed across the pages of the team magazine alongside the headline "Nobody's Little Brother." The accompanying article slobbered over Lindros as "the combination of present and future all rolled up in one player," liberally dropping phrases like "franchise player" and "exceeded all expectations." Maloney kept raving. "He brings everything a championship team needs—character, leadership," he said. "Right now, all he is is big and strong. We think he can develop into more than that." Henning, too, appeared to be pushing Lindros to be the scorer that he never was. "The last thing we want him to think is he has to go out there and be tough," the Islanders' coach said. "There is much more to Brett's game than being a tough guy."[17]

The game featured a subplot, too. If Brett Lindros was the Islanders' future, Flyers goaltender Ron Hextall was the past the team desperately wanted to forget. Hextall had been the Islanders' Swiss-cheese goaltender in the playoff sweep versus the Rangers the previous spring, allowing sixteen goals in three games for a pitiful 6.08 goals-against average and an .800 save percentage. It was a stunning letdown from Hextall's strong regular season, when he backstopped the Islanders to twenty-seven victories and had a 3.08 goals-against average, the best since his rookie season in 1986–87. Eager to move past the Rangers series, Don Maloney traded his veteran goalie for the inexperienced

Tommy Söderström, even though Hextall was a rare Islander who wanted to stay. "He mentioned the fans and how I might be their fall guy," Hextall told reporters. "Well, I've been booed before. You're going to get booed when you are a goaltender. You'd better have a thick skin."[18]

The game matched the hype. Hextall heard the boos from the Nassau Coliseum crowd and played as if he had something to prove. He responded to the Islanders' twenty-two-shot barrage in the first period with twenty-one saves. Eric won the battle of the Lindroses, scoring twice, but the Islanders got goals from their top players, Steve Thomas and Pierre Turgeon. Derek King banked a shot in off a Flyers defenseman. McLennan was strong again. With the score tied at 8:29 of the third period, Benoit Hogue was awarded a penalty shot and backhanded the puck past Hextall for a 4–3 win. The new Islanders had conquered one of the old ones, and they were 2-0-1 in a forty-eight-game season.

The team's early success was a surprise, the sort of fast start that might lead fans to embrace the rebrand. The *Newsday* game story began, "Undefeated. Atop the standings. On a roll. The Islanders? Yep."[19]

Eric Lindros, nursing a body whacked by his younger brother, brooded after the game. The Flyers seemed destined for their third straight losing season, upsetting their superstar captain. "How frustrating do you think it is?" Lindros said. "It's like getting drafted by a team that won't trade you. This is as frustrating as it gets."[20]

Eric's frustration gave Islanders fans hope. For weeks insiders had speculated that Maloney signed Brett for five years to ensure that his contract on Long Island overlapped with the expiration of Eric's deal in Philadelphia. Eric was sure to attract deep-pocketed suitors when he entered free agency, but only the Islanders would be able to offer him a chance to play with his brother. While signing Brett long term could be viewed as clever planning, it may have also weakened the new brand identity in the short term, giving the impression that the Islanders were holding back on signing marquee players now in hopes of building the franchise around Eric down the line. Long-suffering fans were eager to look forward to Eric as the light at the end of the tunnel. "We never believed Eric would spend his entire career in the City of Brotherly Love," declared the *Islander Insider* newsletter. "Sources inform us that the brothers would love to play together at some point. You can see where we're heading . . . Long Island is beautiful in the Spring."[21]

With the 4–3 victory the Islanders had shown Eric Lindros that the grass might be greener for him on Long Island. Asked about his kid brother, Eric added dejectedly, "He's up one-nothing."[22]

The Islanders slipped in their next two games, losing on the road to Washington and at home to Tampa Bay. McLennan looked vulnerable in net, and Söderström wasn't much better. Derek King was benched for taking a double minor penalty that led to a goal. The offense had no punch. For the first time in the season Nassau Coliseum was filled with boos and chants for refunds. Faced with his first losing streak as Islanders coach, Henning called a closed-door meeting and cautioned his players against taking shortcuts. They were about to embark on a four-game, seven-day road trip, and they couldn't afford to dig their hole any deeper.[23]

"What separates the good teams from the bad teams is confidence," said King, who had gone from the Islanders' top line in training camp to Henning's doghouse. "The good teams don't lose it as many times as bad teams do."[24]

Sensing a season-defining moment, Henning sent a message by benching three of his core players, Žiggy Pálffy, Travis Green, and Darius Kasparaitis, for a game against the Panthers in Miami. The team responded with a 5–1 win.[25] Then they flew to Philadelphia to take on the Flyers. The Lindros brothers were not reunited because Brett sat out with a sore wrist. It didn't matter. The Islanders skated away with a 5–4 overtime victory that put their record at 4-2-1. It was only February, but they were still in first place.[26]

"There's a difference in this team from last year and the difference is the guys just don't seem to panic," said Ray Ferraro, who had two assists versus the Panthers and the overtime goal against the Flyers. Added McLennan, "Basically, the guys are just taking the bull by the horns and winning the game."[27]

Meanwhile, the Islanders' marketing staff had not yet picked a name for the fisherman mascot. McDarby, who designed the character, had privately nicknamed him Salty, an allusion to the saltwater off Long Island's shores. *Newsday* proposed Spud. The Islanders ultimately decided to leave the decision to their fans. An issue of the *Blade* included a form for a contest to the name the mascot. Alongside McDarby's sketch the ad encouraged fans, "You can't body slam the enemy. You can't pick the players. You can't kill the ref. But you can name the mascot." The winner was promised a trip for two to an Islanders road game.[28] Entries arrived from across Long Island. One fan proposed Phil D'Net. Another suggested Sam Boni. Some wanted Checkie, Puckie, or Deke.[29] But the Islanders were looking for a name that separated them from other hockey teams.

One night a thirteen-year-old girl in Massapequa named Illana Gazes was watching the game in her family's kitchen when she heard about the contest. She wrote down her choice and asked her mom to mail it in. A few weeks later Gazes received a letter from the Islanders saying that hers was the winning entry. "It was so exciting," Gazes said. "I felt like a kid in a candy shop because I never won anything. It's typical. Yeah, you enter a contest and you never win. You play the lotto as much as you can, and you can never win it." Gazes was one of sixteen fans to suggest a variation of Nyisles (pronounced NIGH-ils), a play on "NY Isles." Her submission was plucked from a hat as the contest winner, and the Islanders threw in free tickets for an upcoming home game to sweeten the deal.[30]

Di Fiore did what he could as mascot to endear himself to the fans. He slid into the net as if he was the puck. He plastered a poster of a swimsuit model against the glass to distract the opposing team. He delivered roses to female fans, switched on his goal light, and placed a hand on his heart like he was in love. "People always remember, Oh, I went to the Islander game, and their mascot, what a goof," Di Fiore said. "Then I used to always ask people, 'Hey, when you went to the Nets game, did you see their mascot?' They're like, 'I don't remember.'"

Still, Di Fiore was limited by the costume. The fifteen-pound head weighed him down, as did the motorcycle battery around his waist that charged the light on the helmet. "I was known as being a hyper guy," he said. "In this costume, it was so big, I couldn't do anything. It hurt. The head was so heavy. The battery pack around my waist was heavy. It was just dreadful. It wasn't made out of what most costumes are made out of. The head was this hard plastic, and so it was heavy. And the body originally was this foamy thing. It was terrible."[31]

Nyisles was also confusing. Unveiling the mascot in the shortened season gave the Islanders several months to gauge fans' reactions to the fisherman brand identity before taking the riskier step of rolling out a radically different logo the following season. Without the context of the fisherman jerseys, however, no one knew what Nyisles was supposed to be. Fans told Di Fiore that he resembled Karl Malden, the character actor who won an Oscar for his role in *A Streetcar Named Desire*. To the *Hockey News*, Nyisles looked like a "fire hydrant with facial hair" or a cross between two hockey personalities, Islanders broadcaster Jiggs McDonald and former Toronto and Calgary right wing Lanny McDonald. "Everybody thought it looked like Jiggs," said Islanders play-by-play announcer Howie Rose.[32]

Some fans even brought complaints about the mascot to management. Calabria used to field inquiries about what Nyisles was supposed to be by describing him as "a beachy kind of character" and pointing out that other mascots, most notably the Phillie Phanatic, were of indiscernible species and professions. In response, the fans griped that a beach bum made a bad example for their children. "I really got that," Calabria recalled. "I said, 'Really? And what is the name of the New Jersey team?'" Calabria was referring to the New Jersey Devils and their new mascot, N. J. Devil, who was clearly not setting a moral example, but N. J. Devil had a name that was an obvious representation of the Devils' brand. In crafting the costume for their mascot, the Islanders made a confounding mistake: they did not put his name on the back of the jersey, only a big blue number 0. The winning contest entry was "Nyisles," and most news media spelled it that way, but some reporters wrote "Nyiles," and the Islanders themselves printed newspaper ads with a third iteration, "Nyles."[33] It was another touch of confusion that muddled the fisherman brand.

Cracks were starting to show throughout the organization. After the rousing overtime victory in Philadelphia, the Islanders lost three straight games, putting them at 4-5-1 and below .500 for the first time that season. The last of the three was a 5-2 loss to the undefeated Penguins in Uniondale that had the Islanders' general manager thinking about breaking up the team. "We can't put up with this kind of performance on our home ice," Don Maloney said. "There is something lacking here. We have to do some surgery and get it the hell out of the system." Off the ice, reports surfaced that the team regretted breaking the bank to sign Lindros, allowing little money left over to re-sign pending free agent Steve Thomas, who had scored forty-two goals the previous season, or sign their first-round draft pick in 1993, Todd Bertuzzi. Losing Thomas or Bertuzzi could be disastrous for a team marketing them as part of the rebrand. Islanders cochairman Stephen Walsh suggested that fans could help pay the players' salaries by coming to games. Through the first four home dates of the season, Nassau Coliseum was averaging only 11,928 seats sold out of 16,297 available. Still, Walsh maintained the Islanders were "one of the stronger franchises in the league" after refinancing over the summer. "Our goal is to build a team that's going to compete for the Stanley Cup year in and year out," Walsh said. "It's up to the hockey staff to do that."[34]

As February wore on the Islanders' early-season buzz vanished. They won one, lost one, tied one, won one, lost one, tied one, lost one. On one painful night they were defeated in overtime when a puck deflected off the left cheek of defenseman Scott Lachance and into the net, leaving Lachance bloodied and swollen.[35] A two-game winning streak at the end of the month put them at a mediocre 8-8-3, looking up at the Rangers in the Atlantic Division standings.[36] They had given up the first goal in seventeen of eighteen games, including fifteen in a row. A string of injuries ravaged the blue line: Vladimir Malakhov hurt his hip flexor, Dean Chynoweth bruised his knee, Rich Pilon pulled his groin, and Lachance broke a bone in his ankle.[37] Then came the biggest blow: sparkplug defenseman Darius Kasparaitis suffered an ACL tear that ended his season.[38] Meanwhile, Henning kept juggling lines to spark the offense. At a time of mounting concern about head injuries in professional sports, Lindros, the face of the new brand identity, missed nine games with a concussion and subsequent headaches.[39] When he did play, he didn't score.[40]

The Islanders' inconsistent play, combined with rumors about their inability to re-sign key players, spelled trouble for the new brand identity. Hockey was already fourth among the major sports in the New York market, behind baseball, football, and basketball. Pretty goals and lots of them were the best ways to grab the media's divided attention, but the compressed NHL schedule ensured that each game meant more. Instead of taking risks to score highlight-reel goals, teams were embracing a boring defensive strategy called the trap, preventing opponents from scoring by blocking them in the neutral zone and forcing them to dump the puck in. As a result, scoring was down a full goal per game.[41] Without marquee players or a winning record, the Islanders, playing in the suburban shadow of the defending Stanley Cup champions, were easy for most of the New York media to ignore.

Islanders fans grew frustrated. The lack of thorough media coverage translated into little accountability for the stewards of a historic franchise that celebrated its fourth straight championship only a decade earlier. With the Internet in its infancy and social media still many years away, fans had few means to connect with each other and vent. Troubled by the organization's decline, a season-ticket holder named Art Feeney put out a newsletter named *Islander Insider*, which promised to "fill a void" left by insufficient coverage by the daily newspapers and sports radio. Feeney, a pharmaceutical salesman from Seaford, Long Island, had the pedigree and the connections to cover the Islanders in a constructive way. He was the brother of sportswriter Charley Feeney, who was about to be inducted into the writers' wing of the National Baseball Hall of Fame and Museum to celebrate his forty years of coverage for the *Long Island Star Journal*, *New York Journal American*, and *Pittsburgh Post-Gazette*. Given his brother's career, Feeney approached the newsletter with a fan's enthusiasm and a journalist's commitment to fairness. He became friendly with an alternate governor for the Islanders, who fed him information from behind the scenes. In the inaugural issue he vowed that *Islander Insider* would not run puff pieces about "Pierre Turgeon's favorite restaurant or Lorne Henning's top ten movie list," nor did it exist only to bash ownership. As evidence Feeney ran a front-page editorial suggesting that Islanders management was ripping off the fans, but he also defended some trades that didn't work out and invited a minority owner to respond in the next issue.[42]

Feeney was purposefully toeing the line on ownership. He grew up rooting for the Brooklyn Dodgers in the 1940s and 1950s, and he was crushed when the team became disillusioned with its aging ballpark, Ebbets Field, and uprooted for Los Angeles in 1957. He feared that the Islanders' situation mirrored the Dodgers'. "As time went by, I started thinking about this new arena and all of this stuff and all the bad owners they had had even up to that point," he said. "I said, 'I'm gonna do everything I can not to let this team move.'" Feeney may have been so worried about potentially losing the Islanders, or so anxious for a return to glory, that he built up the middling roster beyond its potential at times. *Islander Insider* billed the unproven Lindros as a "possible franchise player" and "future captain." McLennan, who was having a pedestrian season, was described as an "NHL starter—may be more than that." Prospect Bryan McCabe, who had yet to play an NHL game, would be a "top two-way defenseman, next season." Inexperienced center Chris Marinucci "may be the real thing," whatever that meant.[43]

Feeney's fears about the Islanders' relocation spoke to the importance of the team branding around Long Island, an assurance the team would stay. The Islanders followed their humdrum February with a hideous March. A disgruntled Henning benched star forwards Steve Thomas and Pierre Turgeon, harming the coach's relationships with two players who had been the core of the Islanders brand for several seasons.[44] Maloney kept squabbling with Thomas over a new contract.[45] The team lost ten of thirteen games. They scored more than three goals in a game only twice in that span. They lost to Ottawa, the worst team in the league.[46] They blew a 3–0 lead in Boston en route to their fifth straight defeat, their longest losing streak of a season spiraling away from them. Even the young players who were supposed to represent the optimism behind the new brand identity were dejected. Marty McInnis said he hoped the Boston game was the worst he would ever play. McLennan called the loss "just the most disappointing game ever in my career."[47] With his team dropping to twenty-fourth in the twenty-six-team league and six points out of the final playoff spot, Maloney fielded offers from rival general managers for the players that the Islanders had been trying to market as the promise of the fisherman era.[48]

Islander Insider provided a forum for fans to let off steam with its "Voices from the Stands" column. With five weeks to go in the regular season, the Nassau Coliseum faithful begged for excitement. "They commit the worst sin any sports team can. They're boring!" said a man from Great Neck. Added another from Garden City, "You have to give people a reason to come. Give us some hope." For a fan from Massapequa Park, the supposedly new-look Islanders had a familiar feel. "At least tell us how you intend to get better," he vented. "We get the same garbage every year."[49]

Despite the downward spiral the new Islanders brand had a chance for positive publicity when the Rangers visited on March 23. A *New York Times* reporter arranged to follow Nyisles around the sold-out Nassau Coliseum. The assignment figured to be lively: many Islanders fans were wary of the mascot, and Rangers fans would be out in large numbers, looking for any opportunity to tweak their archrivals. Islanders-Rangers matchups were known for good-natured ribbing and back-and-forth chanting, but also for expletives, intoxication, and brawls in the stands. Before the game Di Fiore told the reporter, "I love a challenge." He had a plan to deal with the divided allegiances. "With the Ranger fans, to ease up, I would kid around and go, 'Dude, I'm a Ranger fan,'" Di Fiore said. "And they would be like, 'Yo, he's a Ranger fan!' So they would leave me alone." Still, not every fan was kind. As the game proceeded, someone dumped liquid on Nyisles's helmet. When Di Fiore started dancing, a fan shouted that he was blocking his view of the game. When he ventured into a group of children, a ten-year-old boy told the reporter, "I'd like to assassinate him. I think he's stupid. I think he looks horrible, and the Rangers are going to win."[50]

Pat Calabria assured the reporter that Nyisles usually enjoyed a better reception. "You're really not getting an opportunity to see him at his best."[51]

In truth the Islanders had come to expect negative reactions. All mascots endure vitriol from time to time. Some fans forget there's a person inside the costume, or they're too young to know or too drunk to care, and they take liberties. It figures that fans attracted to a violent sport might become physical themselves on occasion, but the fury directed toward Nyisles seemed like more than run-of-the-mill foolishness. Every taunt screamed and every beer dumped onto his enormous helmet was an indication that perhaps the fan base was not open to the team's new brand identity. "He was not terribly popular," Calabria said. "The fans were just angry, and they wanted to criticize almost anything."[52]

The Islanders' poor play probably would have made a scapegoat out of any mascot. At the Rangers game Nyisles tried to entertain the fans while the Rangers swarmed the Islanders' net, outshooting the home team fourteen to five in the first period and fifteen to four in the second.[53] Nyisles had already put up with two hours of verbal and physical abuse by the time the Islanders finally scored halfway through the third period. If the *Times* reporter had wanted to observe the perils of the job, she must have been satisfied. Islanders employee Rich Walker, who escorted Nyisles around the arena, witnessed all that could go wrong with the Islanders mascot. "I'd make sure he wasn't tripping over little kids that might be directly in front of him that he couldn't see," Walker said. "And I'd also be his protection if any fans started to get rowdy." Walker saw fans jab Nyisles with their fingers, poke him with their fists, and, every so often, try to knock his gigantic head off.[54]

One night, a man sitting by the glass motioned for Di Fiore to come to his seat, saying he wanted the mascot's autograph. The request was unusual, since most of Nyisles's admirers were children, but Di Fiore dutifully descended the steps and approached the fan. "The next thing you know, he just punched me in the face," said Di Fiore, who went flying backward over the empty seats in the row behind him. "The funny thing was he hurt his hand because he didn't realize the mascot's head was hard plastic." The Islanders were so concerned about violent fans that Di Fiore was told to stay in his dressing room if the team was down heading into the third. If Nyisles couldn't even survive sixty minutes of action, the Islanders had to wonder how the rest of the new brand identity would be received. They got their first indication when rumblings surfaced about a new logo. Fans didn't know what the new crest was, but they didn't care. A thousand people signed a petition asking the team not to change its look.[55]

The Islanders entered April with dim hopes of a playoff berth. They had fallen to 10-18-4, going eight games under .500 for the first time. They were allowing breakaway goals and soft goals, shorthanded goals and power-play goals. Henning futilely argued with referees. Söderström was pulled in three straight starts, giving up nine goals on twenty-one shots.[56] "There are one hundred ways to lose," Ray Ferraro said, "and we seem to find every one of them."[57]

Saddled with injuries and underachievers, the young Islanders could at least look to the upcoming schedule for inspiration. On April 1 the organization planned to retire number 23 to honor Bob Nystrom, who had served the Islanders in every capacity from player to assistant coach to radio color analyst.[58] Nystrom, who scored 513 points in nine hundred games, was held up as the quintessential no-quit player, exactly the sort of role model that the young, despondent Islanders needed in 1995. "He really typified what that club was all about: hard work, determination, the feeling that you're never out of it," said former Islanders coach Al Arbour. To some observers, raising a banner in tribute of a former player did not jibe with the Islanders' new brand identity. "Events like these can be tricky for the Islanders," *Newsday* pointed out. "The team might look like it is living in the past because it has done little right for about a decade."[59] Still, if anyone could lift the Islanders out of their funk, perhaps it would be Nystrom and his teammates from the Stanley Cup dynasty triumphantly returning to the Nassau Coliseum ice.

During the banner raising the sellout crowd had more reason to cheer than the home team had given them for months. Former Islanders goaltender Billy Smith, whose number was already in the rafters, came onto the ice. So did Clark Gillies, John Tonelli, and Ken Morrow, all cogs in the championship teams. But their presence was not enough to appease the disgruntled fan base. During a pause in the ceremony one fan screamed, "Get rid of Maloney!" The Islanders' play magnified the anger. The Buffalo Sabres easily skated past the Islanders, 5–1, dropping them to 1-9-1 in their last eleven games. Between the second and third periods, fans unfurled a banner reading, "Maloney Must Go." The pregame applause turned to boos. Henning accused his players of quitting. "We were trying to key off Bobby, the hard work, the teamwork," the coach said. "After the second goal, I thought they went into the tank."[60]

With the trade deadline looming the Islanders were seven points out of the final playoff spot. So many rival scouts began showing up at Nassau Coliseum that Henning compared them to "vultures" hovering over the Islanders' carcass, ready to pick apart the remains of a season gone awry.[61] Any trades the Islanders considered would have little immediate impact, but they were heading into a critical off-season that would include the unveiling of new jerseys to complete the fisherman brand identity introduced by Nyisles. The trade deadline presented an opportunity to unload players with high salaries and the stain of the playoff series against the Rangers in exchange for players who could become part of the fisherman era. In two days Maloney pulled off two moves that shook up the Islanders' roster. In the first deal the Islanders shipped first-line center Pierre Turgeon and enigmatic defenseman Vladimir Malakhov to Montreal. In return the Islanders received the Canadiens' point-a-game captain, Kirk Muller, and top-four defenseman Mathieu Schneider, who would replace Malakhov as the power-play quarterback.[62] The next day Maloney sent two draft picks and three-time thirty-goal scorer Benoit Hogue to the Toronto Maple Leafs in exchange for top goaltending prospect Éric Fichaud.[63] The trades cleared $2 million in annual payroll off the Islanders' books, freeing up Maloney to re-sign some of the twelve Islanders entering their option year.[64]

By trading Turgeon the Islanders were giving up on a sweet-skating superstar who led the team with fifty-eight goals and seventy-four assists in the run to the Eastern Conference Final in 1993. Turgeon's 132 points were the third-best in team history and fifth in the NHL that season, within spitting distance of Mario Lemieux. After the season the Islanders rewarded Turgeon with a four-year, $11 million contract, but they privately worried that he wasn't the same player he had been only a few months prior. In the 1993 playoffs, Turgeon was the victim of one of the most notorious checks in hockey history, when he was celebrating a goal and blindsided into the boards by an opponent, separating his shoulder. The play, which drew the longest suspension in NHL history at the time, left Turgeon tentative and gun-shy on the ice.[65] In the 1994–95 season the forward who once scored more than a point and a half per game, drawing oohs and aahs in Nassau Coliseum, was pointless in fourteen of the Islanders' first thirty-three games. He went as many as six games in a row without scoring.[66] "He rarely shows emotion and was not playing with passion," *Newsday* wrote. Meanwhile, the locker room had been turning against Malakhov. "He made it perfectly clear he didn't want to play here anymore," Ferraro said.[67] The time was right for a split.

Muller and Schneider figured to provide the energy and leadership the Islanders desperately needed. As the team underwent a rebrand that had become a rebuild, they were counting on two players who led Montreal to the Stanley Cup in 1993 to mentor promising young talent like Lindros and Pálffy. While *Newsday* derided Turgeon as soft and impassive, the newspaper said that Muller came to the Islanders with toughness and "Mark Messier–style fire in his belly." Before joining the Canadiens he had captained the Devils from 1987 to 1991, so he had experience leading a team in the New York market. He made the All-Star Game six times and scored thirty goals five times. He had missed only 14 of a possible 837 games due to injuries. He won face-offs, killed penalties, hustled to pucks, and worked the boards. Along with Islanders captain Pat Flatley, Muller could be a veteran presence to take pressure off Lindros during his development and build him into the team's next leader.[68]

Meanwhile, the Islanders still needed someone to stop the puck. With McLennan and Söderström struggling in net, Fichaud was brought in as the goaltender of the future. The Leafs selected him with the sixteenth overall pick in the 1994 draft, and he had twenty-one wins and a 3.44

goals-against average in the competitive Quebec Major Junior Hockey League. Several months earlier Maloney had oversold Lindros as the goal scorer of the future and better than his superstar brother. He made similar claims about Fichaud, who had yet to play an NHL game. "I think the guy we got is a franchise player," Maloney said. "He's a clone of Felix Potvin. He was drafted sixteenth overall last year. He's a premier, top-level goaltender. The only way we're going to win here is if we get a Billy Smitty–type goalie in the net." Though Fichaud had promise, it was dubious to compare any untested nineteen-year-old to Potvin, an all-star who had thirty-four wins the previous season, or Smith, a Hall of Famer who backstopped the Islanders to 304 victories and four Cups. Maloney, perhaps thinking that his job security was tied to the success of Lindros and Fichaud, was putting pressure on his newfound goaltender of the future to develop quickly. "I think he could play next year but who knows?" Maloney said. "Felix Potvin jumped into the league at twenty-one."[69]

The fans ate it up. The front page of *Islander Insider* put a twist on the chants that the general manager's critics shouted at Nassau Coliseum, running the headline "Maloney Must Stay!!" The story raved, "Islander fans have more reason to be optimistic now, than at any time in the last decade!" In an open letter to the general manager, the newsletter enthusiastically endorsed the dumping of two finesse players for the hard-checking Muller and Schneider. "We will be calling on all Islander fans to give you the benefit of the doubt and watch this team, a team that more and more is a product of your draft choices and trades, develop over the next two to three years," the letter read. "We are looking forward to the return of an exciting and competitive team to Long Island."[70]

When the Islanders-Canadiens trade was completed, Montreal was only hours away from skating at home against Quebec. Turgeon and Malakhov screeched out of the Nassau Coliseum parking lot and flew to Canada.[71] Their impact was immediate: Malakhov notched two assists against the Nordiques, and Turgeon scored the tying goal and assisted on the winner.[72] Still, one game did not override the disappointing seasons that Turgeon and Malakhov were having on Long Island. The media chalked up their stellar debuts to beginners' luck. Writing in the *New York Post*, columnist Jay Greenberg said he would be surprised if Turgeon played well in the long run. "Your best player has to want to be your best player," he wrote. "If he does not, you cannot win."[73]

Now it was the Islanders' turn to show off their acquisitions, and they had a perfect forum. The day after the trade the Islanders had a Friday-night game against the Rangers at Madison Square Garden. "I really think this deal's going to start a new trend here—that we demand performance out of all our players," Maloney said. "This in my mind is the start of an attitude adjustment. The players we've acquired will set a standard. Consequently, we'll play harder as a team."[74]

On the day of the Rangers game Mathieu Schneider arrived for the morning skate with a smile. Like Turgeon and Malakhov, the twenty-five-year-old Schneider was looking for a new start. He was eager to leave Montreal, where he feuded with star Canadiens goaltender Patrick Roy, and he was excited about making his Islanders debut in Manhattan, where he was born and lived for thirteen years. Schneider also thought the Islanders had some talented players. "I knew the Islanders were a struggling team, but even just a couple of years before we had played them [in 1993], the year we won the Cup in Montreal. We had beat them in five games but they had a very good team."[75]

While the Islanders salivated at placing Schneider on the decimated blue line, they clearly viewed Muller as the centerpiece of the deal. After speculation that Turgeon and Malakhov were disillusioned and perhaps intentionally tanking on Long Island, the franchise looked for Muller to lead his younger teammates by example.

"We have to get people to play every night," Maloney said.[76]

The *Islander Insider* assured, "He *will* show up every night."[77]

It turned out to be a poor choice of words. Muller didn't come to play for the Rangers game. He wasn't even in the country.

Before the game the beat reporters were waiting in the corridor outside the Islanders' locker room, hoping to interview Muller and Schneider. The team's media relations director, Ginger Killian Serby, returned with just one of them. "All of a sudden Ginger comes walking along with Matty Schneider," said Islanders television broadcaster Stan

Fischler. "Where the hell's Muller? And of course it was embarrassing. The guy wasn't there. Why didn't he show? What the hell's the matter with this guy? What kind of pro are you?"[78]

The reasons for his conspicuous absence varied. Muller claimed that he needed time to get his visa approved. The press speculated that he was upset that the exchange rate between Canada and the United States would reduce his salary. Offering yet another excuse, Maloney said that Muller wanted to take care of "personal matters," implying that he was recovering from the shock of leaving the Canadiens, who promised that he wouldn't be traded. Maloney, a former player, professed to understand Muller's situation. "He's the captain of the Canadiens," he said. "He wears that on his sleeve. That's why we got him. I empathize with him. We've all gone through this before."[79]

Initially, the players were sympathetic, too. Schneider was quick to explain the different circumstances facing himself and Muller at the time of the trade. "For me, it was a reset button," Schneider said. "I hit the reset button and I was excited. For Kirk, he was at a different stage in his career. It meant something a lot different for him. He was the captain of Montreal. His family was embedded in the community. I think it caught him by surprise. At the time, I had asked for a trade and he was happy in Montreal."[80]

Without Muller the Islanders played the Rangers down a forward and were losing 2–0 seven minutes into the game. But they struck back before the first period was through. During his first shift on the power play, Schneider swatted a clearing attempt and passed to defense partner Bob Beers, who shot the puck behind the Rangers' Mike Richter for the Islanders' first goal of the night. After two more periods of back-and-forth play, the undermanned Islanders narrowly escaped with a 4–3 victory that plunged the Rangers three games below .500.[81]

The next day the Islanders should have been basking in their triumph for supremacy in New York hockey. Instead, they awoke to headlines about Muller's absence. "Trade Upsets Muller," *Newsday* reported. The wordier *Times* went with "Muller Keeps Islanders Waiting for Now." The *Daily News* made a *Star Trek* reference and blared, "Kirk Tells Isles: Beam Me Up Later." The *Post* was more pointed. "GUTLESS" appeared in huge type on the back page, leading to a story headlined "Distraught Muller May Retire Rather than Report." The article quoted the Islanders' Derek King, one of the best-liked players in the locker room, assuring a reporter that Muller would show up. "He'll be here," King said. "You'll see." The Islanders were about to play for the second time in two days, a Saturday-night game against the Panthers. It should have been Muller's home debut as an Islander. Instead, it was another no-show.[82]

The Islanders were quickly losing patience. They had taken a risk by trading a twenty-five-year-old first-line center for a twenty-nine-year-old second-line center based on the hope that he would serve as a role model for their young players. Now he wouldn't even report. Calabria called the situation "very embarrassing." Lest anyone think that Muller did not want to play for a last-place team, Maloney tried to clarify that Muller was upset about "being traded, not being traded to the Islanders, just being traded." But his prolonged absence gave the impression that respectable NHL players did not want to play for a faltering Islanders franchise. "Muller was a fiasco," said Islanders radio broadcaster Barry Landers. "Players didn't see the Islanders or Long Island, unfortunately, as a place that they wanted to play in."[83]

The day after the Panthers game Muller finally arrived on Long Island. At an awkward press conference at Nassau Coliseum he explained that he needed a few days after the trade to get his "head clear." Infuriatingly, the player who had just missed two games proclaimed with a straight face, "My asset is I come to play every night." His words did little to quell speculation that he did not want to be an Islander. Muller's delay transformed the narrative of a gutsy trade for a veteran player who had captained his team to a Stanley Cup two years earlier. The *Daily News* put him "on probation," and the *Post* tasked him with living up "to the billing he failed to establish while in seclusion."[84]

Maloney did his part to reignite excitement for the trade. "I think Kirk will give us another little jumpstart," he said. "If we're going to go down, we're going to go down with a fight."[85] A few nights later against the Tampa Bay Lightning, the Islanders exhibited feistiness in Muller's Islanders debut, which was also the first NHL game for top goaltending prospect Tommy Salo. Steve Thomas and Mathieu Schneider were involved in a second-period melee that showed the Islanders still had some competitive spirit. However, true to Maloney's comments, they went down with the fight, losing 5–2. Their already improbable playoff push was on the verge of becoming mathematically impossible. Henning called another postgame meeting to ream out his club. Muller said that his new teammates were "all hurting inside."[86] The only consolation was the schedule. Mercifully, the Islanders had just eleven games left.

As the Islanders descended into the NHL basement, the development of their new jerseys was wrapping up. SME had originally proposed evolving the original Islanders logo or replacing it with text-only wordmarks. The Islanders resisted. The Ducks and the Sharks had their success with cartoon logos, not wordmarks. Besides, the Islanders wanted to evoke Long Island's maritime culture. McDarby came up with a character that looked like the Roman sea god Neptune brandishing a hockey stick with a trident on one end, but the team wanted a human figure akin to the baymen from the "Downeaster *Alexa*" music video. SME's designers sketched dozens of potential characters. Some were gruff. Others were jovial. One had smoke curling up from a pipe in his mouth.[87]

After months of deliberations the Islanders selected a design drawn by Andrew Blanco, an illustrator from Venezuela. When Blanco joined SME in 1990, he spoke broken English and lacked a college degree or formal training, and he was tasked with odd jobs. Eight months into his time at SME Blanco got his break when he created a design for a classical music station that the client liked, and he began working on sports brands, including the Islanders.[88] Keeping with the "Downeaster *Alexa*" imagery, Blanco sketched an older man holding a hockey stick with both hands, his body cut off at the waist by "ISLANDERS" in all caps. The man looked to be in his sixties. He sneered so that only a sliver of teeth was visible on the right side of his mouth, framed by a gray beard. He wore a teal slicker and an oilskin rain hat known as a sou'wester. Behind him was a hockey goal.

The Islanders' initial reaction to the fisherman logo is murky. The logo must have had a patron within the organization, or else it would never have been chosen. However, several team executives who attended meetings to choose the new logo have denied or downplayed their roles in its ultimate selection. They may be wary of admitting any culpability, or at least complicity, in a historic sports-branding debacle. "As one of my old bosses said to me, 'Success has many fathers. Failure is an orphan,'" said Fred Scalera, then the vice president of licensing for NHL Enterprises. "When something works, everybody wants to step up and say, 'Oh, I was involved in that. And I did that. And I did that.' But when something doesn't work, they either blame somebody else or they want to tell you that they weren't involved."[89]

No individual was portrayed as the fisherman logo's benefactor in period accounts of the rebranding process. However, several participants in the logo meetings recalled that Islanders cochairman Stephen Walsh, one of the minority owners, set the tone by voicing his approval for the design on the behalf of ownership, an account supported by contemporary sources.[90] According to the participants, Walsh's blessing gave the impression that ownership had no appetite for other suggestions. "He did the Khrushchev banging the shoe on the podium and said, 'No. If we're gonna do this, we're all in or we're not doing it at all,' so options were not an option," said Tim Beach, the Islanders' director of game events. "Of course, when you're in a room with one of the owners who is responsible whether you get a raise or not, or whether you keep your job or not, no one's gonna stand up in the room and say, 'Absolutely not.'" As an outsider, Ed O'Hara, the SME founder, feared that ownership's approach would chill any critical examination of the logo. "When the owner comes in and says, 'Don't you like this?' and the employee says, 'Yes, boss, I do,' I don't think it was a properly run research process. To call it 'process' is overstating what it was." Walsh has never publicly provided his version of events. In 2014 he was sentenced to twenty years in prison for committing fraud at a commodities-trading firm, and his incarceration and tarnished reputation may have emboldened the meeting participants to finger him as the logo's benefactor. Walsh did not reply to a letter sent during the research for this book to the correctional facility where he resides.[91]

Besides Walsh, the Islanders' executive most involved in the rebrand was Pat Calabria. Calabria acknowledged the perception that the fisherman logo was "a whole Pat Calabria production," since he hired the firm that created it and has been unapologetic in his support of its selection. "Trying to be as objective about it as possible, I fail to see what was hideous about that logo," Calabria said. However, he was only one member of a committee that recommended the logo to ownership. "Anybody who was there knows that this was a process," he said. "I didn't decide."[92]

With Walsh and Calabria behind the logo there were few voices in the organization with enough influence to deter them. The Islanders' majority owner, John Pickett, was represented in some meetings late in the process by his son Brett, who grew up in Oyster Bay, Long Island, just fifteen minutes from Nassau Coliseum. Brett Pickett was ten years old when his father took control of the team in 1978 and a teenager during the Stanley Cup run. For a man who described himself as bleeding blue and orange, the teal-and-silver fisherman logo came across as "goofy-looking" and "minor league." Hoping to save the Islanders' original crest, the younger Pickett wrote a lengthy letter to Walsh and the other three minority stake owners who ran day-to-day operations. "I think the crux of it was that Islander fans derive their identity as Long Islanders more than anything from the Islanders' championship past," Pickett said. "Not just the Islanders happen to be located on Long Island and therefore potentially symbolized by a fisherman or some other local culture point, but the Islander fans drew their identity from the championship history, and I think those guys missed that. I think they were trying to connect them to a place, and instead they should have connected them to that timeless concept of those Stanley Cup championships and all the pride that they and their parents drew from that era in the Islanders history. Disconnecting from that was suicide."

Pickett's concerns made little impact. Despite his apparent place in the line of succession of Islanders ownership, he had no official role in the organization and used his background as an attorney to represent the Islanders only in legal matters, not day-to-day affairs. He was bound by his father's agreement to cede operational control to the four minority stakeholders. "It was their decision to make," he said. "With declining attendance and declining performance, you have to give people a chance to try something. And so ultimately I just said, 'Well, this is your call. Let's try it. Let's see what happens.' But I never thought it was a good idea. That's not hindsight twenty-twenty. That's what I said at the time."[93]

With the Pickett family contractually limited, the Islanders' original logo had few other guardians. Most of the franchise's former players had no knowledge of the proposal to abandon the logo they wore, and the few dynasty Islanders with executive roles in the organization, such as former coach Al Arbour, the vice president of hockey operations, and former defenseman Ken Morrow, the director of pro scouting, did not have a voice in the rebranding process. According to the meeting participants, the only alumnus with any say in the matter was Bob Nystrom, the director of amateur hockey development and alumni relations, who played nine hundred games wearing the Long Island map on his chest. "It's the only logo that I played for," said Nystrom, who spent his entire fourteen-year career on Long Island. "It was, I thought, well designed, and needless to say I was pretty fond of it." Two participants in the rebranding process recalled the Islanders running the fisherman logo past Nystrom as a way of gauging alumni opinion. Years later Nystrom said he "wasn't really that keen on the new logo," which was "so totally dramatically different than the original logo that I just felt it wasn't gonna fly." However, Nystrom brushed aside questions about his obligation to fight for the original logo, insisting he "didn't really have much say at the time."[94] It is true that Nystrom was not nearly as involved in the rebranding process as Walsh and Calabria, but it is hard to believe that arguably the most popular player in Islanders history was powerless to prevent the logo change. If Nystrom had voiced reservations, ownership might have reconsidered.

The NHL, for its part, has disavowed responsibility in the Islanders' rebranding process. In addition to the fisherman logo, SME had presented the Islanders with logos based on a brick lighthouse built in 1857 on Fire Island, parallel to the south shore of Long Island. The 168-foot structure was painted with alternating black and white bands, making it a distinctive symbol of coastal living. Scalera said the NHL steered the Islanders away from the fisherman logo and toward a wordmark with the stylized lighthouse as the *I* in *Islanders*. Instead, the Islanders adopted the lighthouse as a shoulder patch and went with the fisherman as their primary symbol. "That wasn't our first choice, and we told the team," Scalera said. "But ultimately, it's their decision." In a 2013 documentary, NHL commissioner Gary Bettman said with a smile, "I expressed skepticism that it would get traction."[95]

Despite the NHL's reticence the Islanders' rebrand moved forward. The team planned to let its humiliating last-place season conclude on May 2 and unveil the fisherman jerseys toward the end of the playoffs in June, just before the hockey media punched out for the summer. The timetable allowed several months for the Islanders to assess how fans would react to the new logo. However, the team ran only a few unscientific tests, cementing the impression that they had already decided on the fisherman. At one point Beach brought the fisherman jerseys to classes at Kings Park High School on Long Island, a forty-minute drive from Nassau Coliseum, and his alma mater, Quinnipiac University in Hamden, Connecticut. Ironically, a university synonymous with public opinion polling was one of the only stops in a token research process that did not include a single poll of Islanders fans. There was Beach, hesitant to contradict his boss, running a proposed Islanders logo past students almost a hundred miles from the Islanders' arena. "I said, 'Hey, let's go around the room here and vote,'" Beach remembered. "Was it 100 percent one way or the other? No. There was probably about 50–50." Apparently, that was good enough.

On the ice the Islanders were trying to wrap up the 1994–95 season with dignity. During one stretch in the middle of April they beat the Florida Panthers by two, lost to the Devils by three, dropped a one-goal game to the Rangers, and defeated the Quebec Nordiques 5–2. It wasn't the most sensational hockey, but the string of competitive performances with Muller and Schneider on board preserved the

Islanders' pride.[96] Fans were impressed by late-season call-ups such as goalie Tommy Salo, who starred for gold-medal winner Sweden at the 1994 Winter Olympics, and left wing Chris Marinucci, the 1994 Hobey Baker Award winner as the top college hockey player.[97] Even Denis Potvin, the Islanders' captain during the Stanley Cup dynasty, expressed hope for the floundering franchise. In an interview with *Newsday*, Potvin praised the team for bringing in the "consistency" of Muller and Schneider and the "real prize," twenty-two-year-old center Craig Darby, a prospect acquired in the same trade.[98] The season was down to its final week, and the Islanders were building much-needed momentum heading into the rebrand.

Then came the horrifying story that pushed hockey onto everyone's backburner. On the morning of April 20 newspapers landed on Long Island doorsteps with coverage of the deadliest terrorist attack on American soil. Some fifteen hundred miles from Nassau Coliseum, a disillusioned army veteran named Timothy McVeigh parked a rental truck alongside the Alfred P. Murrah Federal Building in Oklahoma City. As McVeigh walked away a bomb in the cargo hold exploded. The blast destroyed one-third of the building. The floors collapsed. Cars overturned. Debris buzzed through the air. The human toll was unimaginable: 168 deaths and more than 680 injuries, many of them severe. America's sense of security had been shattered.[99] On Long Island the killings were evocative. Only a month earlier a Jamaican immigrant named Colin Ferguson had been sentenced to two hundred years in prison for a shooting rampage on a Long Island Rail Road train that killed six people and wounded nineteen others.[100] Ferguson fired as the train pulled into the station in Garden City, just ten minutes from Nassau Coliseum. The Islanders helped create a fund for the victims to start the healing process. Now McVeigh's actions ripped open the wound.

The April 20 issue of the *Daily News* was dominated by coverage of the bombing. On page 84, however, the newspaper unveiled a sports scoop. A few days earlier an upstate New York newspaper, the *Schenectady Daily Gazette*, reported that the Islanders were "ready to make a fisherman in a boat their new logo" and change their colors to Atlantic blue with silver, bright orange, and navy blue trim. Schenectady was three hours from Long Island, so most Islanders fans had not seen the blurb. Besides, the *Gazette* did not publish a picture of the fisherman logo itself. Enter the *Daily News*, which branded itself "New York's picture newspaper." It had somehow obtained a copy of the logo and showed off its acquisition in a photo illustration spanning three columns. "Forget about Islander tradition," the caption read. "Here's what Denis Potvin would have looked like with the new 'fish sticks' logo on his sweater." There was the Islanders' Hall of Fame captain, his arms raised in celebration, with the fisherman logo superimposed over the original crest on his jersey. Two months before the Islanders planned to unveil the fisherman logo, it had been leaked to a tabloid with a penchant for sensationalism and puns.[101]

Alongside Potvin's picture the *Daily News* ran a story with the boldface headline "Isles' New Logo Would Be Sea Sick." For nine unrelenting paragraphs beat writer Colin Stephenson characterized the logo change as a flagrant departure from tradition, "the one thing the Islanders have to be proud of in these dark days leading up to their elimination from playoff contention." The article acknowledged the Islanders' weak apparel sales, which ranked them twenty-fourth among the twenty-six NHL teams, lagging far behind the Kings, Ducks, Sharks, and Panthers. "But none of those teams has anything to offer their fans but snazzy uniforms," Stephenson wrote. "The Islanders have four Stanley Cups in their history, which isn't that long. They would move as many replica jerseys next season by building a winning team as by coming out with a new uniform." The story criticized the Islanders for "replacing one of the most distinctive logos in sports with some rip-off of a frozen-dinner symbol" that was "embarrassingly reminiscent of the Gorton's fisherman, the advertising logo used on boxes of Gorton's frozen fish sticks." Stephenson concluded his rebuke of the rebrand by imagining the Islanders' young stars, such as Brett Lindros, Žiggy Pálffy, and Éric Fichaud, trying to draw inspiration from the championship banners in the rafters at Nassau Coliseum. "They won't see their proud logo hanging there reminding them of what is possible," he wrote. "Instead, all they'll see are museum pieces of a bygone era to which they have little or no connection."[102]

For all its bluster, the *Daily News* story was deeply flawed. First, Stephenson overstated the Islanders' abandonment of tradition by erroneously reporting that the team planned to ditch its blue-and-orange color scheme, which matched the official colors of Nassau County, in favor of blue and black. Second, Stephenson was naive to suggest the Islanders could sell just as many jerseys by winning instead of updating their uniforms, ignoring that turning a rebuilding team into a contender would cost many millions of dollars that small-market teams like the Islanders did not have. In addition, the photo illustration put only the fisherman logo on Potvin's jersey, without the lighthouse shoulder patches and ocean waves that SME chose to complete the new look. The *Daily News* did not even feign to uphold the journalistic standard of neutrality in a story that was at turns mocking and hypercritical.

Still, the comparison to the Gorton's fisherman was undeniable. In ubiquitous television commercials, Gorton's advertised its crunchy fish sticks and zesty garlic and herb fillets with the image of a seafarer almost identical to the man in the new Islanders logo. Both characters had gray beards. Both wore rain slickers and oilskin rain hats. In most printed iterations the Gorton's fisherman was gripping a ship's wheel with his hands in front of his chest in the same position in which the Islanders' fisherman was holding a hockey stick. "I mean, it was a spitting image of the Gorton's fisherman," said Eric Mirlis, the Islanders' assistant director of media relations. "Someone should have put two and two together and said, 'Wait a second. This looks too much like something that is established and is out there.'" O'Hara admitted that fans probably would have pointed out the logo's similarity to the Gorton's fisherman if SME had run focus-group testing. "The lessons there are do more research," he said. "If more research was done with consumers, the partners, and the media, it could have taken a different course."[103]

For the Islanders the *Daily News* story worsened a suddenly bleak April. The day the article ran, the team was in Philadelphia for a game against the Flyers, needing to win its last seven games for the slightest hope at a playoff spot. The *Post* was reporting that Kirk Muller would demand a trade after the season and slammed the Islanders for dealing for "the right person at the wrong time," insisting that Muller belonged on a playoff team and that the Islanders would not contend for at least three or four years. And now the *Daily News* was scoffing at the idea of a logo change that the team was not prepared to defend. The Islanders lost that night 2–1 to the Flyers, who clinched their first playoff berth since 1989. Islanders public relations executive Chris Botta, who was in charge of the team's media guide and programs, had trouble concentrating on the action. He figured that Stephenson's story would initiate a stream of negative coverage from other news outlets, putting the team on the defensive long before the official unveiling. "I remember just sitting there during this game in Philadelphia and thinking, Oh my God, the shit's gonna hit the fan," he said. Botta was especially troubled by the photo illustration. By plastering the logo on a beloved former player, the *Daily News* framed the logo change as an abandonment of history, not the refreshing of a worn-out brand. "They got Denis Potvin unwillingly, unknowingly, wearing it," Botta said. "That logo didn't have a chance anyway. It certainly didn't have a chance after it was stuck on Denis Potvin."[104]

Calabria, meanwhile, was angry the *Daily News* called the logo "sea sick" in its headline. "It's an easy target," he said. "As a movie critic, it's like giving a bad review to a movie because you can make fun of the title in a cute way." No matter the validity of the Islanders' protests, the team had little recourse against the *Daily News*. Suing the newspaper for publishing a leaked copy of the logo would only call more attention to the leak and the critical coverage and further preempt the unveiling of the new jersey in two months. Besides, the Islanders figured they probably wouldn't have prevailed in court anyway. Asked if the team ever considered legal action against the *Daily News*, Calabria, a former journalist, recalled the landmark 1971 Supreme Court ruling in *New York Times v. U.S.*, better known as the Pentagon Papers case. How could a hockey team hope to win a lawsuit against a newspaper that published a leaked copy of a logo if the federal government could not stop a newspaper from printing leaked documents on the grounds that publication jeopardized national security? Calabria figured that legal precedent backed the *Daily News*. "They are not bound to keep secrets we want kept," he said.[105]

Calabria was probably right about the Islanders' poor chances in a lawsuit, although he was not citing the appropriate area of the law. Despite the renown of the Pentagon Papers case, any litigation pitting the Islanders versus the *Daily News* probably would have operated within the less glamorous confines of sports trademark law. Working on the team's behalf, an attorney named Anthony Fletcher filed paperwork to register the fisherman logo as a trademark on March 15, more than a month before the *Daily News* published the logo.[106] However, the key event in a trademark squabble is not the filing of the application but the "first use in commerce," or the first day the Islanders planned to sell merchandise featuring the logo, which was listed in the filing as July 1.[107] Since the *Daily News* published the logo before its first use, the Islanders did not have a case. The team couldn't cite common law, either, because they would have had to establish that they publicly used the logo before its publication in the *Daily News*.

Botta's fears about negative copycat coverage were quickly confirmed. A few days after the *Daily News* article, the *Toronto Star*, among the highest-circulation newspapers in Canada, published an item on the fisherman logo that appeared to be based on Colin Stephenson's report. The *Star* cited the same statistic about apparel sales and repeated the same mistake about the team's supposed switch to blue-and-black jerseys. Like Stephenson, the *Star*'s Bob McKenzie approached the logo with incredulity: "The orange-blue map of Long Island combo will give way to a blue-black motif with a bearded fisherman wearing a rain slicker and carrying a hockey stick in front of a net. Really."[108]

The next day the Islanders published the season's final issue of the *Blade*, the official program and magazine. The last page carried a frank full-page column by Botta titled "The Great Logo Debate of 1995." One particularly ruthless passage attacked the *Daily News*. Botta accused the newspaper of "disgraceful" and "more than shoddy tabloid journalism." He called them out for failing to seek comment from the team. He mocked them for publishing a "cheesily-FAXed" copy of the logo. He criticized their erroneous reporting on the color scheme of the new uniforms. "Oh, well," Botta snarkily concluded. "It was the first scoop the *Daily News* has had on the Islanders since the Ford administration."[109]

But the *Daily News* was not the logo's only detractor. One fan hung a banner at Nassau Coliseum reading, "Fish sticks are for dinner, not our logo." Others likened the crest to the bearded character on boxes of Fisherman's Friend cough drops. Many signed a petition to protest the new jerseys. In an open letter to the team that ran in the *Islander Insider* newsletter, a woman from Plainview wrote, "Now you want to change our proud logo; a logo that's been worn by four Stanley Cup champions. At least put the present logo on the shoulder, tie the old in with new."[110]

The team did not listen. In fact, they were about to abandon even more of "the old."

The Islanders followed their April 20 loss to Philadelphia with an April 22 loss to Ottawa that officially eliminated them from playoff contention.[111] A week later they finished the season in last place in the Atlantic Division at 15-28-5, the second-worst record in the NHL. The 1994–95 season had begun with the debut of a new mascot and young stars such as Brett Lindros. It was supposed to mark the first stage of a grand rebrand that would help fans move past the playoff series sweep by the Rangers. Instead, the season ended with the Rangers squeaking into the playoffs, while the Islanders were out of the mix for the first time in three years.[112]

The scapegoat for the disappointing season was the coach. Two weeks after the *Daily News* announced the abandonment of the logo worn during the Stanley Cup dynasty, the team fired Lorne Henning, the center who assisted on the goal that won the Islanders their first title in 1980. The move was shocking. Henning, an original Islanders player who spent eighteen years in the organization, was granted only one lockout-shortened, injury-riddled campaign to prove himself as head coach, even though he still had one year left on his contract. Apparently, the Islanders, who were about to unveil the fisherman logo, wanted a fresh face behind the bench, too. Asked about Henning's replacement, general manager Don Maloney immediately ruled out former coach Al Arbour, another link to the Stanley Cup teams. "A new voice is necessary for us to go forward," he said, advocating for a disciplinarian who would run the players through a grueling training camp in September. "You need a personality to strike fear in the players. If they don't perform, it's going to be hell for them."[113]

If the Islanders hired the sort of taskmaster that Maloney was describing, the next coach could become as much a part of the new brand identity as the fisherman jerseys in the 1995–96 season. But it was only May 3, and the market for prime coaching candidates had not developed. As teams started dropping out of the playoffs in the next few weeks, their head coaches might be fired and their assistants might look to graduate to head-coaching jobs with other clubs. Then the Islanders could start interviewing.

In the interim the team turned to a more pressing problem. The controversy surrounding the fisherman logo threatened to squelch the rebrand before the new jerseys even made their on-ice debuts. The logo was being socked in the stands and battered by the media. After Henning's firing the *Daily News* suggested the Islanders misdirected their ire at their coach, running the headline "Forget Lorne, Fire Logo." Columnist Frank Brown bristled that "some imbecile in Islanders management" had chosen "a guy in a raincoat" for the new jerseys. "The fact is, it's appalling—the logo, that is," he wrote. "It's embarrassing, worse than the just-awful, makes-you-want-to-throw-up mascot."[114]

If the Islanders wanted to salvage their brand identity, they had to hit back.

3

THE BAYMEN AND THE BRUIN

As the Stanley Cup playoffs began in the spring of 1995, the Islanders were in disarray. Lorne Henning, their ousted head coach, turned down another job in the organization, saying that he could not stay on Long Island "as long as Donnie Maloney is still around" as general manager. Pat Flatley, their captain, called Henning's dismissal "unjust" and "completely unfair." Pierre Turgeon, the star they traded away, rejuvenated his career in Montreal, scoring eleven goals in fifteen games, while Kirk Muller, the player they received in return, had only three goals in twelve games and reportedly wanted out. The Islanders' longtime play-by-play broadcaster, Jiggs McDonald, blamed the front office for the turmoil. "The top management has no hockey experience, none whatsoever," he said in an interview with *Newsday*. "Somebody asked me if I thought the team was at a crossroads. Hell no. They've hit the wall." A few weeks later McDonald hit a wall of his own in negotiations for a new contract. The familiar face of the Islanders telecasts was gone after fourteen years, yet another indication of the tumult surrounding the team.[1]

Writing in *Newsday*, columnist Mark Herrmann ran through the list of personnel changes in the Islanders' recent history. "So in the space of six years, they have completely changed their identity three times," he wrote. "And still they don't have one."[2]

The revolving door of players spelled trouble for the Islanders brand. With the fisherman jerseys about to debut, Muller was the closest the Islanders had to the type of marquee name that sold tickets and merchandise. However, as Herrmann pointed out, the team's newest acquisition did not even want to be there. "Shame on Muller for balking at reporting, and mumbling about a trade," Herrmann wrote. "He should be honored to wear the uniform once graced by Denis Potvin, Mike Bossy, and Bryan Trottier (at least it will be an honor, until the Islanders brain trust follows through on plans to replace the noble, title-evoking Islanders crest with a drawing of a hook, line, and sinker or some such gizmo)."[3]

Such potshots at the fisherman logo had become commonplace. The Islanders planned to unveil the logo at a news conference during the Stanley Cup Final in late June, before the hockey press went into hibernation for the summer. But they needed a plan to reclaim their jerseys from the barrage of sniping about the Gorton's fisherman.

Chris Botta's column in the last program of the season offered six talking points to sell the logo. His first point, and probably the strongest, was that the logo was the work of "the best designers." True to Botta's claim, SME came highly recommended by the NHL after a string of branding successes. Botta vouched for the firm's knowledge of which uniforms looked and sold best. As he put it, SME's involvement should end speculation that "some honcho in the Islander office woke up one day, decided he didn't like the current logo, broke out the crayons, and said, 'This is it.'" Regardless of the negative reviews for the fisherman logo, critics could not fault the Islanders for selecting a well-respected design firm.[4]

The second point in Botta's column was dubious. He claimed the Islanders received support for the jerseys from both longtime fans and the target audience of children and young adults. According to Botta, Islanders fans "wanted to hate the thing, broke down and admitted they actually liked it, offered a few ways to tinker with it, and have heartily endorsed it," while younger shoppers "flat-out loved it." On this point Botta was massaging the truth. His suggestion of a rigorous research process was not supported by oral history interviews with several people involved in the rebranding, and period media accounts do not suggest any widespread public excitement. In fact, the fan base had already started a petition for the original logo's return. The only indication that anyone even tolerated the jersey change was when an editor of the *Islander Insider* newsletter responded to a negative letter about the logo by advising the writer "to be patient." It was about as tepid an endorsement as possible.[5]

Botta's third point was similarly unconvincing. He implied the roster as a whole accepted the fisherman jersey. As proof Botta cited his own conversations with three unnamed Islanders. According to Botta, one player said his kids would rather wear the new jersey than the original one, and another player predicted that fans would love the uniform if the team won. Botta also paraphrased a third Islander who said he had "no idea" what the original logo represented. The presentation of the quotes was not compelling. At best they came across as measured appraisals from players unwilling to go on the record in support of the logo they were about to wear across their chests. At worst the anonymity of the statements called their authenticity into question. Even if the quotes were not fabricated, the players may have only been telling management what it wanted to hear, hesitant to contradict the people who paid their salaries and dictated their playing time. In interviews most players framed the team's collective reaction to the logo as skeptical. "When that came in, everybody's trying to find out what they like about it," said defenseman Rich Pilon. "You gotta wear the jersey. Us as players, we're like, Oh my God."[6]

For Botta's fourth point he moved from current Islanders to former ones. To counter the perception that the team was rejecting its heritage, he claimed that two high-profile members of the Stanley Cup teams embraced the new brand identity. Botta figured that evoking Al Arbour, the former coach, and Bob Nystrom, the right wing whose number hung in the Nassau Coliseum rafters, would persuade older fans to accept the change just as their heroes had. "Was it hard at first for Islanders like Al Arbour and Bob Nystrom to see a change in something they represented so proudly? Of course," Botta wrote. "But after making some suggestions, did they get excited over the possibility of a new look? You better believe it." Again, the assertion of support for the logo was flimsy. Neither Arbour nor Nystrom ever voiced public support for the logo. If they were truly excited, the Islanders would have benefited from letting them speak directly to the media. More likely, Arbour and Nystrom may have refrained from criticizing the new jerseys because they worked for the team as executives and did not want to risk their jobs by challenging ownership. Nystrom clearly had affection for the original logo. "There's a lot of good history with that logo," he said. "The Islanders logo of 1972 and '73 is the original, and I think that that means something."[7]

Fifth, Botta proposed that the Islanders' young players needed a jersey of their own. By his reasoning the old uniform associated with four straight Stanley Cups created a staggeringly high standard for Brett Lindros and Éric Fichaud, who already faced the challenge of matching their hype as top draft picks. "Maybe, just maybe, the Islanders' unprecedented early dynasty has overwhelmed some of the next-generation players," Botta suggested. Evoking the NBA's Boston Celtics, who employed team legend Larry Bird as a special assistant, Botta added, "Do you think it is easy to be wearing Celtic Green these days with Larry Bird in the stands?" Botta's argument here was sensible. The constant comparisons to the dynasty players had to place more pressure on the current team. At some point, as Fichaud acknowledged decades later, "You want to start your own history." However, Botta's implication that former Islanders intimidated their successors had the potential to alienate the alumni. Hearing the claim years later, Nystrom bristled. "I totally disagree with that. The people that are in the rafters should be a motivation to the people that are down on the ice."[8]

In Botta's sixth and final point he framed the logo change as an homage to Long Island. To his credit Botta was transparent about the Islanders' desire to increase revenue from jersey sales, which he argued would generate more money to spend on players. "But that could not be the major reason," he continued. "There had to be a cause. Like another famous Long Islander, the hockey team chose to make a stand for an important sector of the community." Then he cited Billy Joel's support for the baymen of Long Island, specifically in the lyrics for "Downeaster *Alexa*" and in a recent interview in which Joel worried about the death of the fishing industry. Botta appealed to fans' identity not just as Islanders fans but as Long Islanders. "That's why anyone who mocks the idea of having a fisherman as part of the change should be ashamed," Botta wrote. "Having a true 'Islander' as part of the logo would be just one step in calling attention to a proud tradition."[9]

For better or worse, Botta's column laid out a strategy for handling questions about the new logo. However, the front office was not in agreement on how to sell the rebrand. A month after the critical *Daily News* article the same reporter followed up on the logo switch in a story that looked like an olive branch. There was no silly photo illustration, no reference to Gorton's fish sticks. This time, the reporter contacted the team for comment, too. It was a chance for the Islanders to change the narrative surrounding the new jerseys. Botta's talking points had been seen by only a fraction of the fan base, while the *Daily News* reached hundreds of thousands of readers across the metropolitan area. However, the Islanders whiffed. Even after Botta wrote a lengthy defense of the logo, the team was bizarrely noncommittal about the change, saying only that the likelihood of new uniforms was "greater than 50 percent." The ambiguous answer gave the impression the Islanders were having second thoughts. Meanwhile, Pat Calabria, the team's vice president of communications, contradicted Botta by saying the character on the logo was a "mariner," not a fisherman.[10] The logo that symbolized the new brand identity would be unveiled in less than a month, and the Islanders couldn't even agree on what it was.

No matter what the Islanders told the press, the character on the new logo was a fisherman. As Botta acknowledged in his column, the team was inspired by Billy Joel's support for struggling East End fishermen, an account supported by O'Hara. When Joel was shooting the music video for "Downeaster *Alexa*" in 1990 he enlisted members of an advocacy group on Long Island's South Shore named the East Hampton Baymen's Association, which was based two hours east of Nassau Coliseum. For the benefit of Joel's cameras the baymen reenacted their routine in Three Mile Harbor, launching a small boat into the choppy water, dragging one end of a net out from the beach in a large semicircle, and pulling in the ends to reveal an ample catch of striped bass.[11]

The efficient technique, known as haul-seining, was a hallmark of commercial fishing. It also angered the influential sportfishing lobby on Long Island, which complained that haul-seining allowed the baymen to take a disproportionate share of stripers. Soon after Joel's music video was shot, haul-seining was outlawed in New York. The state cited the numbers of small fish supposedly killed by the nets, but the baymen viewed the ban as a purely political move to appease the sportfishermen. Sales of striped bass were also forbidden due to contamination from cancer-causing PCBs. It was a double whammy for the baymen. Without bass, even plentiful catches of other species could not support their crews. "You're talking about a people who are the soul of East Hampton," Arnold Leo, the secretary for the baymen's association, told *National Fisherman* magazine. "They draw their life from the water, and that's why they can't stop fishing." To help the baymen wage legal challenges against the state, Joel donated proceeds from "Downeaster *Alexa*" to the association and played benefit concerts that raised $130,000 for their coffers.[12]

By 1995 the baymen were local celebrities. Besides starring in Joel's music video, they had appeared in the well-received book *Men's Lives* and were regularly quoted in the *New York Times*, *Newsday*, and weekly newspapers on Long Island. Leo's previous career as a book editor made him well suited to polish statements for the press. Calabria, seeking an ally to help sell the new fisherman brand, arranged a meeting with Leo at Nassau Coliseum. Leo had never attended an NHL game, and he considered hockey "a brutal, insane sport," full of checking and fighting. Still, he was intrigued by a potential partnership with the region's only major professional sports franchise. Leo thought the fisherman logo folded into his strategy of presenting the baymen as a signifier of Long Island culture. "To me, this was very positive," he recalled. "It was like, Long Island's hockey team wants us to be their emblem. That much more public support." Within days of his first contact with Calabria, Leo sent the Islanders executive a video-cassette of the "Downeaster *Alexa*" music video as well as newspaper articles and television shows featuring the baymen.[13] Each side began learning about the other.

Unlike the fan base, Leo had no knowledge of Islanders history. He thought the original crest with the Long Island map was "crappy" and "one of the lamest logos I've ever seen." The new jerseys, meanwhile, struck him as intimidating. In one fax to Calabria, Leo wrote, "The new design is just great and we are most happy to be a part of all this." Where the *Daily News* saw the Gorton's fisherman, Leo saw his friends who worked the shores of Amagansett. "If you ever were out on a rough day on the water hauling a gillnet or pulling up lobster pots, that's kind of how you'd look. You were in a battle against the rough, chopping sea." For Leo the baymen's conflict with the ocean befitted a coastal hockey team that clashed with opponents. He was the rare arbiter who endorsed the jersey genuinely and without reservation. "I very much liked the entire configuration, the rough, struggling fisherman himself, the lighthouse, the wave," he said. Leo's support came with media savvy. He gave Calabria a list of reporters whose sympathetic stories on the baymen suggested they might cover the jerseys in a positive light.[14] Leo also agreed to act as a media surrogate at the logo's unveiling and called on two baymen who appeared in the music video, Dan King and Brad Loewen, to join him.

King, the association's president, was a logical choice. With an Amish-style beard and meaty hands, he was almost a doppelgänger for the man in the logo. "They used a picture that looked quite a bit like me," King remembered with a laugh. The resemblance made for a neat photo op. However, even Leo worried the Islanders' embrace of the baymen was problematic. While the baymen enjoyed some positive publicity, they also feuded with sportfishermen over the haul-seining ban. From Leo's perspective, the Islanders' newfound connection with the baymen put them in the middle of a contentious issue. "The sport-fishermen, who were virulent fans of the Islanders hockey team, were insulted that their jersey and all their paraphernalia was emblazoned with this bayman," Leo contended. "And they even knew who it was: Dan King, who was a haul-seiner." Leo was probably overthinking the link between the sportfishing lobby and the attacks on the logo. No period account suggests that fans were angry about the alliance with the baymen. Still, the Islanders took a risk by wading into a local controversy. As King said, "A lot of people think that fishermen are just out to rape the sea and kill all the fish in the world."[15]

The Islanders saw more pros than cons in the affiliation. The team was committed to the new logo, and the baymen's attendance at the press conference would demonstrate support from men whose profession was emblematic of Long Island. "We invited them to be part of the event because of the way the mariner was honoring the legacy they were carrying forward," Calabria said. As a gesture of appreciation the Islanders promised to donate to Leo's association. Before *Men's Lives* and Billy Joel, few people cared about the baymen. Now the Islanders were backing them with the cachet of an NHL team, plus a portion of their revenue. "I thought that was a great idea," Loewen said. "The two things that were very obvious about what the Islanders were were a map of where they were or some of the people. It seemed to me that it would be much more appropriate to have a traditional depiction of traditional people."[16]

As the baymen's newest benefactor the Islanders dreamed of uniting with the man the *New York Times* dubbed "the baymen's friend." Billy Joel was so devoted to the baymen that he cut back on recreational fishing for fear of depleting their catches and was arrested with them at a protest over the state's bass-fishing ban. He considered them the last link to a disappearing way of life. "I'm always looking for the Long Island of my childhood," he told *Newsday*. "There's only a little bit of it left out here on the East End. If that disappears, I really don't know that it is my Long Island anymore." In an appeal to Joel's regional identity the Islanders contacted him about appearing in front of the media with the baymen. The potential star power was tantalizing, but Joel's response was disappointing to the Islanders. "He declined to participate in the press conference or in any way support what we were doing," Calabria said. "He didn't say he was against what we were doing. He just did not want to be involved."[17]

The Islanders pressed on. They put out a media advisory inviting reporters to a news conference in the home team's locker room at Nassau Coliseum on June 22 at 1:00 p.m. "Please keep the location and time confidential," the team requested. The subject of the announcement was not specified, but the timing of a press event amid speculation of a jersey change left little ambiguity.[18]

The day before the news conference the Islanders ran a quarter-page ad in *Newsday* to announce a series of upcoming events, including autograph signings by Brett Lindros and Kirk Muller, a volleyball tournament featuring Derek King and Mick Vukota, and a car wash to benefit a charity for children with Down syndrome. At the bottom was the original Islanders logo, representing the franchise for the last time in 1995.[19]

On the day the Islanders unveiled their new brand identity they were not even the top hockey story in the local market. A season after the Rangers ended their fifty-four-year title drought, the Islanders' other geographic rival, the New Jersey Devils, were just two wins away from their first Stanley Cup. Meanwhile, the Islanders had barely made the playoffs in 1994 and finished last in 1995. The franchise that dominated back pages a decade earlier had been supplanted by what Wayne Gretzky once called a "Mickey Mouse organization."[20]

Among its many stories on the Devils' success, *Newsday* found ink for its hometown team. The Islanders were declining comment to preserve a certain mystery before the news conference, so *Newsday* interviewed the designers of the old and new logos instead. In 1972 advertising agency owner John Alogna was contracted on a Thursday to create a logo for the Islanders by Monday. During the three-day design process, Alogna's Long Island map logo did not receive any advance media coverage. It was an afterthought that just showed up one day as the backdrop for a press conference to introduce the Islanders' first general manager. By 1995 sports branding had become more intensive and sophisticated. The Islanders gave SME a year and a half to design their new jerseys and called a press conference specifically to unveil them. SME cofounder Ed O'Hara told *Newsday* that he understood concerns about changing the only logo the Islanders had ever known, but he had overcome similar pushback on previous projects. "Having been through this many, many times, I know the response is always negative. Every time," he said. "I've got pretty thick skin. But I guarantee this is going to grow on people. They are going to like it." Alogna, meanwhile, was gracious about the desertion of his handiwork. "I guess it's the end of an era," he said. "But if it improves the image of the team and brings it back to where it was, I'm all for it. I'm a fan too."[21]

Morning rolled into afternoon, and reporters began arriving at Nassau Coliseum for the 1:00 p.m. press conference. After nibbling on seafood hors d'oeuvres, they toured an unusual display in the team offices. Propped up on easels in conference rooms and hallways were renderings of potential new logos that the Islanders had rejected. The rough drafts may have been exhibited to assure the media that the fisherman was the result of a thorough and thoughtful process. But they also invited second-guessing about whether the logos left on the drawing board were better than the one about to be unveiled.[22]

With anticipation building, the press assembled for the announcement. Islanders cochairman Stephen Walsh, whose early support for the logo change set the tone in meetings with team executives, unveiled the new jerseys of the eighth NHL club to undergo a makeover in the past decade. "This is Long Island," Walsh said, "and this is a new team."[23]

Two months after the *Daily News* slapped the fisherman on the Islanders' old jersey, the press finally saw the new logo in context. Hanging in the players' lockers were the home whites and road blues, featuring the fisherman on the front and two lighthouse shoulder patches. Each had wave patterns across the shoulders and the waist and by the hands. The names and numbers on the back were disjointed to mimic the rolling sea. The gloves and pants were solid blue. At home the Islanders would wear white-and-blue socks with teal, orange, and silver stripes. On the road the socks would be blue and teal with orange and white stripes.[24]

Although rumors of new uniforms had been circulating for months, the confirmation of the switch surprised some members of the organization, especially after fans expressed outrage about a potential change. "It was just such a shock that the cherished and loved logo was going away and being replaced by anything," said Islanders radio broadcaster Chris King. "That to me was the overwhelming feeling. Whether it was better or worse wasn't what was paramount in my mind. It was just that why are you replacing this logo that they've worn for all these years?"[25]

By now the question was familiar to team management. At the press conference Walsh admitted to receiving five hundred negative letters about the logo, and cochairman Robert Rosenthal only half-jokingly added that ownership was "threatened every day." General manager Don Maloney acknowledged that selling the rebrand to the Islanders' core fans would require prolonged effort. "New fans will love it, casual fans will love it, and, for the traditional fans, we'll have to teach them how to love it."[26]

Still, Walsh was firm. "We also are attuned to the winds of change," he said. "And quite frankly, we believe the time for a new uniform has come."[27]

From ownership's perspective the logo switch was one of the only options to improve the club's flagging finances. Among twenty-six NHL teams the Islanders ranked fifteenth in merchandise sales, twentieth in gate receipts, and twenty-fourth in apparel purchases.[28] They spent more than the league average in player costs but earned less than the average in total revenues.[29] Other teams were building new arenas and maximizing their cash flow by installing luxury boxes and boosting ticket prices. Meanwhile, the Islanders were stuck at the antiquated and ill-maintained Nassau Coliseum, nicknamed "Nassau Mausoleum" due to its dark concourses, leaking roof, and long lines for bathrooms and concessions. Under their lopsided lease the Islanders received no share of parking revenue or concession sales, and they ceded 11 percent of ticket sales and 40 percent of revenues from venue signs to Nassau County. The county pocketed its share of the money without upgrading the arena. The Islanders had forfeited their bargaining power, and the unbeneficial agreement did not expire for another two decades, in 2015.[30]

The numbers helped explain the disconnect between the Islanders and their critics. Fans and reporters saw an organization that lagged behind the Rangers in player spending and made an unnecessary logo change out of a combination of ineptitude and greed. Meanwhile, Islanders management thought cost cutting and new revenue streams were essential just to keep the team on Long Island in the postlockout NHL. To settle the dispute with the players in January,

NHL commissioner Gary Bettman sacrificed a salary cap that would have aided small-market teams like the Islanders. Brett Pickett, the son of Islanders owner John Pickett, said the team could not afford to pay the types of burgeoning salaries that its rivals were dishing out. "The Islanders in that era of free agency post-Bettman started year after year to be lucky to be on Long Island at all. All these people were fighting like hell to keep a franchise in a market where it probably didn't belong anymore."[31]

A decade earlier Islanders fans had spoken of the "Drive for Five," the battle for a fifth straight Stanley Cup. With the team unable to sign marquee free agents or retain its own high-profile players, that fifth title seemed a long way off. Instead, Walsh outlined a drive for dollars from fans who were not even old enough to remember the championship years. "The reality is that merchandising is a major part of the sports business," he said at the press conference to unveil the fisherman jerseys. "We're the youngest team in the league. We should give the guys a chance to have their own identity, but I'd be lying if I told you that increasing our sales wasn't a big part of our thinking. Our fan base is the kids growing up. We have to reach them."[32]

The team spun the change as an homage to Long Island history. Dan King, the president of the baymen's association, posed for photographs with an oversize mock-up of the fisherman logo. The association's secretary, Arnold Leo, told the press that he liked "the fighting spirit" of the jerseys. "I truly did believe that it was a tremendous improvement over what they had formerly had," Leo said.[33] For his support Leo was given one of the first fisherman caps ever made, a day before they went on sale at sporting-goods stores.

In addition to the baymen, the Islanders also enlisted surrogates from their past. Original Islanders player Garry Howatt, who wore the map logo for nine seasons and two championships, said the younger players needed a logo of their own. "Every time we go to a golf tournament or something, somebody brings up the old teams, the Stanley Cup winners," he told a reporter. "All the young guys are there too, and I'm sure they're thinking, Enough already. I know I would. I think this is just great."[34]

In the locker room Islanders players wearing shirts and ties slipped on the new uniforms for photographers. Center Travis Green, who was drafted by the Islanders in 1989, chatted with defenseman Darius Kasparaitis, a pick in 1992. They both grew up during the dynasty years and played on the 1993 team that wore the original logo on its surprising run to the conference final. Now they had become the first models for the replacement logo. "I think me and Travis felt a little weird and awkward," Kasparaitis remembered. "I felt like it was a joke in the beginning. It was just some kind of prank. But then you realize that's gonna be our jersey and that's what we're gonna wear."[35]

One snapshot caught Green, hands in pockets, glancing at the logo on Kasparaitis's chest. "Obviously it was something different," Green said. "As players, you can only control the things you can control and try not to worry about other things."[36]

Also in attendance was defenseman Rich Pilon, who was drafted in 1986. Unlike Green or Kasparaitis, Pilon had been on the Islanders long enough to play with one of the dynasty-era stars, Bryan Trottier. Pilon hailed from Saskatchewan in central Canada and grew up idolizing Trottier, who grew up in the same province. He knew Islanders history well. "Anytime you can put on a jersey like that, there's a lot of accountability to you as an individual to be the best you can be for that team," Pilon said. He did not embrace the logo switch. At the press conference to introduce the fisherman jerseys, Pilon told reporters, "They do make us look bigger." Asked about the quote years later he insisted that he was only searching for a silver lining. "That was just trying to find a positive in something that was not good for me," he said. "It's like anything. Whether it's real life or not, you're trying to find something positive. If you're going to be a Debbie Downer on everything, then the whole team's going to be down, correct?"[37]

The Islanders were smart to promote the jerseys with the men who would wear them. Even if fans were skeptical about ownership's justification for changing the logo, they might respond favorably to their favorite players embracing the new look. But the team made a major misstep. The Islanders tried to curry favor for the fisherman jerseys by calling on one of their least popular players, Kirk Muller, whose refusal to report to Long Island a few months earlier embarrassed the organization.

During his surprise appearance at the press conference Muller pulled on his new number-9 uniform and said the right things, calling the jerseys "lively, colorful," and "awesome." But his endorsement meant little to an offended fan base that viewed him as a reluctant Islander. Worse, his presence backfired on the team. Granted rare access to Muller during the off-season, reporters turned their collective attention away from the jerseys and started asking the former Canadiens captain about his future on Long Island. Muller still had two years remaining on the contract he signed with Montreal, but he informed the press that he was renegotiating his contract with the Islanders to compensate for the poor exchange rate between Canada and the United States. The pack of reporters scrambled over to Maloney for a response. Even though Muller had told them he was "redoing" his contract, Maloney insisted, "I've said to his agent, and I've said to him, we are not renegotiating his deal." The general manager was clearly at odds with his top-line center, reigniting the drama that played out when Maloney first traded for Muller in April.[38]

Maybe Muller wanted off Long Island. Maybe Maloney would trade him. The media ate up the speculation. At its own unveiling the fisherman jersey had become an afterthought.

While Muller was probably the biggest name on the roster, the Islanders wanted another player to be the face of the rebrand. Hours after the press conference the team dispatched nineteen-year-old Brett Lindros to sign autographs at the Smith Haven Mall in Lake Grove, marking the Islanders' first public event of the fisherman jersey era. By holding the signing forty minutes east of Nassau Coliseum, the Islanders were bringing their brand farther into Long Island and closer to where the baymen lived. Promoting a young player like Lindros was also an appeal to teenagers and twentysomethings who tended to spend more on apparel than their parents and might be more receptive to a departure from tradition. Like those young fans, Lindros was not even born when the Islanders' original logo was created in 1972. "We're going through changes right now and maybe the new jersey will help the fan identify with the team a little more," he told a reporter. The adoring crowd of three hundred fans lined up to pose for pictures with Lindros in the new road blue. At six-foot-three and a muscular 217 pounds, he had the heartthrob looks that the franchise hoped would help sell the new jersey to female fans. Judging by the fawning looks he received, the strategy was working. "I think it looks very good on him," said a fourteen-year-old girl from Stony Brook. "I like the old one better, but I guess it's time for a change. They have a whole new team, so why not?"[39]

At the same time Eric Mirlis, the Islanders' assistant director of media relations, was an hour and a half away in East Rutherford, New Jersey. He was on loan from the Islanders to help the NHL handle press for Game Three of the Stanley Cup Final between the Devils and Detroit Red Wings, which was nationally televised by ESPN. Sensing an opportunity, Mirlis asked ESPN rinkside reporter Steve Levy if he could show the fisherman jerseys on air. Levy agreed. During a brief stoppage in play Levy appeared with a boy and a girl wearing Pat Flatley's number 26 and Darius Kasparaitis's number 11. "Here is the future of the National Hockey League," Levy said, turning the children around so the audience could see the disjointed lettering on the backs of the jerseys. Color commentator Bill Clement chimed in, "I like those unis. I like the Islanders' new unis." After months of sniping from the local media, the jerseys received a positive national debut.[40]

Local broadcasters were unconvinced. Len Berman, the sports anchor on Channel 4, lived on Long Island and took his children to the championship parades on Hempstead Turnpike in the early 1980s. He did not understand why the Islanders departed from the tradition that fans cherished. "We had an affinity for anything related to the dynastic Islanders," he recalled. "We want to remember the glory years. Why come up with something that takes away from that?"[41]

On the late-night news on Channel 11, Sal Marchiano covered the logo change with a smirk. Viewers could hear the two news anchors laughing off camera as Marchiano launched into his report. "So I see a couple of marketing guys doing lunch and conceptualizing a new look for the Islanders, the hockey team that hasn't done anything since winning four straight Stanley Cups in the early eighties," he began. The fisherman appeared on screen while Marchiano broke down the color scheme. "It's more about marketing, merchandising, and money than it is about ice hockey. Too fishy for me."

Turning to Marchiano, news anchor Jack Cafferty chuckled and added, "Only thing missing was the tuna."[42]

Sports radio poked more fun at the Islanders. On WFAN 660 AM, host Steve Somers, an unabashed Rangers fan, conferred nautical nicknames upon several members of the organization. Dynasty coach Al Arbour became "Al Harbour." His successor behind the bench went from Lorne Henning to "Lorne Herring." The championship players changed from Clark Gillies to "Clark Gills" and from Bryan Trottier to "Bryan Trouttier." The Islanders' former star was "Pierre Sturgeon," not Turgeon, and their much-hyped prospect was now "Cod Bertuzzi," not Todd. Somers needed to swap only a single letter to transform the Islanders' goaltender of the future from Éric Fichaud to "Éric Fishaud." Learning of Somers's pun decades later, Fichaud laughed. Although New Yorkers tended to mispronounce the first syllable of his last name as "Fee-sch," the correct sound was more like "Fish." He even embraced the nickname "Fish" and wore a mask featuring killer whales during his first training camp with the Islanders. "It's kind of funny," Fichaud said. "By making fun of my name, he was probably pronouncing my name the right way."[43]

The tabloids were not much kinder. The next morning the *Post* offered a backhanded review, calling the jerseys "surprisingly" sleek and "better than expected." The *Daily News* referred to two players photographed in the jerseys as "Fisherman's Friends," an unflattering allusion to the character from the cough-drop brand, adding that the uniforms were "somewhat controversial" and would "supposedly" link the team to local history. *Newsday* invited more criticism of the crest by asking fans to complete a mail-in form with leading questions such as "Did the Islanders need a new logo?" and "If you had designed the new logo, what would you have done differently?"[44]

Others in the media walked away impressed. Beneath the headline "Islanders' New Logo Is a Winner," *Newsday* columnist Steve

Zipay admitted that seeing the jerseys in person changed his mind. He criticized the original Islanders logo as "flat" with an old-fashioned blue-and-orange motif that evoked signage for the 1964–65 New York World's Fair. By contrast, he thought the fisherman jerseys had "some zing, some flair." Zipay described the wavy lettering on the nameplates as "cutting edge," and he believed the gray on the fisherman's beard and stick toned down the brighter colors. "Should look great on TV," he mused. "Now, how about a coach?"[45]

The search for a new coach was more than a personnel decision. It was a major component in rebranding a team that wanted to move past its increasingly distant accomplishments. With the unveiling of their new jerseys on June 22, the Islanders had a new symbol to go along with a new mascot and new faces like Brett Lindros, Éric Fichaud, and Kirk Muller. The firing of coach Lorne Henning, who represented the championship tradition associated with the old logo, created a vacancy for a leader to become synonymous with the Islanders' new brand identity.

The team did not produce under the laidback Henning, and general manager Don Maloney wanted the next coach to crack the whip. "I'm not particularly concerned about a popular name choice in June," he said. "I'm more concerned about who's going to get these guys playing in October, November, and December."[46]

Maloney entertained at least eleven candidates, but most of them did not carry the cachet that would elevate the team's brand. Canadian junior coaches Craig Hartsburg and Don Hay had no experience behind the bench in the major leagues. Then there were former NHL coaches with unremarkable records and little star power, such as George Burnett of the Edmonton Oilers, Dave King of the Calgary Flames, Roger Neilson of the Florida Panthers, and Pierre Pagé of the Quebec Nordiques. A seventh candidate, legendary Canadiens defenseman Larry Robinson, was a hot commodity fresh off winning the Stanley Cup as an assistant with the Devils. His market was developing too slowly for the Islanders.[47]

Tellingly, the Islanders also dismissed two strong candidates with connections to their Stanley Cup dynasty. Butch Goring, who played for all four championship teams, had led the Boston Bruins to a playoff berth in 1986 and guided the Islanders' minor league affiliate, the Denver Grizzlies, to a 109-36-17 record over the past two seasons. Another option, Brian Sutter, was the brother of two cogs on the dynasty teams, Brent and Duane, and he had won 273 NHL games and the 1991 Jack Adams Award as the league's best coach. Sutter had a reputation for toughness, exactly the sort of personality that Maloney said he wanted. But neither Goring nor Sutter had much pizzazz, and their associations with the old Islanders identity may have counted against them.[48]

Instead, Maloney was drawn to the two splashiest names on the market. ESPN analysts Barry Melrose and Mike Milbury made regular appearances on the leading sports television network, and each previously took teams to the Stanley Cup Final in their rookie seasons as coaches. At first glance Melrose or Milbury would slot in nicely with the Islanders' rebrand: luring a high-profile television personality would draw media attention and distract from the logo controversy. Both men would also command a lofty salary, so signing one of them would prove the Islanders were willing to spend. However, they lacked experience with rebuilding teams. Milbury went to the Cup Final with the 1990 Bruins, who had all-stars Ray Bourque and Cam Neely in their primes, while Melrose's 1993 Kings relied on the scoring touches of Tony Granato, Wayne Gretzky, and Luc Robitaille. The Islanders did not have the means to supply their new coach with that level of talent. Both men also had short coaching résumés: Milbury became assistant general manager after only two seasons behind the Bruins' bench, and Melrose was fired midway through his third season with the Kings. By the summer of 1995 Sutter had coached 536 regular-season games to Melrose's 209 and Milbury's 160. Melrose and Milbury may have been glamorous by virtue of their television work, but the Islanders brand would have benefited more from winning than razzle-dazzle.[49]

Early in the search Long Island's newspaper made a strong endorsement. Beneath the headline "Isles Need Milbury," *Newsday* columnist Jim Smith openly challenged Maloney to sign the fiery former defenseman. Smith reasoned away Milbury's history of drifting between jobs: his resignation as Bruins coach after only two seasons in 1991, his departure as assistant general manager in 1994, and a two-month stint as coach at Boston College that ended when Milbury quit over "philosophical differences" with the athletic director before a single game. Smith also twisted Milbury's unorthodox tactics with the Bruins. Milbury was once so angry after a playoff loss that he left his players at the dinner table to pay for their own meals and checked them into a fleabag hotel. His actions could be viewed as the mark of a volatile man. Smith held them up as a laudable display of tough love.[50]

Milbury's past was even more checkered than Smith acknowledged. As a defenseman in 1979 he was at the center of one of the most surreal and violent incidents in NHL history when the Bruins climbed into the stands at Madison Square Garden and fought with Rangers fans. At one point Milbury pinned a man across a seat and began beating him with his own shoe in what became the enduring image of the brawl. He was suspended for six games and fined $500.[51] A decade later Milbury was just as unpredictable. By virtue of the Bruins' appearance in the 1990 Stanley Cup Final, he became an automatic coach in the 1991 NHL All-Star Game, allowing him to fill out the majority of the roster. In a controversial decision, he passed up Kirk Muller, a four-time all-star, in favor of a Bruins enforcer with an unsavory reputation. The decision indicated that Milbury did not think much of the man now centering the Islanders' top line.[52]

Still, Smith was unequivocal in *Newsday*. He pointed to Milbury's two playoff runs with the Bruins and labeled him "the best man available" to become the Islanders coach. Given Milbury's aspirations for a front-office job, Smith even wondered if Maloney, with one season left on his own contract, had "the guts" to hire his potential successor.[53]

The media pressure seemed to work. As the Fourth of July approached, news broke that the Islanders were close to signing Milbury. Using the same phrase from Smith's article, a team source was quoted saying, "Everybody thought Donnie didn't have the guts to hire Mike and he did." Milbury understood his role in the Islanders' new brand identity. He told *Newsday* that he appreciated how the team was "rebuilding, everything from a new logo to a new infrastructure."

He signed a five-year contract reportedly worth $3.5 million, making him one of the best-paid coaches in hockey.[54]

On July 5 the Islanders introduced their sixth coach at a press conference in a restaurant in Westbury. Standing in front of a large mock-up of the fisherman logo, the forty-three-year-old Milbury pulled on an Islanders jacket while cameras flashed. For a rebranded organization in desperate need of excitement, the signing was a rare public relations triumph in the short term. The *New York Times* credited ownership with hiring "the best available candidate." Flamboyant television commentator Don Cherry, who coached Milbury in Boston, called him a "tremendous choice for the Islanders." The deal gave the impression that the Islanders could afford top-tier talent without breaking the bank on more lucrative player salaries. Milbury vowed to bring his trademark intensity to Nassau Coliseum. "It doesn't mean you have to be a raving maniac day after day," he said, "although that will happen."[55]

Milbury made clear his intention to move away from the history of the organization. "I've heard enough talk about people wanting to put the past behind them that it must be an issue for some people," he said. "It just doesn't happen to be an issue for me. That was somebody else's past, not mine. In a way, that's maybe why I'm here, and not somebody else. I'm part of a fresh approach to this thing. As much as I respect what was won then, I don't live that day to day. And neither should these guys. And they won't."[56]

In fact, the Islanders' new coach had reason to despise the tradition associated with the Islanders' old logo. His twelve seasons with the Bruins from 1975 to 1987 overlapped with the Islanders' rise to prominence and dominance, including two seasons when New York eliminated Boston from the postseason. As an irritant on a series of gritty Bruins teams, Milbury tussled with the Islanders' Gord Dineen and Bob Nystrom and fought Duane Sutter three times in six days during the 1980 playoffs. Milbury had been such an antagonist during the dynasty era that his hiring as coach threatened to alienate the alumni.

At his introductory press conference Milbury took a shot at the Stanley Cup players by suggesting they overstayed their welcomes on Long

Island. Many of them had remained on the roster long after the last championship in 1983, and their declining production contributed to the gradual deterioration of the brand. "I think it was widely viewed around the league that this team may have fallen victim to its own sense of loyalty to its players," Milbury said. "Perhaps because of the Stanley Cups that were won in the 1980s, they felt the obligation to let that team stay intact until everybody retired. In retrospect, I think it was a mistake for them, and probably for the players."[57] The Islanders later released a commemorative videotape in which the narrator claimed that Milbury was "respectful of the past" from his first day on the job.[58] But the *New York Times* was more accurate with its headline, "New Coach Emphasizes Break with Isles' Past."

In the crowd were veteran Islanders players Pat Flatley, Derek King, and Mick Vukota, who were teammates in the late 1980s with the same dynasty stars that Milbury was knocking. But Vukota was more focused on Milbury's promise of a long-term plan to bring the Islanders back into contention. "I'm that guy that drinks the Kool-Aid," Vukota said. "So I'm in. You got me. I was excited." The *Islander Insider* newsletter announced the hiring with equal enthusiasm. "Hate the new logo? Hate the new colors?" a front-page column asked. "You should love that the Islanders are finally moving in the right direction!" In a conversation with Milbury one reporter pointed out that fans loved the new coach and hated the new logo. "By the end of the season," Milbury cracked, "that will be totally reversed."[59]

Although Milbury's arrival earned instant kudos from players and fans, the rebranding of the Islanders remained incomplete. As the press pointed out, the team had little chance of success unless Milbury was granted the scorers and solid goaltenders that Henning lacked. "The mandate now is for the organization to make the uniform look better by providing the depth that leads to job competition," the *Daily News* opined, "and for the players to make the uniform look better by the performance it should require to keep their jerseys on a nightly basis." Maloney agreed that Milbury alone could not save the new Islanders brand. "The only thing we expect out of Mike right now is to make sure the team shows heart," he said. "It's up to us to get the personnel."[60]

4

NEW TEAM, DASHED DREAM

After unveiling a new logo in June and a new coach in July, the Islanders had three months to assemble a new roster to wear the fisherman
jerseys in their inaugural season. Putting together the right mix of
youth and experience was critical to the success of the rebrand. More
than any other factor, the team's performance in 1995–96 would dictate fans' long-term response to the fisherman jerseys. "Everyone
knew if the team succeeded, everyone would buy into the new logo,"
said Pat Calabria, the Islanders' vice president of communications.
"But if the team didn't succeed, it would be a lightning rod for all
the team's failures."[1]

The Islanders entered the off-season with several holdovers worth
keeping. Still under contract were captain Pat Flatley, who tied for
second on the team in points in the 1994–95 season, and secondary
scorers Derek King and Marty McInnis, who were fourth and seventh.
The team could almost bank on more goals from sophomore forwards
Brett Lindros and Žiggy Pálffy and another year of solid defense from
Scott Lachance, Rich Pilon, Mathieu Schneider, and Dennis Vaske.
Goaltenders Jamie McLennan, Tommy Salo, and Tommy Söderström
all had flashes of brilliance the previous season, and maybe somebody
from the trio would emerge as a number one. Still, the Islanders did not
have the types of stars who sold tickets and merchandise, and a winning
season would require more talent than the core of a team that finished
with the second-worst record in the NHL. In a twenty-six-team league,
the Islanders ended the season nineteenth in goals against and twenty-
first in goals scored. During the season, they waived Troy Loney and
traded away Benoit Hogue, Vladimir Malakhov, and Pierre Turgeon,
who collectively accounted for 21 percent of their goals. Worse, they

played uninspiringly in the home stretch under Lorne Henning. "In the end, they fell apart," Mike Milbury said at his introductory press conference. "I don't know why. There is no question there is good potential in goal. There is a very competent defensive group. As far as the forwards are concerned, I don't know how it's all going to shake out, but last year, they clearly didn't have enough scoring or intensity to make things work."[2]

The Islanders had little means to beef up their scoring. Operating on a tight budget the previous summer, general manager Don Maloney offered one of his best players, pending free agent Ray Ferraro, a 19 percent pay cut.[3] Ferraro rejected the deal, raised his value by leading the Islanders with twenty-two goals and twenty-one assists in the 1994–95 season, and signed with the Rangers for an annual salary more than triple Maloney's offer.[4] Meanwhile, the Islanders' fourth-leading scorer, restricted free agent Steve Thomas, believed Maloney was short-changing him on a new contract. Only two years removed from a forty-two-goal season, Thomas wanted $1.7 million per year, a reasonable bump, but Maloney refused to go higher than $1.5 million. Thomas, the rare scorer who readily engaged in fisticuffs to defend his teammates, was offended. "I'm willing to drop my gloves and fight anybody, and that's considered a major intangible but it's not rewarded," he complained to a reporter.[5] The team was also locked in tense negotiations with its de facto number-one center, Kirk Muller, and sparkplug defenseman Darius Kasparaitis.[6] The Islanders' stinginess prevented them from being legitimate players on the free-agent market in the summer of 1995, as much as a superstar would have buoyed the rebrand.

The Islanders were also too complacent with their goaltending. McLennan, Salo, and Söderström combined for a .891 save percentage, the fourth-worst in the league, with a middling 3.21 goals-against average. The franchise's supposed goaltender of the future, Éric Fichaud, had an alarming 3.44 goals-against average in juniors, and he had yet to play an NHL game.[7] In order for the Islanders to compete in 1995–96, they could have used a veteran goaltender to back up his younger teammates and serve as a mentor. Opportunity arrived when the Oilers shopped all-star goalie Bill Ranford, who won the 1989–90 Conn Smythe Trophy as the best player in the Stanley Cup playoffs, and the Panthers offered John Vanbiesbrouck, winner of the 1985–86 Vezina Trophy as the league's best goalie. Both Ranford, twenty-eight, and Vanbiesbrouck, thirty-one, had some of their best seasons ahead of them.[8] The Islanders passed on both, probably unwilling to pay their premium salaries.

With little money to entice free agents, the Islanders' best chance to improve before the season came at the 1995 Entry Draft. Almost immediately after Milbury was introduced as the Islanders' next coach, he flew with the team's brain trust to Edmonton, where the draft would be held three days later. By virtue of their poor on-ice performance, the Islanders had three picks in the first two rounds, including the prized second selection. In another departure from the Stanley Cup dynasty, the Islanders pulled the draft duties from their longtime head scout Gerry "Tex" Ehman, who selected many of their championship players in the 1970s.[9] Upon Ehman's demotion the *Islander Insider* newsletter waxed, "He helped bring us a team the likes of which we'll never see again. They were the Yankees, Celtics, Notre Dame at their best. They were Ray Robinson, Louis, Ali at their peak." Ehman was also responsible for bringing on board some of the most promising players on the Islanders' current roster. However, two high-profile missteps left him vulnerable under the Maloney regime. Handed the second overall pick in 1989, Ehman bypassed future stars Bill Guerin and Bobby Holik in favor of Dave Chyzowski, who scored only fifteen goals in 110 games. A year later Ehman overlooked Keith Tkachuk and Doug Weight and used the sixth-overall pick on Scott Scissons, who played only three games with the Islanders due to injuries. "Those were two very high picks," said Maloney, who became general manager in 1992. "I'm not throwing daggers at anybody because it's just the luck of the draw. But we just can't do that in the future." With Ehman shelved, assistant general manager Darcy Regier was put in charge of the 1995 draft.[10]

When Maloney arrived in Edmonton he had more pressing concerns than draft picks. After many months of negotiations the team had only a few days left to come to terms with its first-round selection from

1993, twenty-year-old left wing Todd Bertuzzi, or watch him reenter the draft.[11] At an imposing six-foot-three and 222 pounds, the feisty Bertuzzi had good hands, a hard shot, and toughness.[12] His numbers in juniors were tantalizing: Bertuzzi was coming off a breakout season in which he scored fifty-four goals and sixty-five assists in only 62 games. In anxious negotiations with the Islanders, Bertuzzi's agent insisted that his client was among the top three hockey players who had yet to make the NHL, and he was probably right.[13] Placing Bertuzzi on a line with Travis Green and Žiggy Pálffy could give the Islanders a formidable trio for at least a few years until they hit free agency, but both sides were stubborn. The Islanders had until midnight before the draft to strike a deal with Bertuzzi, and they were not even talking at 10:30 p.m. "At 11 o'clock, we thought nothing was going to happen," Bertuzzi said. "At 11:30, we still didn't have a deal," added Maloney. Eventually, they understood they needed each other. Losing a top prospect would have been embarrassing for Maloney, and the new collective bargaining agreement meant that Bertuzzi would make less money if he reentered the draft. With minutes to spare the sides reached an agreement and rushed to the NHL's makeshift office in a nearby hotel to submit the paperwork by the deadline. The contract paid $4.6 million over four years.[14]

Milbury, who had just struck his own deal with Maloney, spent the draft filling out his coaching staff. Milbury was a hard-driving coach, and he wanted gentler voices to balance the bench. He decided to retain Bob Froese, the goaltending coach under Henning, and hired Guy Charron, an assistant coach for five seasons with the Flames, as his right-hand man. A star center in the 1970s, Charron was tired of being passed over for the head-coaching job in Calgary, so he quit and drove three hours north to Edmonton in hopes of landing with a new team at the draft. Milbury was one of the few people to meet with him. "I knew of Mike's reputation and career and he'd had success as a coach with the Bruins and those kind of things," Charron said. "But I have to be sincere by just saying mostly it was an opportunity for me to work and not having to look. Sometimes there's a sense of insecurity, and I guess I had a sense of insecurity."[15]

While most assistants called out line changes, Milbury liked to handle the entire bench himself, rotating forwards and defensemen on and off the ice. Charron would be involved in power plays and penalty kills, but he anticipated playing a more important role as a mediator. Milbury expected the Islanders to play as physically as the Bruins of the 1970s and 1980s, while many of his European and Russian players had been trained to skate smoothly and score with finesse. Even North Americans on the Islanders' roster would bristle at attempts to be molded into the image of a coach who averaged four goals per season and never made an all-star team. "Let's face it, without being harsh about his career, he was a hard-nosed type of guy," Charron said. "He played the game hard. He played the game like Boston Bruin identity. He liked that from a player." Given Milbury's reputation in Boston, his assistants knew they would be expected to reassure players after Milbury screamed, issued challenges, and ran them through demanding practices. "That's what I considered a big part of my role, not so much as a mediator, but as someone who was going to encourage the guys," Froese said. "And it's tough. It's a big man's game, big boy's game, big cities, fans that want to win, but nobody wants to go out there and make a fool of themselves."[16]

At the moment Maloney feared embarrassing himself at the draft. He faced a tough decision with the second overall pick. While the Islanders needed scoring, the best players available were a trio of defensemen. Maloney had the chance to package the second pick in a trade for a proven NHL scorer such as Teemu Selanne or Alexei Yashin, both of whom would have added much-needed star power, or select one of the top forwards in the draft, such as future all-stars Shane Doan or Jarome Iginla. Instead, the Islanders followed conventional wisdom and took eighteen-year-old Canadian defenseman Wade Redden, a strong skater with poise, speed, and a smooth stride. Redden was offensively minded, but he was unlikely to make an immediate impact, and his fourteen goals and forty-six assists in juniors paled against the production that Doan and Iginla could have provided. In the second round Maloney chose Jan Hlaváč, a two-way forward from the Czech

Republic, and another defenseman, D. J. Smith.[17] None of the three would ever play a game with the Islanders.

Although the Islanders failed to land a splashy player in Edmonton, the draft offered an opportunity to publicize their new brand to a large television audience. Viewers watched Redden put on a jersey and a hat with the Islanders' new maritime imagery. "I like that new logo," he told a reporter. On the draft floor the NHL had outfitted every team's table with specially made cord phones covered by a goalie's mask. Eric Mirlis, the Islanders' assistant director of media relations, was smitten with the Islanders' phone, which had the fisherman logo on top, lighthouses on the sides, and a wordmark across the chin, so he took it home. The phone remained on his shelf decades later, still in working condition.[18]

In July twenty-eight-year-old Islanders defenseman Chris Luongo invited teammates to his wedding in Vermont. Luongo had played all but one game for the Islanders in 1994–95, but he had been shuttled among three organizations in the past four seasons and was hardly assured of a roster spot on a team that counted defense as its lone strength. When the Islanders equipment manager arrived at the marriage ceremony with a newly stitched fisherman jersey featuring Luongo's nameplate, the player was touched. It was a gesture intended to show that he had a place on the team that would take the ice in October. "That was pretty doggone neat to me," Luongo said. "I was not as concerned about exactly what the logo looked like and thought that was a pretty neat thing for them to do."[19]

As the summer continued and the free-agent market intensified, the Islanders made no notable changes to their weak roster, even after losing Ferraro to the Rangers. Then August brought a controversial shake-up in their broadcast booth. After the departure of longtime Islanders announcer Jiggs McDonald, SportsChannel hired his replacement, Howie Rose, a radio analyst for the Rangers for six years. An impeccable broadcaster with an encyclopedic command of local hockey history, Rose had been a fixture on the New York sports scene for two decades, voicing updates for the telephone dial-in service SportsPhone, working for WHN and WCBS radio, and joining WFAN upon its inception in 1987. He also hosted pre- and postgame shows for the New York Mets and called two NHL All-Star Games. The only problem was his association with the Islanders' top rival. Rose made the most famous call of his career when the Rangers advanced to the Stanley Cup Final in 1994 on an overtime goal by Stéphane Matteau. Any highlight reel from the Rangers' championship season included Rose's excited call of "Matteau! Matteau!" It was a moment that Islanders fans wanted to forget.[20]

SportsChannel's hiring of Rose was justified, but it created an awkward situation for a franchise trying to distance itself from the smear of the 1994 playoff sweep by the Rangers. As Newsday's Steve Zipay pointed out, "So the opinionated—some say arrogant—Rose, who has raised the hackles of Islanders fans for bashing the team on-air, will be in front of the cameras in Uniondale before you know it." A few months earlier Islander Insider had compiled an unfavorable report card of the hosts on WFAN, calling the station "anything but hockey radio" for dismissing callers who tried to talk about the three local teams. The newsletter issued an A grade to Rose for talking about hockey but said that he could be egotistical and out of touch. "Knocks Islander fans for rooting against the Rangers. (Howie, do you really believe Ranger fans don't root against the Islanders?)." Rose, who grew up in New York City rooting for the Rangers, endured an uncomfortable speaking engagement when a member of the Islanders' booster club asked in an accusatory tone whether he hated the Rangers now that he would be calling Islanders games. Rose responded that he did not, and he was never invited back. "A lot of people made me feel as though I were an outsider infiltrating enemy territory," Rose recalled. "I was getting paid to do a job."[21]

Rose tried to smooth things over with the fan base by writing a full-page column for the Islanders' program. Rather than disavowing the Rangers, he pointed out that he grew up in New York in the 1960s, when there was only one hockey team in town. After the Islanders came into existence in 1972 he covered their games as a college student and for WHN, and then he moved with his wife and children to

Long Island, less than fifteen minutes from Nassau Coliseum and even closer to their practice facility in Syosset. As a clincher Rose said he celebrated his new job with SportsChannel by going out with his wife, Barbara, for a special meal paying homage to Islanders history. In the late 1970s the Islanders ran a promotion that guaranteed fans a free bowl of chili from the Wendy's fast-food chain if the team scored six goals in a game. During a game versus the Rangers the Islanders were running up the score when a Wendy's executive announced that ten goals would mean a second bowl for free. When the tenth goal was scored the scoreboard triumphantly flashed, "DOUBLE CHILI!" Rose remembered the moment well. Describing the dinner with his wife, he wrote, "Barbara took me to . . . Wendy's. For chili. Yeah, a big bowl, too. Twice the size of a regular one. Double chili. I ate the whole thing. The transformation is complete. I'm an Islander, and I couldn't be prouder."[22]

A heaping bowl of beef and beans wasn't enough to convince fans. They were skeptical about an increasing number of former Rangers hired for high-profile positions in the Islanders organization at a time when the team claimed to be differentiating itself from the big-city club with a fisherman jersey. The man entrusted with the franchise, general manager Don Maloney, played eleven seasons for the Rangers from 1978 to 1988, a period when the teams faced each other five times in the playoffs. Some conspiracy theorists questioned Maloney's intentions. "I know there were fans who kept saying, 'What, did the Rangers send him there as a spy to destroy them?'" broadcaster Stan Fischler remembered. "That was a common, common thing, of course." Other former Rangers employees on the Islanders staff included goaltending coach Bob Froese, who manned the nets in Madison Square Garden for four seasons in the late 1980s, and media relations director Ginger Killian Serby, a former member of the Rangers' public relations staff. There was even speculation that two Islanders minority owners, Robert Rosenthal and Stephen Walsh, were Rangers fans. Art Feeney, the editor of *Islander Insider*, said he once glanced into the owner's box at Nassau Coliseum after the Rangers scored against the Islanders. "Rosenthal leaped to his feet and started cheering," Feeney said. "So that's the kind of owners we had here."[23] The appearance of mixed allegiances did not bode well for the rebrand.

As summer wound down the Islanders undertook their first ad campaign involving the fisherman logo. Published in *Newsday*, the ads revealed the Islanders' community outreach efforts in the critical final weeks before the 1995–96 season. One ad announced an upcoming charity softball game involving Travis Green, Darius Kasparaitis, and Marty McInnis in Massapequa and player appearances at banks in Hicksville and Westbury and malls in Massapequa and Lake Grove. Another ad announced a special presentation by the Islanders at a salute to firefighters at the Crest Hollow Country Club in Woodbury.[24] All but one of the events were held in Nassau County, even though the new uniforms were supposedly adopted to encourage East End fans to come to games. The one autograph signing in Suffolk, at the Smith Haven Mall in Lake Grove, was more than an hour's drive west from the baymen's base in East Hampton. Holding events closer to the tip of Long Island would have been a better strategy to grow the fan base.

Tellingly, the newspaper ads positioned three people—Mike Milbury, Brett Lindros, and Mathieu Schneider—as the faces of the rebrand. In August a full-page ad encouraged fans to buy season tickets by offering admittance to an exclusive question-and-answer session with the new coach at Nassau Coliseum. Large type blared, "Go One-on-One with the Coach Next Week." Two weeks later the team unveiled its slogan for the season, "New Team, Same Dream," with another full-page spot focused on Milbury. Across the top of the page was the statement, "This is our new coach," with a close-up of Milbury's face, his eyes staring into the camera, his brows furrowed, and his lips sealed. Beneath the coach was another phrase, "This is our new attitude," and a photograph of nails. The implication was clear: fans would not want to miss the tough-as-nails Milbury changing the culture of the Islanders. The team also forwarded its new brand with ads comparing Lindros to a wrecking ball and Schneider to a panther. A fourth ad showed the jerseys—"This is our new uniform"—above lightning strikes.[25] While many hockey teams try to convey toughness in their advertising, the particular comparisons in the Islanders' ads were strange. A year earlier the Islanders had dismissed the idea of a duck mascot out of fear of brand confusion with the Mighty Ducks of Anaheim. Now they were presenting themselves with imagery that conjured two other NHL teams, the Florida Panthers and the Tampa Bay Lightning.

September brought the Islanders' first training camp under Milbury. During the summer the players received letters from their new coach warning that the upcoming season would be the most exhausting of their careers. The words were intimidating to some, inspiring to others.[26] The day after center Ray Ferraro signed with the Rangers in July, Milbury telephoned the man in the best position to take his place on the Islanders' roster, twenty-five-year-old Travis Green. Green, who blamed himself for being out of shape the previous season, scored only five goals in forty-two games. In a straightforward conversation Milbury told Green to arrive in camp in the best physical condition of his life. "I knew he was going to be a butt-kicker," Green said at the time. "For some people that might not be good news, but for me it was. After the season I had last year, a different approach was probably the best thing for me." Green's response, in word and in deed, illustrates Milbury's skill in motivating certain players. After a summer spent running on the track of a high school in Glen Cove, Green arrived at camp in peak condition, breezing through a two-mile run in under twelve minutes. "Travis showed me a lot," Milbury said. "To be honest, I didn't know what to expect from the guy. But it looks like the work ethic is there, and he has a lot more skill than most people realize." Green ended up having the best season of his career under Milbury, scoring twenty-five goals and forty-five assists. Years later Green remembered how Milbury ignited him. "Mike put a lot of people on high alert that he was gonna challenge players," he said. "He was gonna expect the players were in the right shape. And you knew going in that there was gonna be some tough times. It wasn't gonna be easy."[27]

With Milbury at the helm the Islanders had reason for hope heading into their first season in the fisherman jerseys. Nine players remained from the 1993 team that dethroned the two-time defending Stanley Cup champions on its way to the Eastern Conference Final. Seven others were on the club that made the playoffs in 1994. The Islanders also had Kirk Muller and Mathieu Schneider, two cogs from the Canadiens' championship team just two years prior. The youth movement included an array of highly touted prospects. Ten first-round draft picks were projected to make the roster: Muller (number two in 1984), Scott Lachance (number four in 1991), Darius Kasparaitis (number five in 1992), Brad Dalgarno (number six in 1985), Brett Lindros (number nine in 1994), Derek King (number thirteen in 1985), Dean Chynoweth (number thirteen in 1987), Éric Fichaud (number sixteen in 1994), Pat Flatley (number twenty one in 1982), and Todd Bertuzzi (number twenty-three in 1993). Fans longing for a contender saw just enough talent to convince themselves that the Islanders would make the playoffs. "For the first time in 4 years, I say they'll get in," Art Feeney wrote in *Islander Insider*. "I've been wrong 2 of the last 3 seasons . . . why should I be right now? An obvious reason is Mike Milbury."[28]

A new coach meant a fresh start for players who felt underappreciated under Lorne Henning. Darius Kasparaitis's agent said that the defenseman would have "gone fishing" rather than report if Henning was still the coach. It may have been hyperbole, but it spoke to the possible benefit of hiring a new coach to lead the rebrand. With a lot of open spots on the roster, the Islanders' role players were hungry to perform for Milbury in camp and earn more playing time. "I knew with the new coach you had to make an impression on him," said defenseman Dean Chynoweth. "I was always kind of a bubble guy that was in and out and trying to get myself established still." Under Henning, left wing Niklas Andersson, once a celebrated member of the Swedish team at the World Junior Championships, spent the entire 1994–95 season with the Islanders' minor league affiliate in Denver. When Milbury gave the twenty-four-year-old Andersson a chance to play on the Islanders' top line, he had a career season with fourteen goals. "He was a tough coach for sure," Andersson said. "But on the other hand, he's the guy that gave me the chance too, so I have him to thank for a lot of things." Despite Maloney's inability to add a superstar over the summer, the fall brought about the annual excitement that came with the changing of the seasons and the first sounds of skates cutting into ice at Nassau Coliseum. A year earlier right wing Dan Plante tore his ACL in training camp, an injury that ended his season before it began. "It was something I wanted to put behind myself pretty quickly," Plante said. "I worked pretty hard in the summer and obviously the year before rehabbing, so when you get the opportunity to get on the ice and pull that sweater back on, it's pretty gratifying after all the hard work."[29]

At least initially, the mocking of the fisherman jerseys mattered little to players hoping to stick with an NHL team. After bouncing between Winnipeg, Tampa Bay, and New Jersey in his first six years in the league, right wing Danton Cole signed with the Islanders around the start of training camp in the hopes of extending his career into his late twenties. Although Cole had just tasted success with the Stanley Cup Champion Devils, his disappointing statistics—four goals and five assists in thirty-eight games—left him in no position to dismiss a franchise with a budding jersey controversy. "I certainly wasn't the type of player that I could say, 'I want to play in these three places,' because I liked their jerseys. I didn't have the ability to be that picky. Not really. The NHL is the gold standard. If you're playing there, you're a good player and the guys you're playing with are really good. For a lot of us, we were just trying to stay in the NHL and play as long as we could, regardless of the uniform situation." Cole's addition to the roster gave the Islanders a former twenty-goal scorer only a few months removed from playing on a championship team. "When you're around winners and win, that's a good thing to have around," he said. "That's kind of what I was as a player, and I certainly thought I could bring that to the Islanders."[30]

Still, a quiet off-season left the Islanders without much improvement to the scoring and goaltending that sank them the previous year. At the outset of training camp Derek King and Kirk Muller were the only two forwards who had ever scored more than twenty-five goals in a season. There was such a lack of centers that Milbury put winger Marty McInnis in the middle of a line. Few of the forwards were quick enough to kill penalties. There was no clear favorite to start in goal. Injured defensemen Scott Lachance and Rich Pilon figured to miss opening night, and unsigned free agents Darius Kasparaitis, Steve Thomas, and Dennis Vaske did not even report. In an off-season when they lost leading scorer Ray Ferraro, the Islanders' most significant free-agent acquisitions were Cole, fringe Rangers defenseman Joby Messier, and journeyman left wing Jim McKenzie, who had only seventeen goals in 287 career games. "The signings of McKenzie, Danton Cole & Joby Messier won't turn this team around," the *Islander Insider* stewed. "Maloney's club must show immense improvement this season or else. Don can't sit on his hands this time. If he does, Milbury could move up."[31]

Maloney was constantly reminded that he hired a coach who might soon replace him as general manager. In an interview with *Newsday*, Islanders chief operating officer Ralph Palleschi expressed "full confidence" in Maloney, who was in the final year of his contract, but admitted there had been no discussions about an extension. "We have reached a decision to pay people based on what they've produced," Palleschi said. "Donnie is confident enough in how he's putting this team together to feel the same way." With a new deal dependent on the team's performance in the 1995–96 season, Maloney must have felt pressure to improve the roster immediately. Asked if he could be fired if the Islanders got off to a poor start, Maloney replied, "You'd have to ask my bosses. I would hope not. But on the other hand, maybe I should be. If we flounder, there's casualties. So be it."[32] It was hard to tell whether his comments were an expression of confidence in his handiwork or resignation that his days were numbered.

To his credit Maloney was actively trying to bolster the offense. A few days into training camp he traded a fifth-round pick in the 1997 draft for enigmatic center Alexander Semak, who had scored thirty-seven goals with the Devils three seasons prior before a knee injury derailed his career. Then Maloney looked for a high-profile player to accompany the rebrand. Among his targets were two young all-stars, the Ottawa Senators' Alexei Yashin and the Chicago Blackhawks' Jeremy Roenick. Yashin's demand for $2.5 million per year hindered the cash-strapped Islanders. Chicago offered Roenick in exchange for Lachance, Redden, and Éric Fichaud, but Maloney said he did not want to lose three pieces of the team's future for a single superstar.[33] Running out of options, Maloney agreed to trade Lachance and Redden to Winnipeg for Keith Tkachuk, an all-star left wing who ranked among the NHL leaders with forty-one goals and forty assists in 1993–94. Tkachuk, at twenty-three years old, might have formed a top line for years to come with Green, twenty-four, and Pálffy, twenty-three. The trade also made sense from a marketing standpoint. The majority of NHL players hailed from Canada or Europe, but Tkachuk was born in Massachusetts. His distinction as an American hockey star could help the Islanders sell fisherman jerseys to audiences on Long Island and perhaps throughout the country. Alas, he never arrived. The trade was contingent on the Islanders' ability to sign Tkachuk, and Tkachuk's agent did not return Maloney's phone calls. Instead, the Islanders' would-be left wing of the future signed an offer sheet with Chicago, and Winnipeg matched.[34]

Meanwhile, Milbury was solidifying himself as a media darling, often at the expense of the roster that Maloney assembled. The *New York Times* speculated that Milbury, the most high-profile face of the Islanders' new brand, would "try to draw attention to a team in transition as it fights for visibility in a crowded sports marketplace."[35] Absent a star-laden roster, one way to generate headlines was through offbeat comments to reporters. In an age when most coaches spoke in dull, diplomatic tones, Milbury was authentic and unpredictable. He offered reporters these sorts of assessments of his players during training camp and the preseason:

TODD BERTUZZI: His fuse may be slower to light than others, but he's still got it.[36]

DANTON COLE: If you put it all down on paper, he was more in the fifth-line category than the fourth-line category.[37]

BRAD DALGARNO: The only thing that keeps Brad Dalgarno from being an outstanding player in this league is Brad Dalgarno.[38]

ÉRIC FICHAUD: He seems like a fairly self-confident individual, as in cocky as hell. I don't mind an edge of cockiness as long as it doesn't spread over to arrogance.[39]

WADE REDDEN: If he can't figure out that was the dumbest move he made all camp, then I can't help him out. He could have been whistling, "Whistle While You Work," there. He was mentally stagnant on that play.[40]

ALEXANDER SEMAK: I haven't seen him do a damn thing. I played [his] line until midway through the second period when I couldn't take it anymore. He's supposed to play like a North American in our zone and a European in the offensive zone. He's got it backwards.[41]

While Milbury's act was entertaining and matched the no-nonsense image the Islanders were promoting, his unorthodox ways disaffected the players whose performance would dictate the success of the rebrand. The Islanders' captain, Pat Flatley, called Milbury "intimidating."[42] In one of his first scrimmages as coach, he shoved Redden in the chest for not bodychecking. "It kind of shocked me a bit," Redden said.[43] At another point he played a psychological trick on forwards Marty McInnis and Yan Kaminsky by dressing them for a preseason game only to keep them in the locker room the whole night.[44] When Milbury found out that the parents of a young player were coming to a game to watch their son, he would tell the player that he would not dress that night. "He would give them a practice jersey for the morning skate so the kid would think he wasn't gonna play," Mick Vukota remembered. "Just mind games with kids, young guys. I never thought it was necessary. In the end, it proved to be very unsuccessful."[45] Despite the negative impact on the players, there is no evidence that Islanders ownership ever told the coach to tone down his fiery rhetoric and strange motivational techniques, perhaps enjoying the media attention that Milbury was generating.

Before the season even began Milbury fractured his relationships with the two players who gave the Islanders the best chance to stop pucks and score goals for years to come. Fichaud, the proclaimed goaltender of the future, was itching to prove his worth to his new coach. "If I work hard in practice and keep my focus on my game, I think I'll have a pretty good chance to make the team," Fichaud said. "I make my luck. If I work hard, I increase my chances." Under the tutelage of goaltending coach Bob Froese, Fichaud allowed only one goal in a game and a half in the preseason, showing a quick glove hand and confidence that initially endeared him to Milbury. In one game against the Panthers, Milbury contemplated taking Fichaud out early but the young goaltender held up three fingers, indicating that he wanted to play all three periods. Milbury kept him in, and he earned a thirty-two-save shutout and bolstered his case to make the roster. "There's a job open," Froese said. "There's a jump ball. Let's see who goes up and gets it."[46] Although Fichaud had done more than any other goalie in camp, Milbury cut him from the roster a few days later, saying he wanted to spare him from playing behind an injury-riddled defense corps. The decision was understandable, but the coach's failure to reward Fichaud's strong performance rattled him. "After my shutout, I thought maybe I had a chance to make the team," he said.[47]

Milbury also confronted the Islanders' forward of the future, Žiggy Pálffy. After trading Pierre Turgeon and losing Ray Ferraro to free agency, the Islanders were counting on a breakout season from Pálffy, who scored twice in their opening victory the previous season and potted ten goals in thirty-three games. The laidback Pálffy spent the summer in his native Slovakia and vacationed in Spain, unreachable for six weeks. When he came to camp he could not complete the mandatory two-mile team run in under twelve minutes, nor could he run four miles in thirty minutes, as Milbury instructed. Pálffy saw little point in the exercises. "I don't like to run," he said. "I'd much rather be on the ice."[48] Milbury was livid. He told assistant coach Guy Charron to run Pálffy through a series of grueling drills. "I remember sometimes Mike said to me, 'I want you to work Pálffy until he pukes,'" Charron recalled. "Well, I'm not that kind of a person. You can't ask that of me. But I knew Mike was watching." Charron thought that skating Pálffy to the point of vomiting was "stupid," so he gave him breaks during practices. Veteran players such as Mick Vukota disliked how Milbury treated Pálffy, who was still acclimating to life in the United States. "Think about being a young player, especially a European player like Žigmund Pálffy, who's left his home, learning the language, learning different diets, different foods, and then you come and you got a guy riding you every day about your salary and you got no points last night," Vukota said.[49]

Despite Milbury's concerns about his conditioning, Pálffy was thriving in the preseason. He had a hat trick against Tampa Bay and scored on the power play and shorthanded against the Rangers. Still, a brawl in the Rangers game put the coach and player at odds again. Milbury came up in the gritty NHL of the late 1970s, when most players were Americans or Canadians who grew up practicing in confrontational drills. By the mid-1990s an influx of Europeans such as Pálffy injected finesse into the league. "As we moved along in hockey and more Europeans came in our game, you needed someone that could adapt to what each and everyone's strength was and use them to the best of their ability," Charron said.[50] Milbury was not the adapting type. When fights broke out in the Rangers game Pálffy and Alexander Semak stood to the side with their gloves on, watching while Wade Redden was being pummeled in a mismatch against one of the Rangers' top enforcers. Milbury screamed futilely for Pálffy and Semak to stick up for Redden.[51] On the Rangers television broadcast, announcer John Davidson scolded Pálffy and Semak, but he was more critical of the Islanders coach for putting two Europeans on the ice against the Rangers' toughest players. As the camera lingered on Milbury, Davidson said, "There's got to be some sense of responsibility right there. There just has to."[52]

While Milbury's frustration with Pálffy could be generously chalked up to generational and cultural differences, his mistreatment of the old-school Vukota was puzzling. Vukota, a right wing who led the Islanders in penalty minutes for four straight years, should have been Milbury's type of player. Always down to defend his teammates and give the Islanders a spark, Vukota sparred with the most fearsome fighters of his generation, from Donald Brashear to Rob Ray. Unlike the malcontent Kirk Muller—and much of the rest of the league—Vukota was the rare veteran who wanted to play on Long Island even in the midst of a rebuild. "I would play for less money to be an Islander than I would to go anywhere else," Vukota said. "I just loved Long Island, and that was part of me drinking the Kool-Aid. I believed in it. I believed that we were gonna win at some point, and I wanted to be there to do that."[53]

For no apparent reason Milbury decided to test Vukota's allegiance. Before a preseason game against Tampa Bay, Milbury told Vukota that he would dress only for warm-ups, so Vukota stayed at Nassau Coliseum, skipped his usual afternoon nap, and ate pizza instead of loading up on protein and carbs. As warm-ups began Milbury revealed that Vukota would actually dress for the game, but assured that he would just sit on the bench. Then, in the second shift of the game, Milbury dispatched the unsuspecting Vukota onto the ice. Unfazed, Vukota went out and fought Lightning heavyweight Rudy Poeschek, served his five minutes in the penalty box, and returned to the bench. Then Milbury sent out Vukota for a second shift, and he fought Brantt Myhres, who was two inches taller. The two scraps left him exhausted. "I've never been that dehydrated. Holy shit," Vukota remembered. His performance, though, made Milbury radiant. "Kid, you got some balls," the coach told Vukota. "You got one more in you for me?" Vukota was stunned that Milbury had invoked himself rather than the other players. He shot back to the coach, "I have one more for the boys." Milbury smirked, walked away, and benched Vukota for the rest of the night. Their relationship was irretrievably damaged. "It was, for me, a slow transition to self-destruction," Vukota said. "I never had played for a coach, meaning Mike, that wanted you to play for him."[54]

In the final days before the season, Maloney made two moves to improve the Islanders' underwhelming forward corps. First, Maloney used the waiver draft to claim veteran checking center Bob Sweeney from Buffalo. The Sabres lost confidence in Sweeney after he underwent off-season surgery on a torn rotator cuff, but he had scored as many as twenty-two goals in a season, was strong on penalty kills and face-offs, and had experience playing under Milbury for two seasons in Boston.[55] The next day Maloney pulled off one of the most significant trades of his tenure, a three-way deal with the Devils and Avalanche that sent disgruntled center Steve Thomas to New Jersey and Colorado's holdout left wing Wendel Clark to Long Island. Clark, a former Maple Leafs captain with 220 career goals and a reputation for hard hits, was by far the Islanders' biggest off-season acquisition. He had exceeded the thirty-goal mark three times in his career, including a career-high forty-six with Toronto in 1993–94. The Islanders hoped that Clark would become a team leader and a mentor for young, gritty forwards like Brett Lindros, and Maloney promptly signed him to a three-year deal, insisting that he transformed the Islanders "from playoff pretenders to playoff contenders."[56]

Adding former all-stars like Muller and Clark in the span of a few months enthused the role players on the Islanders' roster. "It was exciting to play with them," said defenseman Milan Tichy. "It was something special because I was playing with very good stars over there." Cole, who spent much of the season in the minors, appreciated Clark going out of his way to include him in team outings. "That's why everybody who played with him really liked him." Although Clark was only five-foot-eleven and weighed 194 pounds, he played with power and enthusiasm that impressed Milbury. When Clark arrived in Islanders camp a reporter asked the coach if his newest winger would play in the season opener a few days away. "Unless he's crippled, he's playing," Milbury responded. Clark laughed when he heard the promise. "I guess I'll be playing Saturday then." Milbury put Clark on the Islanders' top line with Muller and Lindros.[57]

The media was more skeptical about Maloney's only major trade of the summer. Clark was about to turn twenty-nine and had missed 276 games over ten seasons to suspensions and injuries to his hands, feet, knees, ribs, and back. *Newsday* called the signing "a $6-million dice-throw on an injury-prone player." Clark's passion for the game was indisputable, but he was too banged and bruised to make the sort of impact the Islanders expected. A few seasons prior the Maple Leafs coach criticized Clark for taking a Caribbean vacation while he was injured over the All-Star Break, and opposing players mocked him as "Wendy" for passing up chances to fight their enforcers.[58] By 1995 Clark was no longer a player to build around. Neither was Muller or Sweeney. "It was more players that could have been more complementary on a real good team," said assistant coach Guy Charron. "And now all of a sudden we bring these guys into a situation that we know success won't be turned around by just acquiring these guys." Clark said he was happy to be traded, but jumping from perennial contenders in Toronto and Quebec to a cellar dweller on Long Island had to be demoralizing. "The veterans didn't really want to be there because the team was so bad," said Eric Mirlis, the assistant director of media relations. "A guy like Wendel Clark was so out of place on that team."[59]

As hockey reporters began filing their season previews, a general consensus emerged that Maloney had not done enough to ensure a positive season. *Sports Illustrated* predicted the team would finish tenth in the conference. The *St. Louis Post-Dispatch* said the Islanders had "a decent defense and a few useful forwards, but not nearly enough of anything else." *Newsday* called them "a bottom-third-of-the-league club that can aspire to win about 30 games and should miss the playoffs for the fourth time in six seasons." Even the normally measured *New York Times* predicted that Milbury would become so frustrated by the lack of talent on the roster that he "might explode by Halloween."[60] Successful rebranding depended largely on winning, and Maloney's failure to build a contender—due in large part to the tight fists of ownership—would doom the fisherman jerseys.

The Islanders' front office ignored the media chatter. All teams play up their prospects to build excitement and sell tickets, but the Islanders raised expectations so high above what the hockey media had predicted that fans would either tune them out or buy in and be disappointed. Incredibly, the first Islanders program of the season called the team "one of the strongest in the league." Their playoffs chances were "very real." Milbury brought "instant credibility." Clark was "everything they have been looking for." The program even suggested that Maloney had built a team capable of winning a string of championships: "There is an obvious commitment to the current and future success of the franchise so that perhaps one day, this season will be remembered as the rebirth of the New York Islanders. Or the beginning of a new dynasty."[61] By overselling themselves, the Islanders had almost guaranteed a letdown for the fan base.

For the players the rebranding effort was cause for optimism. If the Islanders lost, young players stood to receive more ice time and cement themselves as regulars in the world's greatest hockey league. If they won, success would be its own reward, and they would be credited with outperforming the media's low expectations. "You're optimistic all the time whenever you start the season," said Travis Green, who was heading into his fourth NHL campaign. "You're anxious. You're looking for new opportunity." Twenty-four-year-old Niklas Andersson, whose NHL experience amounted to just three games with the Quebec Nordiques in 1992–93, was hoping to stick on Long Island. "I was actually just focusing on doing my part at that time and didn't really know and think about winning games that much. I just thought about playing my best hockey, but we for sure had some talent on the team that I thought we had a chance to win games." Even Darius Kasparaitis, still an unsigned free agent on the eve of the season, was eager to rebound from tearing the ACL in his right knee eight months prior. "I felt like we're shifting towards [a] different direction," he said. "We were rebuilding. We had a lot of good first-round draft choices and we had a lot of young talent."[62]

If the players needed further inspiration from their doubters, they could look to the pages of the *Daily News*. The same newspaper that mocked the Islanders' new jerseys with "sea sick" and "gone fishin'" headlines in April continued its maritime mockery in October. One headline read, "Championship Hopes? For the Isles, None Atoll." The accompanying article contended that the Islanders had "a not-ready-for-prime-time cast that will challenge for a playoff spot and earn respect, but will ultimately fall short."[63] Even that dim prediction turned out to be too generous.

After months of controversy surrounding the rebrand, the Islanders opened their first season in the fisherman jerseys in a Saturday-afternoon game against the Bruins in Boston on October 7, 1995. The media had an embarrassment of subplots to choose from. In his first game as Islanders coach, Mike Milbury was returning to the city where he was a defenseman for fourteen years, coach for two, and assistant general manager for two more.[64] The Bruins were christening their new arena, the FleetCenter, after almost seven decades at the fabled

Boston Garden. Milbury named disgruntled center Kirk Muller an alternate captain, but Muller said he might sit out the opener if he could not come to terms on a new contract by game time. Scott Lachance, arguably the Islanders' best defenseman, made a surprise return from a groin injury that cost him almost all of training camp. Wendel Clark was scheduled to make his Islanders debut, and can't-miss prospects Todd Bertuzzi and Bryan McCabe would lace up for their first-ever NHL game.[65] The Bruins, led by future Hall of Famers Cam Neely and Ray Bourque, threatened to steamroll the inexperienced Islanders, but Milbury assured the press that his current team was prepared for his former one. "They'll have all they can handle with us," he said. "I promise you. The guys are ready to play."[66] With so many compelling side stories, the rollout of the fisherman jerseys was barely mentioned by the press.

The players who cracked the season-opening lineup reflected the mixture of youth and experience the Islanders wanted to usher in the fisherman era. Pat Flatley, the longest-tenured Islander, remained the captain for the fifth straight season, while Milbury designated two of the newest Islanders—Muller and offensive defenseman Mathieu Schneider—as alternates. For the top line Milbury went with veterans: the twenty-nine-year-old Muller would center the twenty-eight-year-old Clark and twenty-five-year-old Marty McInnis. On the second he went with three promising young forwards: the twenty-year-old Bertuzzi and twenty-three-year-old Žiggy Pálffy would flank twenty-four-year-old Travis Green. Tellingly, Brett Lindros, who was presented as the franchise's face of the future for months, dispatched to autograph signings and appearing in newspaper ads, was reduced to third-line status. Tommy Söderström, entering his fourth NHL campaign, started in goal. The Islanders would begin the season with three players who were legitimate candidates for rookie of the year: Bertuzzi, McCabe, and back-up goaltender Tommy Salo.[67]

In the broadcast booth, new Islanders play-by-play announcer Howie Rose joined color commentator Ed Westfall, an original Islanders player who was the franchise's first captain. After the Bruins took the ice the SportsChannel camera caught Islanders players approaching the bench.

"Here they come, the new-look Islanders," Westfall announced.

Out skated Muller, then Flatley, McInnis, and Pálffy, until all the Islanders were present.

Except for one.

"Mike Milbury, of course, will be behind the bench for the first time as a New York Islander," Rose said. "And, um, he doesn't seem all that anxious to get out there, you know. His players are on the ice. The Bruins coaching staff is assembled behind their bench."

Rose paused.

"Where's Mike Milbury? He's gonna answer the bell. Won't he?"

The Islanders' assistant coach Guy Charron appeared in the dimly lit runway leading from the locker room to the bench. But Milbury, the face of the rebrand, remained absent.

"I'm sure Mike will come out once the national anthem and so on has been played," Westfall said. "He probably feels a little more comfortable not coming out onto the bench at this time."

The sellout crowd let out a cheer at the sight of singer Rene Rancourt, who had been intoning the national anthem at Bruins games for twenty years. The Islanders stood on the bench, swaying from side to side, still without their coach.

As Rancourt reached "land of the free," Milbury finally emerged on the runway, glanced at the scoreboard, and briskly walked to the bench, much to the announcers' amusement.

"Don't think Mike Milbury wasn't trying to low-key this," Rose said. "While everybody was on their feet for the anthem, that's when Milbury sort of snuck in from the runway leading to the Islander dressing room and winds up behind the Islander bench."

Rose laughed while the television broadcast replayed Milbury's unconventional entrance. Westfall narrated, "All of a sudden, attention is somewhere else, he appears behind the bench." Most viewers probably dismissed Milbury's stealthy appearance as last-minute nerves before his debut as Islanders coach or an attempt to avoid the television cameras from catching his first walk to the bench against his old team.[68]

Something else was amiss, though. Both goaltenders were in their creases, and the starting forwards and defensemen were skating at center ice as if the opening puck drop was imminent, yet nothing happened. The cameras zoomed in on Tommy Söderström, wearing his signature oversize cage, and the Bruins broadcast blamed the puzzling situation on a problem with his equipment. Little did they know that Milbury, after waiting till the national anthem to emerge on the bench, was now slowing down the game itself. According to Charron, Milbury had inexplicably loosened a knot that tied shut the door where the players entered onto the ice.

"Mike had different ways," Charron said. "He knew that there was gonna be a lot of emotion. He wanted to delay the game. He found a way to undo the knot of the door so that he would bring attention to the referee that the door wasn't closing properly and it would delay the game and somehow psychologically would change the outcome of the game. Mike had always different things, different ways."[69]

The season hadn't officially started yet, and the Islanders were already sensing why their coach was nicknamed Mad Mike.

When the game began the Islanders' play reflected Milbury's approach. Early in the first period the Bruins scrambled for a loose puck in the slot, while Söderström sat in the crease. Conventional strategy would have the Islanders looking to clear the puck away from their fallen goaltender, but the three Islanders in front of the net, Travis Green, Bryan McCabe, and Brent Severyn, all played the bodies of their opponents, not the puck. Bruins color commentator Derek Sanderson was incredulous. "Get a look at Mike Milbury's philosophy of 'take your man in front of the net.' If you start focusing on just 'take the body,' you can be in trouble. Mike Milbury likes to do that in his career, but there's a time and a place to play the puck."

A minute later the Islanders' Bob Sweeney was called for holding. After Sweeney skated to the penalty box Milbury caught the announcers off guard again. "This has the appearance of a time-out by the Islanders," said Bruins play-by-play commentator Fred Cusick, right before the public address announcer confirmed Milbury's unusual decision. "And that's hard to believe and a rarity in this game, but it is called by Mike Milbury."[70]

The strange strategy didn't help. Boston scored twice in a twenty-six-second span, igniting the crowd of 17,565. The Islanders responded with a Travis Green goal on their first power play of the season before the period was through. Then the teams traded goals. Forty-two seconds into the third period, Cam Neely netted his third of the game to put the Bruins up four to two. The Islanders skated away dejectedly. Black and yellow caps descended onto the ice to celebrate the first hat trick in FleetCenter history. New season, new coach, new jersey, same old Islanders.

But the team didn't quit. First, Kirk Muller, whose appearance in the game signaled a possible thaw in contract negotiations, knocked in a rebound to bring the Islanders within one. Then Green banged home his second goal off a slapper from Pálffy. A scoreless overtime gave New York its first point of the season, a feel-good tie on the road against their coach's former employer. By most accounts the season opener was a success. Milbury's charged-up team had rallied from two goals down on three occasions and overcome the emotion of the opening of a new arena for an Original Six franchise. Lachance returned unexpectedly early from injury. Bertuzzi scored his first NHL goal. The *New York Times* described the line of Pálffy, Green, and Bertuzzi as dominant. The usually critical *Daily News* ran the headline "Milbury Savors Boston Tie Party." *Newsday* proclaimed, "Handsome Tie."[71]

During an interview on the Bruins broadcast, Milbury said the Islanders' trade for Clark confirmed their commitment to winning. "As long as we're working hard, and we have been, some good things are gonna happen," he said.[72]

Maybe there was hope for the fisherman jerseys yet.

Heartened by the tie against the Bruins, the Islanders headed to Toronto to face the Maple Leafs in their second game of the season. For the second straight game the Islanders would oppose an Original Six franchise in its home opener. After the first game saw Milbury face the team that he coached in a Stanley Cup Final, the second pitted Wendel Clark against the club he captained for three seasons. It was Clark's first game against the Maple Leafs since he was traded away fifteen months prior. Emotions were heightened further because the more tenured Islanders would skate versus their former teammate Benoit Hogue, a three-time thirty-goal scorer on Long Island, for the first time since his trade in April. The cause of the trade was perplexing: general manager Don Maloney made the deal after reading an article in which Hogue expressed disappointment that he was not included in an earlier trade, but Hogue insisted his words were misinterpreted.[73] As with game one of the season, the many subplots surrounding game two diverted attention from the new jerseys.

While in Toronto the players figured they would spend game day eating together in the team hotel, stealing afternoon naps, and heading to the rink. To their surprise Milbury, ever unpredictable, canceled the team meal, a fixture for traveling NHL teams. His players were handed per diems and sent onto the streets of a foreign city to find their own food.

"Instead of going to the hotel that we were staying at in Toronto, we were forced to go out to try and find a place that would serve twenty guys chicken and pasta at 11:30, 12 in the morning," Mick Vukota remembered. "We did it, but it threw off everybody's routine and schedule. And that's in Toronto, so the media is writing about it in the *Toronto Sun* the next day, how the Islanders don't do a team meal anymore before the game. You talk about division? Guys just want to eat and get to bed. We're all breaking up into groups of five 'cause you can get served quicker than if you walk in as a group of twenty-five."[74]

Team spirit, which had been buoyed by the come-from-behind tie against Boston, suffered another blow when Milbury scratched Derek King, depriving perhaps the best-liked man in the dressing room of playing in his hometown. The Maple Leafs came out to a raucous crowd revved up by a laser light show and fireworks. The Islanders, meanwhile, looked like a mess. They took stupid penalties and were outshot fifty to twenty-one. Söderström allowed six goals in two periods, raising his goals-against average to 5.71. Salo let in another. Brett Lindros recklessly hit a Leafs defenseman from behind and was punished with a five-minute major penalty and an automatic game misconduct. The game ended with a lopsided score of seven to three.[75]

After Lindros's dangerous check, the Leafs responded with explosive hits and gritty goals. "We stuck together as a team," Leafs coach Pat Burns said. Meanwhile, Milbury's Islanders were falling apart. *Newsday*'s back page nicknamed the beleaguered starting goaltender "Sieve Söderström," and beat reporters speculated that the team might have to call up Éric Fichaud. Clark mustered only two shots in his much-hyped homecoming. Sparkplug defenseman Darius Kasparaitis, a restricted free agent, was threatening to play in Europe unless general manager Don Maloney offered him a $1 million contract.[76] Behind the scenes Maloney was also frustrated by the slow pace of negotiations with Kirk Muller. "I'm getting a little tired of it," Maloney said. Added Muller, "Right now, I'm not happy the way the talks have gone."[77] As the Islanders flew home for the opener at Nassau Coliseum they looked every bit of the disaster that preseason reports made them out to be.

At the time the front office was coming up against a key deadline that would dictate the length of the rebranding campaign. The Islanders were committed to the fisherman jerseys for the remainder of the 1995–96 season, but they could still opt to abandon the logo in time for the start of their silver anniversary season in October 1996. They just had to make the decision fast. The NHL did not want licensees and retailers stuck with racks of jerseys that were about to be obsolete. As a safeguard teams were mandated to notify the league of a logo change for the 1996–97 season by October 15 to give stores at least one calendar year to deplete their stock of outgoing uniforms. That date fell on the day after the Islanders' home opener.[78]

Only a few games into the season the reaction to the fisherman logo was mixed. Since the jerseys hit stores on August 1, anecdotal feedback was largely positive.[79] The owner of a major sporting-goods chain said that he expected strong sales.[80] The manager of a store in the Roosevelt Field Mall, the largest shopping center on Long Island, said that a shipment of 120 T-shirts and hats with the new logo was almost completely depleted in a week's time.[81] The manager of another store in Westbury said that the new jersey was selling "like hotcakes."[82]

Still, many Long Islanders were vocally opposed to the logo. The day after the new jersey was unveiled in June, *Newsday* invited fans to mail in their reactions with a form that contained the sort of leading questions that encouraged second-guessing.[83] Not surprisingly, more than one thousand responses flooded into the newspaper, the vast majority of them negative. Asked if the team even needed a new logo, a whopping 74 percent of respondents said no. When queried more specifically about the fisherman logo, 78 percent said they did not like it. One person suggested the logo be shipped to Nashville, which was rumored to be the next landing spot for an NHL expansion team. Another proposed placing it on a can of clam chowder. Some wondered about the connection between fishing and hockey. Others said the fisherman looked too mean, too old, like Santa Claus, and, of course, like the Gorton's fisherman. For comparison, *Newsday* ran a photograph of a box of Gorton's crunchy, breaded fish sticks, with the fisherman at the top.[84]

Other objections to the logo came alive in a series of quotes and letters to the editor that the newspaper published over the summer. Chris Goltermann of Seaford called the change a "disgrace." Douglas Guarino of Islip Terrace claimed the Islanders had "lost their last bit of dignity."[85] Jeanne Schumacher of Bethpage suggested that Gorton's sue the Islanders for copyright infringement.[86] And John Mateer of Wantagh called for a boycott of any fisherman merchandise.[87]

The feedback in *Newsday* was far more extensive than what the Islanders had bothered to seek. However, the team maintained its public defense of the logo. Pat Calabria, the Islanders' vice president of communications, told *Newsday* that the skeptical feedback "flies directly in the face of the reaction it got here and the reaction it got out in the street." The respondents in *Newsday* constituted a small sample size, and the critical messages were written before the Islanders wore the jersey in a single game. Ownership did not know how the reception might play out in the coming months. "At the beginning of the season, there was a vocal minority of diehard fans against the logo," said Islanders cochairman Robert Rosenthal. "We thought, If this continues, we will readdress it."[88]

The deadline to submit a logo change passed without any action. No matter what happened in its first season, the fisherman would live to see a second.

5

DEAD IN THE WATER

On the verge of their first home opener in the fisherman jerseys, the Islanders were still looking for their first victory. At a time when the franchise needed consistent faces to represent the new brand, Tommy Söderström, who started the season as the number-one goalie, was usurped by Tommy Salo only two games into the season. Brett Lindros, hyped in preseason newspaper ads, was awaiting a possible suspension for his dubious check in the Maple Leafs game. Fan-favorite defenseman Darius Kasparaitis became so disgruntled over contract negotiations that he walked out. The Islanders suspected that top center Kirk Muller, who was insisting on a four-year deal that would pay him as much as superior scorers like Theo Fleury and Cam Neely, had little interest in playing on Long Island and was trying to trigger a trade to a contender. Coach Mike Milbury named Muller an alternate captain just days earlier. Now Milbury wondered if Muller would even be in the dressing room much longer, let alone a leader. "If a contract problem is going to be a distraction," Milbury said, "I'd just as soon he go away."[1]

A few days before the home opener the pun-happy *Daily News* ran a headline saying the Islanders were "lost at sea."[2] If so, their arena was not the shining beacon that they needed. By 1995 Nassau Coliseum was an albatross. Located in the middle of a parking lot, with a bland, concrete facade and a height of only seventy-five feet above ground level, the Coliseum never had an imposing appearance. Still, its seats were filled in the early 1980s because the Islanders won nineteen consecutive playoff series and four Stanley Cups. When filled to capacity the sixteen-thousand-seat Coliseum was the epitome of the old barns erected in the 1970s, with "Let's go, Islanders!" chants bouncing off the low ninety-seven-foot ceilings.[3] "It was great," said Bruce Bennett, the Islanders' team photographer from 1982 to 2004. "Any of those old NHL arenas, which were more intimate and smaller and less the big, cavernous arenas that many of the teams play in now, the fans are closer to the players." As late as 1993, when the Islanders made an unlikely run to the conference final, the volume of the crowd made up for the unattractive sight of garbage bags and trash cans strewn about the Islanders' locker room to catch dripping water, the result of a lack of maintenance by the local government. "You went in there and you knew that the home team had an advantage with the fans," said defenseman Bob Halkidis. The old-school atmosphere, which included terrific sight lines, counted as a plus for winger Mick Vukota. "I loved that opposing teams felt like it was confined and it had two locker rooms and it wasn't modern-day showerheads. Everything was a little old about it. I thought that was part of the intimidation factor."[4]

As the Islanders faltered in 1994 and 1995 the Coliseum's shortcomings became more difficult to overlook. Thousands of fans stopped coming, so crowd noise decreased. Corridors were poorly lit. Years of shoehorning seats into the arena bowl reduced legroom so much that fans in the nosebleeds sat with their knees pressed against the hard metal backs of the chairs in front of them. An insufficient number of concessions and restrooms produced long lines in the narrow concourse. After a game the logjam meant fans were packed against each other stomach to back as if in a crowded subway car. Besides the installation of luxury boxes in the 1980s, no major changes had been made to the arena in its two-decade existence. There were none of the frills of more recently constructed NHL venues, either. "By the mid-'90s, it had just become an outright dump, just a dump," said Brett Pickett, the son of Islanders majority owner John Pickett. "Depends on what you care about. If you care about an incredible, raucous environment and great sight lines, people will remember it that way. If you care about a half-an-hour wait for the bathroom and shitty food and dirty, scummy seats, then people will remember it that way. It was all of the above."[5] Incredibly, the Islanders charged the second-highest average ticket price in the NHL—$42.64—behind only the Boston Bruins, who were coming off a playoff season and unveiling a new arena.[6] At the press conference to announce Milbury's hiring, Islanders ownership said that a new arena would be too costly but assured fans that Nassau County was considering the addition of a level of luxury boxes halfway up to the ceiling, the expansion of the seating capacity to almost nineteen thousand, and the construction of a restaurant overlooking the ice at one end of the rink.[7] None of those features would come to fruition.

Lacking the amenities of most professional sports venues, the Islanders had few options to improve the atmosphere at Nassau Coliseum besides updating their game presentation. Before the home opener on October 14, 1995, a new sound system was added and several steps were taken to accentuate the new fisherman brand inside the arena. The team decided that the wailing siren that signaled an Islanders goal would be followed by a foghorn familiar to seafarers in the waters off Long Island. The scoreboard was outfitted with fisherman logos on the corners and smoke machines to simulate fog, becoming the only smoke-producing scoreboard in the NHL. The flowing beard of the mascot, which originally covered the front of his jersey, was neatly trimmed to showcase the fisherman logo. The back of the jersey, previously adorned only with a zero, saw the addition of a nameplate with "Nyisles" in wavy lettering. The bulky costume was also slimmed down for greater mobility. The man inside the mascot suit, Rob Di Fiore, joked, "He went to Weight Watchers and Mike Milbury's training camp."[8] Still, the beard continued to make Nyisles an easy mark. Ousted Islanders broadcaster Jiggs McDonald, whose bearded face drew comparisons to the mascot's, suggested that Nyisles looked more like one of his former colleagues at SportsChannel. "That thing looks like Stan Fischler on steroids," he cracked.[9]

Despite the skepticism toward the rebrand, many fans arrived at Nassau Coliseum in bright moods. After a summer without hockey they were excited to catch their first live glimpses of Milbury behind the Islanders bench and highly touted rookies such as Todd Bertuzzi and Bryan McCabe. "It's a young team with bigger players, and they're going to play a physical style," one fan said. "Good things can happen when you play a physical style." Another fan predicted the Islanders would finish as high as fourth in the conference and "open a lot of people's eyes." The players were excited, too. "It's totally different this year because of all the changes," said captain Pat Flatley. "There are a lot of reasons why this should be a big night."[10]

A few minutes before game time, the lights inside Nassau Coliseum dimmed. Spotlights projected six images of the new logo onto the rink. At center ice Nyisles waved his arms, and the red light atop his helmet flashed. A near-sellout crowd of 15,222 began chanting, "Let's go, Islanders!" Television viewers could sense the electric atmosphere. "Of course, opening night is always special," said Islanders broadcaster Ed Westfall. "And this one has an extra special flavor as you get a look at the Islander logo, the new logo of the New York Islanders."[11] An animated video played on the scoreboard to excite the crowd, taking them on a bird's-eye tour of Long Island. Three of the region's most recognizable landmarks were highlighted: the Montauk Point lighthouse commissioned by George Washington, a duck-shaped roadside attraction named the Big Duck, and the Jones Beach water tower, a symbol of Long Island's sand and surf. The clip ended at the arena, where the fisherman logo graced center ice. Play-by-play announcer Howie Rose recognized the video as a rebranding tool. "It seems that part of the marketing scheme now, and I think the graphic you're watching is a good example of that or of this, is to portray the Islanders as Long Island's team. You know, they had the NY on the old logo before and they would seem to be almost obsessed with getting their fair share of the New York market coverage. But it seems to be a little bit different now."[12]

As the fisherman logo lingered on the scoreboard, the voice of public address announcer Alex Sioukas, working his first season at Nassau Coliseum, reverberated through the arena. "And now, ladies and gentlemen, it's time to meet your New York Islanders!"[13]

Milbury was the first to be introduced. A loud cheer went up, and fans banged the palms of their hands against the boards as he passed. Milbury acknowledged the crowd with a quick wave. He was followed by the assistant coaches, the trainers, and the equipment manager.

Then Islanders players emerged one by one from the locker room and passed through machines that tossed sparks for dramatic effect. Almost all the players skated out to applause. The only exceptions were Kirk Muller, whose ongoing contract negotiations fed speculation that he did not want to play for the Islanders, and Derek King, whose production had declined the previous season. When Žiggy Pálffy came out, Nyisles dropped to his knees and waved his arms as if greeting a king. Especially boisterous reactions welcomed Bertuzzi and McCabe. With the entire lineup on the ice, Sioukas announced, "Ladies and gentlemen, the 1995–96 New York Islanders!" Pinwheel-shaped fireworks exploded above the ice. Vigorous clapping followed. The crowd buzzed with breaking news that the Islanders had agreed to a four-year contract with Darius Kasparaitis. The reaction suggested that the performance of the players, not aesthetics, would dictate the success of the fisherman logo. "At first I didn't like it," one fan said. "But if they win, I don't care if they wear pink."[14]

The Islanders were too flawed to break out the pink just yet. Playing in their home whites for the first time, they kept pace with the visiting Philadelphia Flyers through two scoreless periods. The defense looked sharp, Tommy Salo made twenty-two saves, and Brett Lindros nearly barreled his older brother Eric over the boards in front of the Flyers bench. As the game wore on, however, the lack of talent was exposed. The Islanders did not register a shot on goal in the second period until fifteen minutes had passed. They went scoreless in six tries on the power play. Early in the third Travis Green fanned on a one-timer, and Bob Sweeney failed to convert on a break-in. The Flyers scored twice in four minutes and added an empty-netter for a 3–0 victory. "We continue to repeat the same mistakes," Milbury said after the game. "A number of guys still haven't got it in terms of how much commitment it takes to win." The only other time the Islanders had been shut out in a home opener was 1973, when the franchise was only in its second year of existence. The team was now winless in its first three games of the season. A sportscaster on Channel 11 delivered the sort of snarky characterization that had become typical for the franchise: "For two periods, the Isles looked just like a pro hockey team."[15] The implication, of course, was that the third period outed them as bush league.

The Islanders' tight finances contributed to the sense of amateurishness. At one point Di Fiore asked if he could receive free tickets for games for his friends. Rather than provide him the tickets outright, the team countered that he could receive two free tickets to every home game if he agreed to drive the new organist, Eddie Layton, to and from each one. Layton, best known for playing the organ at Yankee Stadium for decades, lived in Queens and was accustomed to the Yankees sending a car service to pick him up. By contrast, the Islanders dispatched the man who played their mascot from his home in Westchester County to pick up Layton at a diner in Queens and drive him out to Nassau Coliseum. In an image that epitomized the team's frugality, the organist would puff away on cigarettes while the mascot took the wheel in a Suzuki Samurai, an off-road mini-SUV with a soft top that made for a chilly commute in the fall and winter. "The Islanders were so screwed up," Di Fiore said.[16]

A quirk in the schedule shipped the weary Islanders from their home opener on Saturday night in New York to a road game in Miami on Sunday. Due to inclement weather their charter plane landed in South Florida only three hours before game time, and they fell to the Panthers 5–3. The Islanders' postgame reactions suggested complacency with their third straight loss, as if coming within two goals of an opponent was sufficient progress. Milbury told reporters that his players "did a good job" and gave "better effort" than in the Flyers game. Defenseman Mathieu Schneider said the Islanders were "in great shape." Derek King proposed the team "travel that way all the time."[17] While teams often make positive statements after losses to build up their confidence for the next game, the Islanders' optimistic responses came across as oblivious and unaccountable to outsiders. "It is sad that the Islanders, despite weather-related travel problems, seemed satisfied with their effort Sunday," columnist Jim Smith wrote in *Newsday*. "Has it come to this? Are they really happy to lose 5–3 to a third-year expansion team? So far the only direction this team has gone is south." In an especially alarming sign for the Islanders' marketers, the media was waning in its adoration for Milbury, one of the faces of the rebrand. Smith, who had written a column headlined "Isles Need Milbury" in May, criticized the coach for adopting a system of aggressive forechecking that allowed too many opposing odd-man rushes and breaking up his best line of Pálffy, Green, and Bertuzzi.[18]

Two days after the Panthers game the Islanders flew home for their first rivalry game of the season against the Rangers at Nassau Coliseum. No matter the Islanders' sins in the first four games of the season, a victory versus the Rangers was a surefire path to forgiveness from the fan base. The rivalry was so fierce that the Islanders-Rangers game sold out all 16,297 seats, which had not even happened for the home opener. The stands would be filled with trash-talking and warring chants that had historically energized both teams.[19] "Every time I played the Rangers, it was like a playoff game," Kasparaitis said. "We hated the Rangers. We want to beat them so bad."[20] It would be appropriate to notch the first win in the fisherman jerseys against the team whose ousting of the Islanders in the 1994 playoffs sparked the uniform change.

Surprisingly, the Islanders came out flat. Only 1:23 into the game, former Islander Ray Ferraro blew by defenseman Dean Chynoweth and fired a wrist shot past Tommy Salo. Two minutes later Todd Bertuzzi took an inexcusable penalty for closing his hand on the puck, and the Rangers scored again on the power play. Žiggy Pálffy had a third-period goal to break the Islanders' scoreless streak of nearly 178 minutes at Nassau Coliseum stretching back to April, but the Rangers coasted to a 5–1 win. In what was supposed to be a new chapter for the franchise, the Islanders were 0-4-1, their worst start in team history. *Newsday* called them "dead in the water."[21]

Frustration mounted in the locker room. The Islanders were repeating the same mistakes through their first five winless games. "Right now, to be candid with you, it looks like the worst-coached team in hockey," Milbury said. "I take responsibility for disciplinary problems, for taking foolish penalties, and for not shooting the puck at the net when we cross the blue line."[22]

The media agreed the Islanders' coach was to blame, although they added another reason—his unusual off-ice persona. Most coaches avoided making critical comments about opposing teams for fear of motivating them. Milbury, meanwhile, had a preseason meeting with reporters during which he called the Islanders' archrivals arrogant and blurted out, "Fuck the Rangers." Rangers captain Mark Messier acknowledged that Milbury's words inspired him. "If anything, it alerts us to how he and that team feels about us," Messier said. "If anything, it made us pay more attention to the rivalry and how much it means to them to beat us. If anything, it helped us."[23] After the Rangers game Milbury made another faux pas. Upset over a dubious penalty call against the Islanders, he gave a thinly veiled critique of the referee by saying, "We all know the official in question," implying that he had a reputation for inconsistency. Milbury could get away with criticizing referees when he was analyzing games for ESPN, but as a coach he risked angering the officials who would dictate his team's power plays and penalty kills. By contrast, veteran defenseman Mathieu Schneider wisely deflected when reporters inquired about the same penalty call, placing the onus on the players. "We're just coming up with one excuse after another," he said. "Enough is enough. We better do something, and quick."[24]

Luckily for the Islanders, their next opponent was the 0-4-0 Montreal Canadiens, off to their worst start to a season since 1938. Montreal was a rare NHL franchise in even more flux than the Islanders. Days earlier the once-proud Canadiens, only two years removed from a Stanley Cup, had fired their coach, general manager, and assistant general manager.[25] Behind twenty-six saves from Tommy Söderström and unlikely goals from defensemen Dennis Vaske and Scott Lachance, the Islanders managed to blank Montreal 2-0 for their first victory of the fisherman era. Unfortunately, few fans were around to see it. In a sign of waning enthusiasm for the rebrand, the Islanders attracted a dismal Friday-night crowd of only 9,253 for the Canadiens game, even though they were playing an Original Six team featuring former Islanders marquee center Pierre Turgeon. Newspaper headlines framed the victory not as an accomplishment worth celebrating but as an interval of relief during an embarrassing season. They also reported on the familiar speculation that Kirk Muller was disgruntled and general manager Don Maloney might be fired. Ralph Palleschi, the team's chief operating officer, seemed to target Muller and Clark when he was quoted accusing veteran players on the roster of not "pulling their weight."[26] A single victory did not erase years of disappointment about the direction of the franchise.

Predictably, the Islanders lost any momentum from the Montreal victory with five losses in their next seven games. Their only victory during that stretch was hardly reassuring, coming in overtime in Florida after the Islanders gave up a two-goal lead in the third period. Rather than rejoicing in the locker room, Bob Sweeney, who scored the game-winning goal, told reporters, "You could say we deserved to lose the game."[27] The crowds on Long Island hovered around nine or ten thousand, and the summertime excitement about Milbury evaporated as he tried to mold the players into his own tough likeness. In his latest verbal tussle with a player, Milbury accused Dennis Vaske of not hitting hard enough and having a "laissez-faire attitude," leading Vaske to point out that he was not the type to pile up penalty minutes.[28] Perhaps as a by-product of Milbury's emphasis on aggression, defenseman Brent Severyn was so eager to jump into a fight in Philadelphia that he wrestled with a linesman and received a three-game suspension for abusing an official, the first suspension of his career.[29]

Shockingly, one journalist saw what had transpired and concluded the Islanders were underachieving because Milbury was too soft. In a biting column *Newsday*'s Jim Smith tried to goad Milbury—whom he labeled "Mike Milquetoast"—into making the Islanders' practices more intense and roasting his players more often. "This Milbury seems so concerned with not destroying a young team's confidence that he tolerates ineptitude," Smith wrote. After encouraging the Islanders to hire Milbury in the summer, Smith hammered away at him in story after story, sometimes contradicting his own reporting. In the same article he accused Milbury of "using a soft hand" with his players and then noted that he had gone hoarse from yelling at them. The Islanders had one of the worst rosters in the NHL, so it would be misleading to compare Milbury's record against the first-year coaches of more gifted teams. Smith did it anyway. "As far as I'm concerned," Milbury told Smith at the end of October, "eight or nine games is not enough for me to be condemned or for them to be put up for coach of the year honors." Perhaps Smith, frustrated with covering a lousy team, was hoping for a livelier beat by prodding Milbury to be more forceful. He was not alone in thinking Milbury was treating his players too gently. Islanders broadcaster Howie Rose told an interviewer, "He's been much more patient with the team than I thought he'd be."[30]

Whether a result of the pointed media commentary or not, Milbury became harsher with his players. The night after a loss to Vancouver in early November, the coach summoned the team to Nassau Coliseum for an unorthodox film session and meeting, breaking down defensive mistakes against the Canucks and talking about the pride of being an Islander. He said he would have held a second practice too but couldn't because of a college basketball game at the arena. Asked why he called the forty-five-minute meeting, Milbury sounded like Smith's criticism had registered with him. "I can't go on forever saying, 'That's okay. I know you're nervous. That's okay. We've got a lot of new faces. That's okay. I know you're still getting used to me.' It's not okay."[31] In his twenty-year career in professional hockey, Milbury belonged to only one losing team that missed the playoffs, and his early adversity with the Islanders and the famously critical New York media may have pushed him to a new level of ferocity that further damaged his relationship with the players.

Besides Milbury, the most obvious scapegoats for the Islanders' misery were Don Maloney and the two established players he traded for, Kirk Muller and Wendel Clark. In interviews that may have been too forthright, Milbury and Maloney did not defend their two most talented players against widespread accusations they were tanking. Muller and Clark had averaged almost a point per game in their careers, but through thirteen games in the 1995–96 season, Muller had seven and Clark had six. Milbury said he had "no overt sense" they were going through the motions until they were traded, but he added, "I'm not that deep. Have they played very well? No. Read into that what you can." Maloney was even more cryptic. "At some point," he said, "the real story will come out." Muller offered a similarly vague response when asked the straightforward question of whether his heart was into playing for the Islanders. "I don't want to get into anything," he said. "The day will come. I'm just not allowed to say anything right now." For his part Clark came across as resentful that Milbury had not put him on the power play. "You can't get points if you're not on the power play," he protested. The quotes contributed to the notion of a wayward organization. The reporters who nicknamed Nassau Coliseum "Fort Neverlose" during the dynasty years now called it a "temple of doom." The positivity in the fan base in the summer of 1995 quickly turned to animosity. In the *Islander Insider* newsletter, fans pushed for the trades of Muller and Clark and blamed Maloney for failing to acquire a playmaking center. A front-page story in the November issue began, "Thus far the Islander management team has shown the foresight of George Armstrong Custer, the empathy of Marie Antoinette, the flexibility of Czar Nicholas II, & the inventiveness of Wil E. Coyote!"[32]

With the season slipping away, the Islanders had a final opportunity to turn around their fortunes, and save the fisherman rebrand, on November 10. Instead, the night sealed the fate of one of the worst branding failures in hockey history. The Islanders, mired in a three-game losing streak and dropping out of playoff contention, were scheduled for their second game against the Rangers, this time on enemy turf at Madison Square Garden. Uniting to defeat a common foe could be just the right salve to ease tensions between the increasingly agitated Milbury and the malcontents Muller and Clark. Alternately, a loss was sure to shatter any confidence left in the locker room and increase speculation about firings and trades. Salo and Söderström had been so inconsistent in goal that the Islanders handed the net over to Jamie McLennan, recently called up from the minors. "It's a big rivalry and I've been able to experience it," said McLennan, who had played parts of the past two seasons with the Islanders. "I know the intensity. It's going to be a good challenge." In the Rangers' net was former Islanders goalie Glenn Healy, unbeaten in five games that season.[33] McLennan received scant support from his defense and allowed two goals each in the second and third en route to a 4–1 loss.[34] Yet again Muller was ineffective, registering just one shot on Healy. Clark was scoreless and minus two. Meanwhile, Milbury's penchant for trash-talking haunted him for the second time in two meetings against the Islanders' archrivals. After the game the Rangers again made clear that Milbury's preseason statement about their arrogance had motivated them. "We played an arrogant game tonight," Rangers coach Colin Campbell said. Asked for clarification, Campbell said, "You caught that, eh? Well, it was just an arrogant win. Little things catch up and statements catch up to people. We remember that."[35]

The second straight loss to the Rangers set the tone for the remainder of the season both on and off the ice. For decades Islanders fans had tormented Rangers fans with singsong chants of "Nineteen-forty," referring to the last time the Rangers won a Stanley Cup. Then, in the course of sixteen tide-turning months, the Rangers' championship in 1994 deprived Islanders fans of their favorite taunt, and the fisherman jerseys gave Rangers fans convenient fodder to verbally mock their rivals. "We just gave the Rangers a big gift to abuse the team," Kasparaitis said. During the November 10 game, some Islanders players felt uncomfortable in their new-look uniforms. Among them was Brent Severyn, an enforcer whose duty was to jaw and jab at opposing players. "You're playing the *Rangers*, you know what I mean? The *Rangers*. And you've got a fisherman on your jersey."[36]

Rangers fans had historically returned the "Nineteen-forty" chants with cries of "Potvin sucks," directed at former Islanders star defenseman Denis Potvin. As McLennan stiffed the Rangers in the first period the home crowd stuck with Potvin taunts. Once the Rangers went ahead in the second, their fans began mocking the Islanders logo with a new, full-throated chant of "We want fish sticks!" Two Rangers fans drew laughter by marching through the arena wearing yellow rain slickers and fake gray beards. As *Newsday* pointed out, "The frozen-dinner fisherman on the visitors' sweaters might not have seemed so funny if the game had been hotly contested." Instead, the Rangers dominated, and there was little for Islanders fans to do but slump in their seats and bear the barbs. "The 'fish sticks' and all that, I felt bad for the fans," Vukota remembered. "It's more of an embarrassment for an Islander fan than it was for the players."[37]

Eventually, the "We want fish sticks!" chant followed the Islanders to Nassau Coliseum, uttered by the very fans who were supposed to spark the team. The fans associated the fisherman with a struggling, volatile coach and dissatisfied, underachieving players, while the original logo evoked the glory days the fan base longed to return to. "Maybe that's the reason why they jumped on the bandwagon too with that chant," said Islanders radio broadcaster Chris King, "just to try to move the process along to get back to the logo that they all loved." Fans conveyed their disgust by tossing fish sticks and raw fish onto the ice. "It was a pain in the neck to get it off," recalled Lance Elder, then the Coliseum's assistant general manager. According to Elder, a piece of fish was once scooped off the ice with a shovel, tossed under the bleachers, and forgotten until it began to smell a few days later.[38]

Islanders players generally said they did not pay much attention to the backlash against the logo because they had no say over what they wore. "As a player, you're just a soldier," said Mathieu Schneider, then a seven-year veteran. "You put on your game face and try to make the best of a situation." Travis Green, in his fourth season with the Islanders, agreed. "You don't overthink things that aren't in your control." For the bubble players on the roster, wearing any NHL jersey, no matter fans' opinions about it, symbolized the attainment of a lifelong goal to compete at hockey's highest level. After years of paying dues in college and the minor leagues, they said they were not fazed by vitriol from the stands. "You're playing for the Islanders," said Dan Plante, who played his first full NHL season in the fisherman jerseys. "It doesn't matter what symbol is on the front of your jersey." Others said they were too focused on wrapping up their professional careers to be concerned with the failed rebranding of the team. "I certainly didn't understand the need for it, but I wasn't asking that question either," said twenty-eight-year-old Chris Luongo, playing his last season in the NHL. "That wasn't in my area." Danton Cole, another twenty-eight-year-old playing his last NHL season, said he did not let reactions to the uniform distract him from trying to earn more playing time. "If that gets you off your game, then boy, you got bigger problems than a jersey."[39]

Nevertheless, the fans' reactions confirmed the players' skepticism toward the jerseys. Week after week of hearing fans unleash derisive chants and throw fish onto the ice must have tested the motivation of men already coping with the annoyance of losing and playing under a hard-driving coach. "You felt the fans' frustration with it and you read articles and so forth," Plante said. "That was somewhat frustrating as a player, that they're more worried about that than maybe the play on the ice." While marketing was beyond the players' domain, they had heard the common mantra in sports to play for the logo on the front of the jersey, not the name on the back. The adage reminds players to place team over self, but the debacle surrounding the fisherman jerseys damaged their faith in the organization's judgment. "The pride that you need to have in the jersey and the logo is important," said Dean Chynoweth, "so obviously when they made such a drastic switch, it was with mixed emotions." The chants challenged players including Rich Pilon to draw pride from wearing the fisherman. "When teams used to yell 'Fish sticks!' at us, it was kind of, Oh my God. How could you take the Islander logo and change it to that?" Defenseman Jason Holland remembered fans asking for his thoughts on the logo as he walked between Nassau Coliseum and the nearby Long Island Marriott. "It was awkward," he said. "I did have my own opinion and I didn't like it either, but it wasn't something that you were going to openly share during that period of time because that's what you were wearing on your chest." The insults at Madison Square Garden gave pause to assistant coach Guy Charron. "Where it became more obvious is when we'd go to New York and they'd scream during the game, 'Fish stick!' That's when you come to terms: Was the logo thought out as well as it should have been?" Similarly, goaltending coach Bob Froese questioned the organizational decision to change uniforms instead of players. "I would sooner change the numbers and the names on the back of the jersey than I would change the crest or the logo and the identity of the team."[40]

Like the fans, the players drafted into the organization were upset that the fisherman had pushed out the original Islanders sweater. The

Long Island map crest was the first and only NHL logo that many of them had worn. "It meant a lot to me because when I came in I didn't know a lot about [the] Islanders," said Darius Kasparaitis, who slipped on the original jersey the day he was drafted fifth overall in 1992. "That's what I knew. I didn't know anything else. There were no third jerseys in those days, so that's all we had." Other players grew up as hockey fans in the early 1980s, when the map logo was associated with the success of the dynasty teams, and they entered the Islanders organization hoping to wear the symbol they recalled from their youth. As a teenager in Sweden, Niklas Andersson watched fellow Swedes Tomas Jonsson, Anders Kallur, and Stefan Persson contribute to the Stanley Cup runs. "I learned to like that [logo] pretty early when I was younger," Andersson remembered. "With their success earlier and some Swedes playing there, it was very familiar to me before I got there." Disappointed by the fisherman jerseys, the players privately shared laughs in the dressing room. "Honestly, we all had a bit of a chuckle at it," Chynoweth recalled. "It was kind of like, Oh really? That's what we're gonna wear? It wasn't inspirational by any means."[41] If even the players being paid to wear the jerseys did not like them, the Islanders had little hope of convincing fans to buy their own.

Within the franchise the logo quickly became a scapegoat for the Islanders' poor play. Only two months into the season the team already had two four-game losing streaks, and the players' dislike for the jerseys had them searching for other motivations to get through a long season. Rich Pilon said that he stayed driven by focusing on the men sitting beside him on the bench. "You put the jersey on for the team, so to look past that when you're wearing that jersey that I didn't care for on my side—lots of players didn't either—then you're playing for your teammates, right?"[42]

Islanders executives said they did not remember any player complaining directly to management, but the simmering dissatisfaction over the uniforms reached them anyway. Pat Calabria did not understand the objections. "What is it about it as a player don't you like about it? It's not Goldilocks on the front. It's not something effeminate. It's very similar to a pirate, wouldn't you say? So what is so offensive about it?" At one point Calabria was approached by a trainer who claimed to have run an unusual experiment involving the jersey. The trainer said he placed the old and new uniforms in pails of water and weighed them. He found the fisherman jerseys were heavier and concluded that they were slowing down the players on the ice. Calabria was incredulous. "That's hardly scientific, okay? Hardly scientific," he said, still annoyed years later. "How much more could the patch of a new jersey weigh over the old jersey? A hundredth of an ounce? A fiftieth of an ounce? That's the reason the team was on an eight-game losing streak? The patch? Really?"[43]

As the personification of the logo, Nyisles continued to have trouble connecting with fans. The abuse began to wear on the man inside the costume, Rob Di Fiore, who had spent years battling personal demons that the Islanders knew nothing about. Before his stint as Nyisles, Di Fiore worked at Barneys, the luxury fashion store in Manhattan, and he became so concerned that he did not fit in there that he resorted to drinking and drugs. At twenty-one he overdosed and almost died.[44] Di Fiore said he had been sober for eight years by the time he began the Islanders' mascoting gig, and he was comfortable enough in his identity as a recovering addict that he broke his anonymity as an alcoholic to Islanders defenseman Darius Kasparaitis, who had admitted to his own struggles with drinking.[45] However, Di Fiore was still suffering from depression, and the reactions that Nyisles received in the Nassau Coliseum stands did little to lift his spirits.

Some fans who abused the mascot were repeat offenders. Game after game the same boy approached Nyisles, punched him in the ribs or kicked him in the groin, and ran away before Di Fiore could catch him. On one occasion Di Fiore finally saw where the boy was sitting. He went to his dressing room, changed out of the costume and into street clothes, and headed back to the arena bowl in a nasty mood. "I went right to where that kid was sitting," Di Fiore recalled. "Obviously, you can't do anything to a fan, but I just whispered in his ear, 'I know who you are.' I think I scared him. He never bothered me again." Another time Nyisles was working a street hockey fair in the Nassau Coliseum parking lot when a teenage boy took a stick and whacked the mascot between the legs, sending Di Fiore crumpling to the blacktop. "I just went down, and I just thought, Forget it. I just got hit big time. That hurt." From then on Di Fiore wore a cup every time he put on the costume.[46]

On the ice the Islanders continued to tumble through November. After the Rangers game that spawned the "We want fish sticks!" chant, the Islanders fell to St. Louis the next night to run their losing streak to five games. Interest in the team brand waned. After attracting 15,222 and 16,297 fans for their first two home games, the Islanders averaged just 9,902 over the next six.[47] Meanwhile, Kirk Muller, supposedly the best player on the roster, had a team-worst minus-ten rating. In the latest sign of the turmoil in the organization, Don Maloney told the sulking Muller not to accompany the team on a three-game road trip to California. "We have decided to ask Kirk to go home," he said. "He will not play for the New York Islanders again."[48] Muller's overdue exit eliminated a distraction in the dressing room but did little to spark the team, which dropped two of the three games on the trip, including one by an embarrassing 9–2 margin in Los Angeles. The Islanders ended November at 5-15-3.

The Islanders' disavowal of Muller highlighted the disconnect between players and management. Maloney and Milbury criticized Muller for betraying the organization. "Any player that doesn't want to play for us, we'll get them out of here as soon as possible," Maloney told reporters. "We want everybody to be united behind the Islanders crest." Striking a similar tone, Milbury said, "You've got to have twenty guys in the room and on the ice that care about each other and want to be on the Islanders hockey club."[49] The players, who were already skeptical about the front office's decision to rebrand, sympathized with their castaway teammate. From their perspective Muller was understandably jarred by the trade from the Canadiens, a franchise he led to a Stanley Cup, and longed to play for a contender again. Decades later Islanders players spoke about Muller almost unanimously in glowing terms. Brent Severyn called him "very gifted" and "a guy that would battle and not take any guff from anybody." Asked if Muller's refusal to report affected the team, Mick Vukota blamed the Islanders for fostering a bush-league atmosphere that made the veteran Muller want out of Long Island. "I'll tell you," Vukota said, "it's a direct reflection of [how] the organization was perceived at that time." Darius Kasparaitis said he too understood why Muller requested a trade. "I think it was hard for him to come to a team that was rebuilding. Nobody wanted to play for the Islanders in those years between having a funny jersey and having a rebuild."[50] Muller declined a request to be interviewed for this book.

For Maloney the devolution of the Muller trade proved ruinous. Once other teams realized how badly the Islanders wanted to unload Muller, they were unlikely to offer players of comparable value in a trade. Maloney suggested that he could ship out Muller before Thanksgiving, but he could not close a deal with any of the several teams rumored to be interested.[51] Muller, the most notable acquisition of Maloney's tenure, relaxed in sunny California and continued to collect his full salary while his team struggled to compensate for the scoring he was supposed to provide.[52] The lack of a first-line center crippled the Islanders. "It's tough," Derek King admitted. "You look around and every team has that kind of player."[53]

At the same time, Maloney's most significant import of the off-season was proving to be a bust behind the bench. Reporters referred to Milbury as "Captain Queeg," the eccentric commander in the novel *The Caine Mutiny*. Due in part to Milbury's reputation, some players made clear they would rather stick with the Islanders' minor league affiliate in Salt Lake City, Utah, on the verge of winning back-to-back International Hockey League championships, than be promoted to the big club. "We actually said when we got sent down, you're getting called up, and when you get called up, you're getting sent down," remembered center Chris Taylor, who bounced between Utah and Long Island frequently. Maloney was the highest-ranking executive of an organization that had become a laughingstock on and off the ice. When the Colorado Avalanche visited Nassau Coliseum the *Denver Post* called the fisherman jerseys "the joke of the league," describing the logo as "a crazed-looking 'Islander' who looks more like the Gorton's fisherman after eating too many of his own fish sticks." Had Maloney built a winning roster, the uniforms might not have mattered, but the piling losses under his watch doomed the rebrand. On many nights the half-empty Nassau Coliseum resounded with chants of "Don must go!"[54]

On December 2 the fans got their wish. During a long-distance phone call, Ralph Palleschi, the Islanders' chief operating officer, told Maloney that he had been fired. "He failed," Palleschi told reporters.[55] Maloney took responsibility for the team's poor play. "At some point in time, enough is enough. The bottom line is the job didn't get done." Maloney also understood that his failure to ice a winning team affected the fledgling brand. "The idea is to be competitive and entertaining," he said, "and we weren't." The Islanders had paid for Maloney's inexperience. Since becoming the NHL's youngest general manager at age thirty-three in 1992, he had handed an overgenerous contract to an unproven Brett Lindros on the foolhardy notion that he would be as dynamic as his superstar brother and engineered unsuccessful trades for Muller, Wendel Clark, and Tommy Söderström. In fairness, though, Maloney had also been hamstrung by a cash-strapped ownership that could not afford to green-light pay increases for Ray Ferraro and Steve Thomas or dish out lucrative free-agent contracts. The same small-market money troubles that drove the Islanders to unveil new jerseys paralyzed them from acquiring the star power necessary for a successful rebrand. "Money is such a factor," Maloney acknowledged. "We're not working with unlimited resources."[56] In retrospect, it was hard to dissociate the general manager from the logo controversy. As one fan said, "To me, the logo thing was done to try to make fans forget how the team, under Maloney, has been allowed to fall apart."[57] The Islanders promised to conduct a thorough but expeditious search for Maloney's replacement, appointing former coach Al Arbour to lead the selection process.[58]

On the day Maloney's firing was announced, Islanders ownership identified Milbury as a possible successor. His inclusion on the short list was surprising. Although Milbury was an assistant general manager with the Bruins and aspired to control player personnel someday, he coached the Islanders to a last-place record that had just gotten

Maloney fired. Among the more qualified options were Maloney's assistant Darcy Regier, a former Islanders defenseman who was credited with designing a computerized system for scouting and drafting, and former Winnipeg Jets general manager Mike Smith, who presided over several winning seasons in Manitoba and expressed interest in coming to Long Island.[59] Alternately, the Islanders, under criticism for abandoning their original logo, could have embraced their heritage and appeased their alumni by hiring Hall of Fame defenseman Denis Potvin, who was lobbying for the job.[60]

Two months into the season Milbury's erratic behavior was hard to ignore. As the general manager search got under way he compared the banished Muller to three other NHL players who voiced problems with the management of their clubs. "Every team's got it these days," he said. "The inmates are officially running the asylum."[61] Suggesting that one of his players was mentally ill did not eliminate Milbury from consideration for the franchise's most high-profile job. In fact, the media presented him as the most obvious candidate.

Only ten days after Maloney's firing the Islanders added the GM duties to Milbury's plate. "At the end of the day, we strongly believed, with the support that he has in this organization through Darcy and Al and others, Mike would help us make the progress we hadn't made in the past," said Islanders cochairman Robert Rosenthal. As with most Islanders moves, the team probably chose Milbury because he was the most cost-effective hire, so eager to control player personnel that he agreed to take on added duties even though he would not receive a raise on top of his five-year coaching contract. Rosenthal assured fans that Milbury would have a "flexible" budget, but in truth the Islanders had no clearer path to resurgence than when Maloney was in charge. In one headline *Islander Insider* raged, "Don Maloney's Firing Solves Nothing! The Organization from Top to Bottom Doesn't Have a Clue!" A franchise that won four straight titles the previous decade seemed content just to escape the NHL cellar in the 1990s. "If I said we were going to win the Stanley Cup in three years, that would be a load of bull," Milbury said. "We have to get better, and the sooner the better."[62] In his first major move Milbury hired former Bruins and

Senators coach Rick Bowness to join his staff as an assistant, providing the team with an experienced replacement behind the bench to fill in when Milbury's new role required him to travel.[63]

In the short term Milbury's new responsibilities had little effect on the on-ice product. The Islanders ended the calendar year last in the seven-team Atlantic Division at 9-22-6, thirty-two points behind the first-place Rangers. It was the third-worst record in the league. They also led the league with twelve losses within their division. The roster that Maloney assembled had scored only 105 goals, coming in at twentieth in the twenty-six-team NHL, and allowed 141 goals, the fifth most.[64] There were still three and a half months left in the regular season, but the Islanders' hopes for a playoff berth were dead.

The Islanders bridged 1995 and 1996 with their best games of the season. During a three-week stretch from December 21 to January 15, the team went 5-1-4, picking up fourteen of a possible twenty points. Lessening the embarrassment of the Kirk Muller trade, Mathieu Schneider, who was acquired in the same deal, had acclimated to life on Long Island, contributing regularly on offense and defense and buying a home for his family in Huntington Bay. "We love it," he said, offering a refreshing change of pace from the Islanders' disgruntled veterans. "It's a great place to raise a family. It's beautiful."[65] Schneider was an established player who spoke openly about wanting to sign long term with the Islanders, making him a perfect candidate to become the face of the rebrand. He ranked third on the team with twenty-nine points, filled in as captain in games when Pat Flatley did not dress, and was selected for his first NHL All-Star Game, notching an assist for the victorious Eastern Conference.[66] (The Islanders' only other all-star representative was Nyisles, who worked the crowd in Boston with other mascots.)[67] In the Islanders' last contest of January, Schneider scored in overtime against fellow all-star Dominik Hašek to defeat the Sabres in the thrilling conclusion of a game that marked the NHL debut of supposed goaltender of the future Éric Fichaud.[68] As the cameras scanned the raucous crowd at Nassau Coliseum, a teenage fan in a fisherman jersey was spotted clapping wildly against the blare of the foghorn-like goal horn.[69] It was a brief glimpse of how the rebrand might have been received if the Islanders won more often.

Another feel-good moment involved the call-up of twenty-five-year-old defenseman Jason Herter from the minors. Drafted eighth overall by Vancouver in 1989, Herter had yet to skate in the NHL in the six years since his selection, making him the highest-drafted player in NHL history to never play in the league. His first action as an NHL player was participating in warm-ups before a game against the Penguins at Nassau Coliseum, with Mario Lemieux in the opposite end.[70] "What I remember is skating off the ice after warm-up and some guy yelling out, 'You look great, Herter. Hope you stick.' That was it. I thought, Well, that was nice of him." Herter did not play versus Pittsburgh, but he traveled with the Islanders to Hartford and finally made his NHL debut the next night against the Whalers. Paired with Schneider, Herter was on the ice for three Islanders goals and got an assist on one of them. The *New York Times* called him "a bright spot, one of the only ones on defense for the Islanders." While some regular players mocked the fisherman jersey, Herter was proud to wear any NHL uniform with his nameplate on the back. He was sent back down to the minors and would never skate again in the NHL. "For that one day or the two days I was up, that was outstanding," he said. "I felt I played well and my dad saw me play on TV. There's a lot of things to be proud of."[71]

Around the same time as Herter's debut the Islanders scored a rare public relations coup when photographs of the fisherman jerseys appeared in two major fashion magazines. In *Mademoiselle* a two-page photo spread of NHL players involved in their communities showed Schneider, clad in his fisherman uniform, reclining on a bench alongside Ottawa's Alexandre Daigle, Dallas's Mike Modano, and Boston's Cam Neely. In another shoot for *Cosmopolitan*, a female model draped her arm around the Capitals' Joe Juneau and the Islanders' Scott Lachance. Gleeful over the mainstream coverage, Islanders programs reported the jersey was "in fine fashion."[72]

The Islanders brand took another step forward in January when Milbury finally found a taker for Kirk Muller, ending a nine-month saga involving probably the most talented yet most despised player to put on a fisherman sweater. In a three-team trade with Toronto and Ottawa, the Islanders sent Muller to the Maple Leafs and defense prospect Wade Redden to the Senators in exchange for defenseman Bryan Berard, who had been selected first overall in the 1995 draft, as well as center Martin Straka and enforcer Ken Belanger. The key to the deal was Berard, the first player in the history of the Ontario Hockey League to win rookie of the year and defenseman of the year honors in the same season. A steady blueliner who liked to join the rush, Berard had nineteen goals and thirty-five assists in just thirty-seven games in juniors.[73] The day after the trade, the famously hasty New York media was already comparing the eighteen-year old to future Hall of Famers Chris Chelios and Brian Leetch.[74] The Islanders, burned before when they overhyped young players, had reason to be more cautious in promoting Berard. Only a few weeks earlier Brett Lindros, whom the team once billed as its scorer of the future, ended his season after sustaining his third concussion in nine months.[75] Lindros would never play another game in the NHL. What should have been a learning experience for the Islanders, however, did not affect their hyperbole about Berard. "We think he has the upside of a superstar nature," Milbury told the press.[76] Bowness was just as enthusiastic. "With the offensive skills and the fire with which he plays the game, he should become a franchise player."[77] The *Blade* ran a cover photograph of Berard, who was born in Rhode Island, next to the headline "American Dream."[78]

Belanger, a rookie who had spent most of the season playing for the Maple Leafs' minor league affiliate in Newfoundland, knew nothing about the jersey controversy until he played his first home game at Nassau Coliseum on January 30. By then Islanders fans had amended the "We want fish sticks!" chant to more accurately convey their opinion of the uniforms. "I could hear the crowd chanting something," Belanger remembered. "I couldn't make out what they were chanting, so I asked a guy. I don't remember if it was Berard or Lachance. I said, 'What are they saying?' The crowd was chanting, 'No more fish sticks!' I go, 'What the hell are "No more fish sticks!"?' He goes, 'Our logo. It's a fisherman.' That was my first experience with the logo." At six-foot-four and 225 pounds, Belanger had compiled a whopping 222 penalty minutes in just thirty games in the minors, and he realized his role was to bring a measure of toughness and respect to a team with a flagging brand. Similar to his new teammates, Belanger disliked almost every aspect of the new uniform. "There's nothing that I would want to go buy that jersey on a shelf in a sporting-goods store," he quipped, "other than my name on the back of it."[79]

Although Muller's departure rid the team of its biggest distraction, the results on the ice remained mediocre. The trade came amid a stretch in January and February during which the Islanders dropped ten of thirteen games, including a five-game losing streak. On February 8 the Islanders fell 6–2 to the Rangers, their fourth loss to their rivals in four games, while "We want fish sticks!" echoed through Madison Square Garden. As further embarrassment for the Islanders brand, Milbury was so irate over late-game taunting by the Rangers' Ulf Samuelsson that he spit at the defenseman when he made a second pass by the Islanders bench. Samuelsson, who had a reputation as one of the dirtiest players in the league, relished the chance to school the uncouth Islanders coach on manners. "Right now I'm trying to teach my two kids not to spit at each other at home," he said. "It's going to be tough now that they saw it on TV."[80] Even though several Rangers players witnessed the incident, Milbury denied spitting, calling the accusation "ridiculous" and "ludicrous" and claiming he was "really offended."[81] *Newsday* dubbed the minor scandal "Watery Gate."[82] Decades later, Milbury, returning to his role as a hockey analyst, admitted on air that he had indeed spit at Samuelsson. "I did spit at Ulf Samuelsson, at least in his direction. I lost all sorts of respect for him when he told the press about it afterwards. It was just a gesture." His broadcast colleagues looked incredulous that Milbury would claim to have lost respect for a player who was the target of the coach's own saliva.[83] The quote epitomized Milbury's odd perspective on appropriate behavior in hockey.

With five minutes remaining in the Rangers game, the jerseys again became a target for derision when a fan tossed a fish on the ice. "We'll definitely remember that the next time we come in," Schneider told the *New York Times*. Asked years later to elaborate, Schneider said, "Those are things that as a professional athlete you store it in your memory bank, and you try to use it as motivation when you're playing, whether it's a fan or something that a player says in the paper or on the ice. It becomes motivation. For us, that rivalry was huge." The games were just as intense for Islanders fans, who had to endure constant ribbing in the stands over the fisherman logo. Belanger sympathized. "You could see how people would be upset about it, because now that logo's representing—it's making a joke of all the people of Long Island, right?"[84]

Incensed over the state of the franchise, the men behind the *Islander Insider* founded the Save the Islanders Coalition, known as STIC, with the primary goal of pressuring ownership to restore the original logo and sell the team. Leading the coalition were the newsletter's editor, Art Feeney, and Tom Croke, a computer consultant from Huntington. At its apex STIC had about four hundred members who attended weekly meetings, many of which included heated rhetoric about the new jerseys. "I won't say everyone, but a lot of the fans were embarrassed to wear it," Croke said. "The biggest complaint was, 'What was wrong with the original uniform? There's nothing wrong with it.'" To the chagrin of Islanders management, *Islander Insider* became a powerful mouthpiece of outrage against the logo. At one point the newsletter offered a twenty-seven-dollar deal for an annual subscription and a hat with the original logo. Citing sources, the *Insider* reported that a sporting-goods store in Westbury had sold only one fisherman jersey and was considering removing all new Islanders merchandise from its shelves.[85] The newsletter criticized Nyisles for dancing through the national anthem and blocking the views of spectators, and it openly wondered whether a new policy prohibiting fans from bringing banners into Nassau Coliseum was adopted to minimize criticism of the uniforms. It documented negative media coverage of the rebrand, including ESPN anchors reporting scores with wording such as "Kings 9, Fish Sticks 2."[86] Not content to grumble among themselves, the members of STIC even coordinated letter-writing campaigns to ownership, met with local politicians, and organized rallies to protest the jerseys.

The Islanders were clearly frustrated over STIC criticizing their new brand. When Croke appeared on a sports radio program in January, Pat

Calabria unexpectedly called in and criticized the *Islander Insider* and another newsletter, IFAN, an abbreviation for *Islander Fans Awareness Network*. In a subsequent issue of the *Blade*, Calabria wrote a full-page column ridiculing *Islander Insider* for its tendency to "take discredited stories, warmed-over gossip, and far-fetched rumors, and then dress them up and masquerade them as fact." He dismissed Feeney's sources as "about as reliable as someone's brother-in-law's cousin's girlfriend who works in the mail room." In return, Feeney wrote that Calabria was suffering from "Fonzie's disease," refusing to admit when he was wrong. The back-and-forth continued for weeks, with the jerseys at the center of a deepening rift between the team's top public relations executive and the editor of a newsletter read by much of its fan base. Calabria told Feeney that he was particularly sore over *Islander Insider* spreading the rumor that Gorton's was suing the team claiming trademark infringement over the fisherman logo. Feeney claimed the rumor had been circulating online for months and asked Calabria if he had ever published a rumor in his many years as a sports reporter. According to Feeney, Calabria said that he printed rumors only if he confirmed their veracity. "After hearing that, I expected Pat to tell me he had a bridge he wanted to sell me," Feeney wrote sarcastically. "He didn't, maybe next time."[87]

With the rhetoric ramping up, Islanders chief financial officer Art McCarthy and general counsel Bill Skehan met privately with Feeney and Croke and agreed to speak at a STIC meeting on February 28. Two hundred fans attended, and most of the crowd grew hostile when McCarthy and Skehan defended the fisherman jerseys. "McCarthy tried to tell us that some people like the new uniform," complained one fan, Sandy Kreple of Patchogue. "Some guy had to tell him that the point is not to have some people like it, but most people. You can find kids in kindergarten who know more about marketing than these guys." In an effort to gauge the fan base's opinion on the jerseys eight months after they were unveiled, Feeney polled 108 people at the meeting. Only 21 said they liked the new uniform, and a mere 12 came out in favor of the fisherman logo. There was a general feeling that management was out of touch. "This bunch changed the uniform without even considering the fans," said one man from Long Beach. A fan from Bellmore remarked incredulously, "Now they are having focus groups to see if the uniform should be changed again. They need a focus group for that?" Eighty-four percent of those polled suggested that STIC should demonstrate publicly. In the next issue of *Islander Insider* the group announced plans to hold a rally outside Nassau Coliseum on April 6.[88]

As their fans complained about team management in newsletters, the Islanders used their own mouthpiece, the *Blade*, as a channel to vent their frustrations over the failure of the rebrand. The franchise was surprisingly unrestrained in employing its official program to attack its critics. One item pleaded with *New York Post* columnist Larry Brooks to stop defending Kirk Muller for wanting off Long Island.[89] When Wayne Gretzky ridiculed the selection of one player from every team for the All-Star Game, which gave Mathieu Schneider a spot despite the Islanders' last-place record, the *Blade* charged the league's greatest player with "egotistical grandstanding."[90] In another issue the Islanders knocked one of their own players for his "gutless, very-unIslander-like move" of granting two anonymous newspaper interviews that were apparently critical of the team.[91] Not surprisingly, the Islanders took most exception to any backlash against the fisherman jerseys. At one point the *Blade* expressed disappointment in former Islander Ray Ferraro, then playing for the Rangers, for criticizing his former team's uniforms in a television interview.[92] Another time the organization called out MSG Network anchor Bob Page merely for asking Islanders dynasty winger John Tonelli about the new jerseys on air.[93] In retrospect the Islanders' constant protestations seem unbecoming for a professional sports franchise.

Meanwhile, the team continued its poor play into the spring, drawing even more volatility from Milbury. During a loss to the Devils on March 1 Milbury was so angry over a questionable penalty call against the Islanders that he threw two sticks and two water bottles on the ice, cursed at the referee, and was ejected. Afterward, the irate coach and general manager ignored the risk of a fine or suspension for criticizing the officials, treating the postgame interview more like the outspoken television analyst that he once was. Milbury let loose on referees in general for calling more penalties at key times against the Islanders because the team had a losing record and less at stake than their opponents. "I've said it since the beginning of the year," the coach said. "We're easy targets."[94] Milbury was just as short-tempered with his own players. Once, according to Dean Chynoweth, Milbury called out Scott Lachance in front of his teammates.[95] Lachance suffered a groin injury in training camp and rushed back to play in the regular-season opener, but his body had not healed, the injury grew worse, and he missed twenty-seven games in a row.[96] Despite Lachance's well-advised caution in rushing back a second time, Milbury questioned the heart of one of his top defensemen. "He more or less said he was faking his injuries and challenged him: 'Do you even want to play? Are you even hurt?'" Chynoweth recalled. "Then he came unglued and they were at one another." Milbury apparently thought that Lachance would be motivated to prove his coach wrong, but instead the locker room bordered on mutiny. "There were just so many things at that time that were starting to unravel," said Mick Vukota.[97]

Milbury's skewed approach to player relations found its next target in Wendel Clark. Toward the end of his career Clark resorted to daily medical treatments for his cranky back. "I haven't had a day since my third year [in 1987–88] when I haven't been sore," he confided to a reporter, "and I will be for the rest of my life."[98] Teammates respected the twenty-nine-year-old Clark for sacrificing his body with bruising body checks and viewed his daily routine of acupuncture, stretching, and massages as a sign of his commitment. Milbury was unconvinced. Players recalled a tense confrontation between the coach and Clark at the team's practice facility. Milbury questioned whether Clark wanted to play hockey anymore, noting that he sat at the end of the bench instead of the middle. When Clark defended his dedication to the Islanders, Milbury questioned it again, and Vukota thought that Clark was about to punch Milbury in the face. "Wendel stood up, and Wendel goes, 'You think you're God? 'Cause you're not.' And then a couple guys stood up and intercepted Wendel." At a team party later that day Milbury stunned Clark by pulling him aside and making light of the incident, as if it was just another act intended to spark the team. "Mike's there and everybody's having a few beers," Chynoweth recalled. "He grabs Wendel and was like, 'Well, we got a real rise out of them today, didn't we?'" The incident forewarned the departure of the most accomplished player left on the roster. On March 13 Milbury cut a deal with Toronto to ship out Clark, who had twenty-four goals, and Mathieu Schneider, the team's top defenseman and lone all-star. In return the Islanders received a package that included twenty-one-year-old defense prospect Kenny Jonsson.[99]

While the trade made some sense for the future, the short-term effects on the Islanders brand were devastating. The partings of Clark and Schneider deprived the team of its two best players, aside from Žiggy Pálffy, and continued the revolving door of athletes in fisherman jerseys. It also gave the impression that the Islanders were dumping the salaries of promising players at a time when the franchise desperately needed to win to sell its fans on the rebrand. By trading away Clark and Schneider and putting Martin Straka on waivers, the already low payroll dipped from $17.8 million to $15.03 million in a matter of three days.[100] Soon after, the Islanders saved another $70,000 by sending center Bob Sweeney to the Flames in exchange for journeyman left wing Pat Conacher and a draft pick.[101] For the thirty-six-year-old Conacher, the fisherman jersey was his seventh uniform in thirteen years and his third of a season that had previously included stints in Los Angeles and Calgary. It was also his last jersey in the NHL. "I didn't like it 'cause I'm a traditionalist," Conacher said. "Just like, why would you ever change the Montreal Canadiens jersey? It's one of the most beautiful jerseys in the league. It was like the Islander jersey to me. Why would you change it with all the winning they've done behind it and the people that played in those jerseys?"[102]

As expected the change in personnel damaged the on-ice performance. In two and a half weeks after trading Clark and Schneider the Islanders did not win a single contest. Mired in an eight-game losing streak, they faced the Rangers at Nassau Coliseum on the last day of March. The disparity between the rival brands was apparent even before puck drop. Fox prefaced its broadcast of the Saturday-afternoon game with footage of a world-famous scene from the Rangers' backyard, Times Square at night, with taxis zooming past bright lights. An unseen narrator sang the first few bars of "New York, New York," but stopped abruptly, recognizing the game would take place in unglamorous Nassau County. "Aw, forget it," he said with exasperation. "This scramble's not in the Apple." Lacking obvious imagery for Long Island, Fox settled for slang that evoked an altogether different type of island—"It's out on the Island, mon"—accentuated with an image of a hand stirring a tropical drink.[103] In the game the Islanders, trying to market a team of the future, used fifteen players between ages twenty and twenty-five, while the Rangers, selling a playoff-bound team of the present, had thirteen players at least thirty. Fichaud and Söderström, two young, inexperienced goalies, manned the Islanders' net; the Rangers had Mike Richter, already a two-time all-star and Stanley Cup champion. Not surprisingly the Islanders dropped the game 4–1, cementing their ninth straight loss, thirteenth in their last fifteen, and fifth in six tries against the Rangers that season. Adding injury to insult, Kenny Jonsson left the game with a concussion due to an errant Mark Messier elbow to the jaw.[104]

The Rangers brand was built around superstars such as Richter, who notched his twenty-second win of the season, and Messier, who scored his forty-sixth goal. The Islanders brand could not compete with that star power, especially in the absence of Clark and Schneider. Bertuzzi, hyped as a scorer who might sell tickets someday, may have actually damaged the team's image during the Rangers game. Two months after Milbury spat at Ulf Samuelsson, and later called for Bertuzzi to engage in "some sort of physical activity that might include a fight," Bertuzzi sucker-punched Samuelsson late in the game, exchanged punches with another Rangers player, and wrestled with a linesman trying to pull him away from attacking Samuelsson again.[105] With an opportunity to raise his national profile on the Fox broadcast, Bertuzzi instead came across as reckless. Rangers coach Colin Campbell said, "It's on national television. It's disgraceful." Even Milbury criticized the behavior. "Todd showed some fire, but I think he may have crossed the line there a little bit. There's no place for frustration, as much as that would be a natural reaction. It's an emotion that serves no good purpose." The unrepentant Bertuzzi was suspended three games.[106]

As the calendar turned to April, the merciful final month of the season, the Islanders' losing streak reached eleven games, one shy of the franchise record, and they had dropped an astonishing sixteen of their last eighteen. Management was resigned to finishing in the NHL cellar in the first season of the fisherman jerseys. As the April 6 rally against the new logo approached, perhaps the Islanders' most prominent alumnus, Stanley Cup captain Denis Potvin, was quoted saying, "It's unbelievable how much I don't like those uniforms."[107] The team had to choose between sticking with a widely criticized logo and sacking the signature element of a brand that was supposed to endure for years to come.

The mounting pressure from fans, media, and former players proved too difficult to ignore. On April 4 *Newsday* reported that the Islanders were seeking permission from the league to ditch the fisherman logo for the upcoming 1996–97 season, which marked the team's twenty-fifth anniversary. As a compromise the Islanders proposed retaining most of the elements of the new jerseys, including the color scheme, the lighthouse shoulder patches, and the waves, while replacing the fisherman with the old Long Island map logo. The timing suggested that the team wanted to defuse the fast-approaching rally led by the Save the Islanders Coalition, which was urging fans to wear apparel with the old logo.[108] Fans flooded the Islanders' offices with phone calls supporting the change.[109] However, the switch seemed uncertain the next day when word came out that the league was reluctant to leave merchandisers with racks of fisherman jerseys that were about to become obsolete. The abandonment of the fisherman logo would require the unlikely four-month extension of the December deadline for teams to notify the league about a uniform change.[110] Amid the uncertainty, Feeney said the rally would go ahead as scheduled.[111]

Unable to announce the desertion of the fisherman logo before the rally, the Islanders tried to appease the fan base by making their first public acknowledgments that dumping the traditional uniform was a mistake. Appearing on SportsChannel, chief operating officer Ralph Palleschi called the logo change "a bad decision" and placed blame on the NHL, saying the league "prompted" the Islanders to make the switch because of their low merchandise sales.[112] The explanation came too late to prevent more bad press. Two hours before the Islanders skated against the Sabres at Nassau Coliseum on April 6, three hundred people marched from the Long Island Marriott to Hempstead Turnpike, carrying signs scrawled with resentful messages such as "Restore the Original Uniform" and "Give Gorton's Back Their Logo and Give Us Ours Back."[113] Most fans wore the original Islanders uniform. One was dressed as the Grim Reaper. A boy held up a sign for the cameras with a hand-drawn fisherman logo and the common observation "It's Stan Fischler." The antagonistic atmosphere brought out reporters from two newspapers and three television stations, more media than the last-place Islanders were used to receiving.[114] "We're just ordinary people," one fan from Farmingdale told a *Newsday* reporter. "And those jerseys—the old jerseys—mean a lot to us." In an interview with the *Daily News* a season-ticket holder from Malverne insisted, "The entire jersey has to come back."[115]

For the designers at SME, the scene was humiliating. Never before had a jersey created by the agency resulted in such an outpouring of disdain. "They had riots in the street over the damn thing," remembered illustrator Pat McDarby, laughing in disbelief. "People protesting over a logo that we did was pretty funny and embarrassing." The company's cofounder Ed O'Hara thought the mockery of the logo overshadowed how carefully SME had analyzed industry trends when developing the new jerseys, even if the firm had misjudged the affection for the original Islanders crest. "It's really easy to look back and say that was ridiculous. Everybody involved and I think the entire industry has learned something from that, but I think you've got to be sensitive to what was going on. What were the trends? What were the objectives?" Islanders management, meanwhile, viewed the protests as a lack of gratitude for ownership's efforts to keep the Islanders on Long Island. Brett Pickett, the son of the Islanders majority owner, said he understood the fans' desire for different jerseys and better players but thought they did not appreciate the existential threat facing the club. "I knew at that point in time that the franchise on Long Island itself was a dubious proposition," Pickett said. "You could see the new markets and the new ownership coming into the league, and it just had substantially better buildings, deeper pockets, more glam than the Islanders did. The creeping suspicion started to grow that this franchise is really in a struggle to make it on Long Island. Those protests, from my vantage point, I thought, Gosh, if these people could see what I see."[116]

The contentious crowd continued to express itself inside the arena. In the second period the fans began chanting, "No more fish sticks!" Soon after, the Islanders took a 1 0 lead. They added another goal in the third. Then Travis Green iced the game with an empty-netter.[117] The clinching of the Islanders' twenty-first victory of the season and the conclusion of an eleven-game losing streak brought a roar from the crowd of 13,225, cheering the players wearing the uniforms they had protested a few hours earlier. "I think the question we got to ask is, Were they making fun of the jersey because we had a bad team, you know what I mean?" said goaltender Éric Fichaud, who earned the first shutout of his NHL career in the game. "It usually goes with it. If you're winning, you can play with pink jerseys. It wouldn't matter because you're winning games."[118]

On April 12 the Islanders called a much-anticipated press conference led by cochairman Robert Rosenthal. "We realize we made a mistake and we're here to admit it," he said. "Our fans and alumni have been heard." To the fan base's chagrin, Rosenthal announced that the NHL had rejected the request to discard the fisherman logo for the following season. However, the league granted the Islanders permission to wear their original logo for as many as fifteen home games in 1996–97 and eliminate the fisherman entirely starting in 1997–98. In response to fans' complaints about the team turning its back on tradition, the Islanders promised to raise banners to the rafters in honor of Al Arbour and Clark Gillies and named Gillies, Bob Nystrom, John Tonelli, and Ed Westfall as special ambassadors in the twenty-fifth anniversary season.[119] "There's a sense of frustration on the part of the fans, and the logo is part of that," Nystrom said at the time. "It would appear that was a mistake, and they're revising it. Is that because of pressure from the fans? Probably."[120] Asked about the return of the original logo, albeit for a limited number of games, Denis Potvin told a reporter, "I'm thrilled. I'm absolutely thrilled."[121] The next day the Islanders' 1995–96 season ended with a 5–5 tie against Montreal. That put their record at 22-50-10, last in the Atlantic Division and twenty-fourth out of twenty-six teams in the league.[122]

The phasing out of the fisherman jerseys placed the Islanders in an awkward marketing position for the next year. The team had admitted the logo was a mistake and shipped out prominent players associated with the fisherman such as Clark, Muller, and Schneider, but players would still be wearing the logo for the vast majority of their games the following season. Other elements of the rebrand also figured to remain, from Nyisles roaming the stands as the mascot to Milbury standing, and perhaps spitting and tossing hockey sticks, behind the bench. The New York press was unlikely to let go of the rebranding debacle, either. A premature obituary for the logo in *Newsday*, which sarcastically credited the logo for a "boom in sales of fish sticks" and increasing interest in *Moby Dick* across Long Island, exemplified the sort of media criticism the Islanders would have to endure for another season.[123]

At the same time the Islanders were ridiculed for adopting the fisherman logo, they also faced criticism from a small but vocal minority of fans who actually liked the jerseys and were sad to see them go. Despite the many failings of the rebrand, the homage to the baymen resonated with some Long Islanders from the East End, and they were disappointed by its abandonment. *Dan's Papers*, a resort newspaper based in the Hamptons, ran a front-page story that took exception to the sacking of the fisherman: "For the legendary Long Island Islanders hockey team to choose a bayman as their symbol to take them into the future was a great compliment to the East End. Last week, however, they fired him." To absolve the baymen from the controversy surrounding the jersey, *Dan's Papers* blamed the logo's failure on poor design that made the fisherman come across as too mellow. The article complained, "They might have said he did not look ferocious enough in a league that was filled with new teams with logos bearing pictures of Raptors, sharks, cougars, or black panthers. The peaceful Long Island bayman, even with the grimace, might even have had a hard time fending off an Anaheim Mighty Duck." A sarcastic editorial cartoon mocked the lack of other viable options for the Islanders logo. A hockey player in a jersey reading "The Brown Tides," a reference to the smelly waters off Long Island, was quoted saying, "We stink." Another player, wearing "The Ticks" across his chest, added, "We Suck!"[124]

To their credit the Islanders did not forget their pledge to the men who inspired the outgoing logo. The team made a preseason promise to the East Hampton Baymen's Association to donate all proceeds from messages that fans and sponsors paid to put on the scoreboard during the 1995-96 season. In May the association's secretary, Arnold Leo, received $3,770 from the Islanders.[125] In a response to Pat Calabria, Leo wrote that the baymen understood "how important tradition can be" and why the team reverted back to its original crest. "Well, we certainly thought the new Islanders logo was appropriate and beautifully designed," Leo continued in the letter. "The baymen are very fond of funny nicknames, and actually Old Fishsticks is not a bad one for the logo bayman, but probably it would only be funny in an acceptable way if the team was having a little better luck. But that's another thing about the baymen: they know that bad luck is just part of the grand scheme—good luck eventually shows up."[126]

In requiring the Islanders to wear fisherman jerseys in 1996-97, the NHL had cited its obligations to stores with the uniforms in stock. For all the negative publicity, the Islanders had actually profited from the switch over the past year, selling ten thousand jerseys and increasing sales of team apparel to seventeenth in the league, up several slots.[127] Still, merchandisers on Long Island remained skeptical about clearing their inventory, no matter how long the Islanders planned to skate in the controversial jerseys. "All the fans who come into my store say they love the jersey and love the lighthouse patch—they even like the wavy numbers," said the president of one sporting-goods shop. "They just all hate the fisherman."[128]

FIG. 1. Brett Lindros (*right*) wearing the original Islanders logo during the lockout-shortened 1994–95 season. Photo by Marc A. Weakland.

FIG. 2. Islanders general manager Don Maloney (*left*) introducing Mike Milbury as head coach on July 5, 1995. Photo by Joe Tabacca for the Associated Press.

FIG. 3. (*opposite top*) A Starting Lineup statuette of Kirk Muller, the only mass-produced figurine of an Islanders player in a fisherman jersey. Photo by Nicholas Hirshon.

FIG. 4. (*opposite bottom*) Rob Di Fiore as the Islanders' mascot, Nyisles. Photo courtesy of Rob Di Fiore.

FIG. 5. (*above*) Wendel Clark shooting on the Lightning's Daren Puppa on November 3, 1995. Photo by Al O'Meara for the Associated Press.

FIG. 6. (*above*) Darius Kasparaitis skating off the ice after cutting his hand in a fight on December 9, 1995. Photo by Bill Kostroun for the Associated Press.

FIG. 7. (*opposite top*) Žiggy Pálffy breaking away from the Senators' Steve Duchesne (*left*) en route to scoring on January 6, 1996. Photo by John Dunn for the Associated Press.

FIG. 8. (*opposite bottom*) Éric Fichaud making a save versus the Rangers on February 6, 1996. Photo by Ron Frehm for the Associated Press.

FIG. 9. Tommy Söderström blocking a shot against the Flyers on March 19, 1996. Photo by George Widman for the Associated Press.

FIG. 10. Nyisles taping a segment with Rangers goaltender Mike Richter at an Extreme Championship Wrestling event that aired on April 2, 1996. Photo courtesy of Rob Di Fiore.

FIG. 11. (*opposite top*) Jean-Pierre Dumont (*right*), selected by the Islanders with the number-three pick in the 1996 draft, with number-two pick Andrei Zyuzin of the Sharks (*left*) and number-one pick Chris Phillips of the Senators on June 22, 1996. Photo by James A. Finley for the Associated Press.

FIG. 12. (*opposite bottom*) Todd Bertuzzi (*left*) wearing the reimagined Islanders jersey that debuted during the 1996–97 season, which combined the original logo with the color scheme, lighthouse patches, and wavy numbers from the fisherman uniforms. Photo by John Dunn for the Associated Press.

FIG. 13. (*above*) Žiggy Pálffy (*left*) battling for a loose puck with the Maple Leafs' Jamie Macoun on October 31, 1996. Photo by John Dunn for the Associated Press.

FIG. 14. (*above*) Rick Bowness in his first game as head coach of the Islanders on January 24, 1997. Photo by Steve Miller for the Associated Press.

FIG. 15. (*opposite top*) Bryan Berard warming up in Calgary on January 28, 1997. Photo courtesy of Chris Krystalowich.

FIG. 16. (*opposite bottom*) Tommy Salo before a game against the Flames on January 28, 1997. Photo courtesy of Chris Krystalowich.

FIG. 17. Rich Pilon (*left*) skating past a goal celebration by the Devils' Doug Gilmour on February 26, 1997. Photo by John Dunn for the Associated Press.

FIG. 18. Pat Flatley, the first player from the fisherman jersey era inducted into the Islanders Hall of Fame, revealing his name on a banner on January 14, 2012. Photo by Nicholas Hirshon.

FIG. 19. A fisherman logo hoodie for sale at Nassau Coliseum in 2014.
Photo by Nicholas Hirshon.

FIG. 20. The Islanders' Cal Clutterbuck wearing the fisherman logo in
warm-ups as part of a one-night promotion on February 3, 2015. Photo by
Irene Jedrlinic Hirshon.

6

SPANO FOR PRESIDENT

After the ignominy of the 1995–96 season the Islanders went out on as high a note as a last-place team could muster, with a win and two ties in their final three games and the anticipation of the return to their traditional logo the next season. In five months as dual coach and general manager, Mike Milbury had rid the team of Kirk Muller and Wendel Clark, two high-salaried veterans who were out of place on a rebuilding roster. As the 1995–96 Islanders skated off the ice for the final time, their supposed goaltender of the future, Éric Fichaud, tapped helmets with their defenseman of the future, Kenny Jonsson, and their forward of the future, Todd Bertuzzi. It was one of the final images that fans saw before the off-season. "Fichaud, Jonsson, Bertuzzi, such important parts in the future of this hockey club, handling the puck for the final time as the final few seconds wind down," analyst Howie Rose said on the television broadcast. "And although the season did not end anywhere near the way Mike Milbury wanted it to, people you just saw handle the puck will be a large part of what you'll see from the New York Islanders next year and beyond."[1]

Entering their second season in the fisherman jerseys, the Islanders had reason to expect their young talent would keep developing. Žiggy Pálffy had scored forty-three goals, tied for fourteenth in the league, while linemate Travis Green broke out with twenty-five. They had a respectable winger in Niklas Andersson (fourteen goals); a solid defense corps with Jonsson, Darius Kasparaitis, Scott Lachance, and Bryan McCabe; and a potential number-one goaltender in Fichaud, who sported a .897 save percentage in his rookie year. In 1995–96 the team suffered through the distraction of a tanking top-line center who never wanted to play on Long Island and the misfortune of a league-leading 528 man-games lost to injuries. Now Muller was gone, and Milbury fired the team's orthopedist, two trainers, and an equipment manager, whom he held accountable for the injuries.[2] With any luck the 1996–97 Islanders would be healthier and free from soap-opera drama. "Next year," Pálffy said with confidence, "we'll have a chance to make the playoffs."[3]

If the Islanders were going to live up to Pálffy's prediction, they had work to do. Any attempt at salvaging the rebrand depended on winning, and the existing roster was too inexperienced and inadequate to escape the NHL cellar. In a stinging announcement in May, Brett Lindros, once positioned as the face of the franchise, confirmed that he was retiring at just twenty years old due to concussions.[4] The Islanders reached a three-year deal with defense prospect Bryan Berard in June, but that would still not be enough to push them into contention.[5] Milbury acknowledged that he needed a veteran NHL goalie, a solid defenseman, and three forwards for the top two lines, but he assured reporters that the Islanders could attract elite players by offering opportunity and the chance to live on Long Island.[6] "I can see it—the good things that are coming ahead for this team," he promised.[7] If Milbury's vision was correct, skeptics might finally be sold on the fisherman jerseys. A *Post* reporter contended that if the Islanders made the playoffs, fans would not care "if Travis Green was dressed in a toga."[8]

For weeks Milbury emphasized the importance of the Islanders' third overall pick in the 1996 draft.[9] With little money to offer free agents and few chips for trades, the Islanders' best route to improvement was the draft, and Milbury was intent on securing a player ready to make an immediate impact or trading the pick for one.[10] The Islanders had little to show for their high picks in recent seasons, selecting busts such as Dave Chyzowski (second overall in 1989), Scott Scissons (sixth overall in 1990), and Brett Lindros (ninth overall in 1994), so there was pressure on Milbury to select wisely in his first draft as general manager. "If we don't make the right call, it sets us back a lot, one or two years," he admitted.[11] Nonetheless, in a bizarre move only days before the draft on June 22, Milbury told his four full-time scouts, whose recommendations were crucial to the selection process, that he would let them go when their contracts expired on June 30. Milbury's decision put the organization in an awkward position of entrusting the future of the franchise to four men who knew they would not be around to see it.[12] At the draft Milbury chose right wing Jean-Pierre Dumont, coming off a forty-eight-goal season in juniors but lacking the intensity or defensive awareness of most NHL players. Despite his previous mantra that the Islanders had to translate the pick into an instant-impact player, Milbury said he did not think the eighteen-year-old Dumont would play right away.[13]

With the erratic Milbury at the helm, the organization descended into the same sort of chaos that unraveled the previous season. During a negotiating stalemate with the team's best player and leading scorer, restricted free agent Žiggy Pálffy, Milbury publicly insulted Pálffy's agent, Paul Kraus, for asking for what appeared to be a reasonable salary bump. "We hope that Žiggy will come to his senses," Milbury said. "We have no hope Paul Kraus will."[14] He also called Kraus a "moron."[15] (The nasty tenor climaxed two years later amid another round of negotiations between Pálffy and Milbury. Speaking of Kraus, who lived in Edmonton, Milbury cracked, "It's too bad he lives in the city. He's depriving some small village of a pretty good idiot.")[16] Negotiations were equally contentious with the Islanders' second-leading scorer, restricted free agent Travis Green, and Milbury stubbornly said that he was prepared to play the season without two-thirds of his top line.[17]

In a sign that Milbury was pushing out veterans in search of young players to fit the hard-hitting Bruins mold, the Islanders bought out the contract of their captain, Pat Flatley, ending his thirteen-year career on Long Island.[18] Flatley's departure concluded a poor relationship between captain and coach that included an incident when Milbury, incensed by the team's poor play, told the players they were unworthy of practicing in Islanders uniforms. According to Mick Vukota, a disobedient Flatley retrieved the jerseys from the trainer's office and put them in every stall, firmly telling Milbury that he had sacrificed his body for the Islanders and was not about to give up his jersey. Milbury reluctantly relented. "He thought we were some college team that you just strip the jersey off my back. No," Vukota said. "There's far more commitment than he realized."[19] In Flatley's absence the Islanders would play the 1996–97 season without naming a new captain. Milbury was assured an uncontested position as the face of the franchise.

Besides his tension with the players, Milbury was losing his coaches. After one year on Milbury's staff, goaltending coach Bob Froese resigned in the off-season, leaving the Islanders' young netminders without one of their first mentors in the NHL. Froese wanted to care for his father, who had been diagnosed with cancer, and his mother-in-law, who had Parkinson's disease, but he had been limited by a demanding travel schedule as a coach, going on the road with the Islanders and visiting their minor league affiliate in Salt Lake City. "The morning I had to give my answer, I wept at my kitchen table for about two hours, because I just loved hockey and I loved what I was doing," Froese said. In an emotional phone call with Milbury, Froese said he had decided to join the pastoral staff of a church in upstate New York. Thirty seconds of dead air ensued, as Milbury pondered losing a respected coach whose gentler style complemented his own rough approach. Finally, Milbury, sensing a negotiating ploy, asked, "How much are they offering you?" Froese laughed. "I said, 'Mike, if I told you what they were offering me, you'd think I was absolutely crazy.'" In a last-ditch attempt to retain Froese, Milbury arranged for him to meet Al Arbour at the draft. "Al Arbour told me that he was going to take me out and talk me out of this," Froese recalled. "He said, 'But Bob, I know you,' and he said, 'You're doing what is best.'" With that Froese was gone.[20] Around the same time, one of Froese's protégés, Tommy Salo, requested a trade. Milbury refused to ship him away.[21]

Meanwhile, another assistant coach, Guy Charron, was becoming disenchanted. In order to infuse the Islanders with the Bruins mentality, Milbury had not only fired the Islanders' four scouts in favor of former Bruins chief of scouting Gordie Clark but also hired former Bruins goalie Gilles Gilbert to replace Froese and promoted former Bruins coach Rick Bowness from an assistant to associate coach, even though Charron had seniority. While Charron had the unglamorous tasks of running specialty teams and serving as a mediator between the hard-driving Milbury and his mutinous players, Bowness became the coach's right-hand man, the first choice to fill in when Milbury traveled and in prime position to take over the bench someday if Milbury ever decided to focus solely on his GM duties. Charron felt slighted. He had been a much better NHL player than Bowness was, and he was still sore from being passed over for the head-coaching job in Calgary, where he had been an assistant for five seasons. "I felt [with] my loyalty to Mike and some of those things, I would have at least been given an opportunity or had discussions prior to the hirings and knowing what the direction Mike wanted to take was," Charron remembered. "I didn't think it was the right communication to me."[22]

With holes in their lineup and behind their bench, the Islanders were desperate to finish the off-season with at least one top-flight forward. Opportunity arrived when restricted free agent Jeremy Roenick, an all-star center who twice scored fifty goals in a season for the Blackhawks, could not come to terms on a new deal. Long Island appeared to be an unlikely landing spot: Roenick was one of the game's biggest offensive threats, and any team that signed him would have to pay about $4 million per year and compensate Chicago with five first-round draft picks, a high cost for a rebuilding team that was relying on the draft.[23] Besides, Roenick had little incentive to rush from a contender to a cellar dweller. Still, Milbury set up Islanders fans for an almost inevitable letdown by playing up the possibility. "As a coach, I keep hearing myself say, 'You're up, Jeremy, you're up, Jeremy, you're up, Jeremy,'" Milbury told *Newsday*, which ran optimistic headlines like "Roenick Deal Near" and "Isles Close In on Roenick."[24] In his autobiography *J.R.*, Roenick recalled that Milbury carried an offer sheet in his briefcase for weeks. He never sent it, and Roenick was traded to Phoenix on August 16.[25] Meanwhile, a potential trade to reacquire goalie Glenn Healy broke down when Milbury insisted that Healy take a pay cut.[26] After setting an April agenda to obtain an established goaltender, a steady defenseman, and three elite forwards for the 1996–97 season, Milbury added only one impact player to the roster by signing Bryan Berard, who was already in the system. In an uninspiring first off-season as general manager, Milbury's most notable acquisitions were little-known forwards such as right wing Brent Hughes, coming off a meager five goals the previous year, and center Claude Lapointe, who had only four.[27]

Milbury tried to spin the failed pursuit of Roenick as proof the Islanders had money to spend. "We had a chance to get in there, in the whirl, and we showed we're a credible player in the game," Milbury said, claiming that agents for several NHL free agents had called him over the summer after hearing about his willingness to pay top dollar for Roenick. But the general manager's ringing phone was little solace to the fan base. In the pages of the former *Islander Insider* newsletter, redubbed the *7th Man*, the Roenick courtship was framed as merely a public relations ploy to generate media coverage in a generally unproductive off-season. "The fans will be angry," the newsletter predicted. "Some already believe the Roenick affair was concocted by the minority owners and Milbury. The goal: Make it look like they'll spend money without actually spending any."[28]

Milbury's inability to wrangle star power was another blow to the Islanders brand. *Newsday* estimated that acquiring Roenick would have added at least one thousand new season-ticket holders.[29] Without a marquee name to help them stand out in the competitive New York City market, the Islanders assumed the role of laughingstocks once more. On WFAN one afternoon mischievous host Steve Somers announced on air that the station was about to cut to live coverage of "a major press conference at the Nassau Coliseum."[30] Hoping for a big signing, fans called the Islanders to inquire about the nature of the event.[31] In fact, the team had nothing to announce, and Somers was only setting up another bit at the Islanders' expense. WFAN's listeners heard Somers's producer, Eddie Scozzare, impersonating an Islanders executive at a supposed news conference to announce the signings of no-name free agents the team had picked up days earlier. Scozzare thanked Islanders fans for coming—"both of you"—over the sounds of snoring and crickets.[32]

By then the Islanders had come to accept Somers's good-natured barbs, which usually involved puns based on the names of their players or playing songs from the Broadway show *Oklahoma!* to emphasize the rural heritage of Long Island. His taunts tended to be harmless.

This time, though, Somers's promise of a major press conference raised the hopes of Islanders fans just for the sake of cheap laughs, and the influx of phone calls bothered the team's receptionist. Islanders public relations executive Chris Botta normally viewed Somers as a decent person. "That was the only time," he said, "where I can say I was genuinely annoyed." Apparently, so was Milbury. A few weeks later Islanders players gathered for a charity softball game against WFAN employees in Massapequa Park. When Somers approached the plate the Islanders player on the mound suddenly feigned injury. In came Milbury to relieve him—and promptly throw a knockdown pitch. Recounting the incident two decades later, Somers recalled being frazzled. "If I didn't back off and duck, that thing hits me in the head—he threw it hard," Somers said. Informed that Somers was actually frightened, Botta replied, "Good. I'm glad he was."[33]

Despite Milbury's missteps and Somers's shtick, the Islanders managed a pretty good off-season in public relations. In June the team kicked off an annual tradition by hosting a free party at Nassau Coliseum during the draft, featuring live television coverage of the selections, appearances by Islanders players past and present, and complimentary popcorn and beverages.[34] Despite the team's last-place finish, three thousand fans showed up, and the normally critical *7th Man* newsletter raved, "It was a booming success!"[35] Among other attempts to foster goodwill, the Islanders judiciously promoted their past in concert with their future by sending Bryan Berard and Bob Nystrom in tandem to youth hockey clinics in Hauppauge and Syosset. Berard was also dispatched to autograph signings in Massapequa and Kings Park.[36] As part of a new charitable campaign named Isle Make a Difference, the Islanders announced food drives and player visits to cancer patients and abused children.[37] The Islanders finally landed some positive media coverage, too. In July Robert Smith, the front man for the postpunk band the Cure, was photographed wearing a fisherman jersey during a concert.[38] In September Milbury appeared alongside Bertuzzi, Fichaud, Lachance, and Mick Vukota on *Good Morning America*, where the players led the local weather forecast.[39] The team even signed a three-year deal to broadcast its games on a popular radio station whose signal stretched from Manhattan to Montauk.[40] Although the Islanders would still be stuck wearing the fisherman jerseys on the ice, no rule forced them to use the much-maligned icon in other media. The club took advantage by developing a secondary logo, pulling the all-caps "ISLANDERS" wordmark off the uniform, for use in newspaper ads.[41]

Still, the Islanders were weighed down by familiar problems. As new NHL arenas went up across the country, Nassau Coliseum remained subpar, with a leaky roof, insufficient luxury boxes, and concessions limited by an outdated ventilation system. "It's like a grand old lady that needs to have a makeover," Milbury said.[42] On the ice the team also did not have much to offer fans. In his increasingly hostile negotiations with Pálffy and Green, Milbury issued an ultimatum on August 22, telling his players they could either sign the next day or face significantly reduced proposals.[43] Once again Milbury's rhetoric set into motion a war of words. The agents called his bluff and ignored the deadline. Pálffy threatened to play in Europe. Milbury told the press that Green had demanded to be traded. Green angrily denied it.[44] Asked about interest in Green among other teams, Milbury snarkily told a reporter, "If I said none, it would be insulting. I don't want to be insulting. It's not my style."[45] League sources suggested the Islanders were trying to hammer out trades for replacement forwards such as Keith Primeau, Brendan Shanahan, Bryan Smolinski, and Doug Weight, any of whom would have added name recognition and offensive punch.[46] But as the preseason dragged deep into September, the team's two leading scorers remained home, with no new acquisitions to offset their loss.

Then, in the span of two weeks, the evolving Islanders brand got a series of boosts. First, Pálffy agreed to a two-year pact worth $3.1 million, giving the top-line winger just enough time to fly from his native Slovakia to Long Island, get in a few practices, and travel with the team to the regular-season opener in Los Angeles on October 4.[47] Although the Islanders lost 1–0 to the Kings, they kept the score close behind strong goaltending from Fichaud, who made thirty-eight saves. Derek King said his teammates were out to prove they were more than "just the same roll-over-and-die Islanders."[48] They sent that message in their next two games, tying the Sharks in San Jose and the Senators in Ottawa to earn their first two points of the season.[49] Then Green came to terms for one year at $1.1 million and headed to Uniondale to take his spot in the lineup for the home opener.[50]

For Islanders fans, though, the most exciting news had more to do with dollars and cents than sticks and pucks. After five years of the absentee ownership of John Pickett and the day-to-day management of the shareholders known as the Gang of Four, news surfaced that the team was on the verge of falling into new hands. The prospective buyer was everything the fan base wanted: he came with deep pockets, New York roots, and a pledge to keep the team on Long Island. The day before the Islanders' first home game of the season, *Newsday* ran the story on its front cover. "Texan Ready to Buy Islanders," the headline blared. "His Promise: The Puck Stays Here."[51] Inside the newspaper Pálffy summed up the reaction of the players and the fans with two words: "Holy schneikes!"[52]

Nobody knew much about John Spano. The first reports had this much down about the man willing to spend $185 million on the Islanders and their cable television rights: Spano was only thirty-two years old, grew up in Manhattan, owned a house on Long Island's East End, and spent most of his time in Dallas, where he had season tickets for the Stars. He was the president of a firm that leased aircraft and heavy equipment, and he owned companies that sold beverages and cookware. He was married with no children, and friends called him shy and never flashy. Most important for the fans, Spano said his immediate priorities were to build a new arena for the Islanders and improve the team. The promises came with a red flag: Spano had previously pursued two other NHL teams, the Stars and the Florida Panthers, only to have the deals fall through. Reporters also had trouble confirming his net worth. As one newspaper columnist presciently warned, "You always have to worry about the devil you don't know."[53]

The questions about Spano's inability to acquire the Panthers and the Stars did not matter to a long-suffering fan base that craved a savior. Besides, the Panthers absolved Spano, saying his prospective purchase fizzled because their owner decided not to sell the team, and the owner of the Pittsburgh Penguins said, "I would certainly vouch for John Spano's character." Islanders management had already announced a verbal agreement to sell to Spano, pending a rubber stamp by the NHL Board of Governors in December. Spano had the backing of NHL commissioner Gary Bettman, and the league released a statement saying it would start the approval process "as quickly as possible." The *New York Times* reported that the deal could be finalized as soon as the end of October. *Newsday* heralded the "dawning of a new era" on Long Island.[54]

When Nassau Coliseum opened its doors the next night for the home opener against the Flyers, Spano's emergence as the presumed new owner of the Islanders added electricity to the sellout crowd. In another sign that the team was turning a page, the fisherman jerseys were not invited. The Islanders would still wear their home and away uniforms with the fisherman logo throughout the season, but on this night they debuted what was known as a "third jersey," which NHL rules allowed them to use for a limited number of games. The third jerseys paired the beloved original logo with the ocean waves and lighthouse patches that fans said were their favorite elements of the fisherman uniform.[55] Fans settled into their seats for a video that commemorated the team's silver anniversary season with clips from the glory years, followed by the returns of former stars Ed Westfall, John Tonelli, and Clark Gillies to the Coliseum ice. Fireworks soared to the catwalks lining the roof of the arena. Roman candles illuminated the glass when the 1996–97 Islanders were introduced, skating out to the roar of 16,297 throats. Spano watched intently from the owner's box.[56] The players were charged up. Marty McInnis and Derek King each scored twice. Derek Armstrong added another. Fichaud came within 30.9 seconds of a shutout. The 5–1 final score gave the Islanders their first win of the season. "This is like a dream come true," Spano said.[57]

After a crushing season in 1995–96, the Islanders no longer expected their fan base to embrace the fisherman jerseys, nor did they put much effort into promoting the outgoing logo anymore. The jerseys would be history in seven months anyway, or maybe eight if the team somehow squeaked into the playoffs. In fact, the organization was so eager to move past the fisherman as its symbol and renew the association with the classic crest that team vice president Al Arbour offered a frank assessment when a reporter asked about the two logos. "You don't see countries changing their flags because it's a good marketing tool," Arbour steamed. "I don't like the idea that teams, and that includes us, change their jerseys because some marketing guys say it will sell better. I like tradition."[58]

Nevertheless, the Islanders were not giving up entirely on the fisherman brand. The team picked a telling slogan for 1996–97: "A Season to Remember." For a franchise with little to show for itself but its legacy, some success in 1996–97 could at least improve public memory about the rebrand and prevent the fisherman-era Islanders from going down as one of the worst sports-branding failures of all time. With a 1-1-2 record and Spano in the owner's box, the franchise had reason to hope. A few days later the team released an anniversary promotional film titled *Never Say Die: The Story of the New York Islanders*, which made bold comparisons between Milbury's crew and the teams that won four straight Stanley Cups. "It's just a matter of bringing that kind of dynasty back to the nineties now," Todd Bertuzzi said in the tape. "We got the same kind of mix, different names though on the back, and no reason why we can't do the same thing that they did in the eighties."[59]

Privately, the players were optimistic but knew better than to expect a championship anytime soon. Amid the postgame revelry of the home opener, a veteran Islanders player pulled aside the nineteen-year-old Berard, high off his first NHL victory. The player spoke words of caution: "Don't think they're all like this here."[60]

Five days after the home opener, the Islanders returned to Nassau Coliseum to face Keith Primeau, Paul Coffey, and the Hartford Whalers. Now they were without their classic jerseys, the fanfare, and the sellout crowd that rocked the home opener. Milbury warned his players about a letdown. "I think that maybe that kind of got us thinking about it," Berard told a reporter.[61]

Before a much quieter crowd of 8,019, the Islanders dragged through the game. They did not have a shot on their first four power plays and went scoreless in seven tries with the man advantage. They registered only four shots in the second period. Scott Lachance and Darius Kasparaitis were caught behind the net for a Whalers goal. Tommy Salo allowed a softie. The Whalers, playing without number-one goaltender Sean Burke, managed a 3–1 victory.[62]

The *Times* said the Islanders skated "as if they had hangovers." *Newsday* riffed that they "played Jonah" to the Whalers. The *Daily News* called them "flatter than Kansas."[63]

Of more concern to the players was Milbury's assessment. "It's always disappointing as a coach when you try to implement something, or at least make a point on something, and it falls on deaf ears," he told the beat reporters. "Maybe that's because I didn't deliver the point properly. Having not listened to it this morning, they'll probably have to hear it from me again tomorrow."[64]

Milbury left the postgame press conference with an ominous guarantee: "I'll find a way. I promise, I'll find a way."[65]

Milbury was still ticked the next day at practice. As the players finished an hour-long skate at Nassau Coliseum, he went onto the ice carrying a hardbound edition of *Webster's New World Dictionary*, its pages marked with yellow slips of paper to note words of importance. He defined them one by one, words like *commitment, compete, desperation, fear, hustle, intensity, pain, ready, sacrifice, communication, consistency, discipline, focus, insecure, motivation, react, resilient, support,* and *team*. After Milbury finished each definition, the players skated the length of the ice. This went on for twenty-five tiring minutes.

"They can't just be empty words," Milbury said. "I just wanted to make sure I was very clear on every word, on each meaning of every word. These are things that I believe in."[66]

The players left the ice sweaty and exhausted. A reporter overheard Mick Vukota saying "uncle" as he skated off. "I remember thinking, How many letters are there in the alphabet?" Vukota said.[67]

The players did not publicly complain about the unconventional practice. "We needed a little butt-kicking," Bryan McCabe said. Added Scott Lachance, "We have to understand we're not good enough, ever, to lay back." Derek King even compared Milbury's tactics to Al Arbour drills when players were forced to skate without pucks. "It's never fun getting skated, but I think it's an eye-opener for everybody," he said. "The words he did bring up, we've talked about them before. When we lose that edge, forget about some of those words, it's Mike's job to bring them back to us."

Privately, however, the practice bred more resentment for Milbury. Söderström, who had played only twenty-six seconds in the Whalers game in relief of Salo, was not inspired by the coach's reading. "On A, he said, 'Attitude.' And then he screamed, 'You have no fucking attitude,'" Söderström remembered. "And then we needed to skate back and forth to the other side. And then after one time he comes to B. And it was something on B. And then he comes to C, D, E. I don't know if he went all the way, all the letters, but I remember that. And then I was joking about, 'Maybe he should have said on A, "Asshole," that he was an asshole.'"[68]

Milbury's lesson only weakened the confidence of his young players. After one win and two ties in their first four games, the Islanders slumped, going 0-4-2 in their next six. Again, the relationship between the coach and his team was strained. In Detroit Milbury benched Bertuzzi, the latest player in his doghouse, even though Bertuzzi's in-laws drove three hours from Ontario to see him play. "I'm furious," Bertuzzi told *Newsday*.[69] After another loss against Tampa Bay, Milbury threatened to trade some players and said they were driving him to drink—"about three vodkas," to be precise.[70] Milbury also renewed his rampage versus the referees, earning another fine when he colorfully criticized officiating that "makes me just want to puke."[71] The fan base had a similar reaction to the Islanders' stomach-turning performance, resulting in a 1-5-4 record at the end of the month. During a loss on Halloween to the Maple Leafs, which marked the return of public enemy Kirk Muller, Islanders fans switched from serenading the forward with shouts of "We hate Muller!" to booing the home team to chanting, "Help us, Spano!"[72] At the next game the Nassau Coliseum sound system piped in the Midnight Oil song "Blue Sky Mining," with the chorus, "Who's gonna save me?"[73]

Spano was not around to answer, not yet, and the Islanders spent the first few weeks of November mired in mediocrity, winning three games, losing three, and tying two. The team crumbled. Angry that Berard was straying too often into the offensive zone, Milbury punished the rookie defenseman by using him at left wing in one game.[74] In practice the players were shooting pucks at each other when Bertuzzi shot high at Dan Plante's head, leading Plante to ram Bertuzzi into the boards and wrestle him until the men were separated by their teammates.[75] Through eighteen games the Islanders were averaging only two and a half goals. The only promising development involved their new third jerseys. At the time, the team was 2-8-4 in the fisherman jerseys but undefeated when wearing the original logo, going 2-0-2.[76] Although the sample size was small, it was enough to fuel speculation among the Islanders about the curse of the fisherman logo. "In general, hockey players are superstitious," Pilon said, although he added that he never blamed the losses on the fisherman. "It has nothing to do with the logo. It had everything to do with the team, probably who are we playing, right? That's just superstitious, and all athletes are like that."[77]

On November 17 Milbury finally pulled off a trade for some offense, albeit at a high price. The general manager sent hard-hitting defenseman Darius Kasparaitis and a prospect to Pittsburgh in exchange for holdout center Bryan Smolinski. At age twenty-four Smolinski had already played four NHL seasons and developed a reputation for a quick release, accurate shot, and crafty playmaking. His twenty-four goals and sixty-four points the previous season would have placed him third on the Islanders behind only Pálffy and Green. Smolinski said the right things to reporters, expressing hope that he would find his "calling" by leaving the Penguins, where he was stuck behind Mario Lemieux and Ron Francis on the third line, to what figured to be a more prominent role with the young Islanders.[78] On the other hand, Pittsburgh was coming off a trip to the conference finals, while the Islanders were in last place. "I knew they did not have a chance to win," Smolinski said.[79]

The deal was bittersweet. Losing Kasparaitis, a former fifth-overall pick who manned the Islanders' blue line for five seasons, diluted a defensive corps that had been the team's lone strength. Kasparaitis was only twenty-four, the same as Smolinski, and his up-tempo, feisty play made him a fan favorite. For a team trying to rehab its brand, shipping out one of its most popular and longest-tenured players was a dicey proposition. Milbury admitted the front office was divided on whether to make the trade, but he said the need for offense forced him to pull the trigger. Another factor, as with so many of Milbury's moves, was Smolinski's upbringing with the Bruins when Milbury was their assistant general manager. No matter the reason, the trade caught Kasparaitis off guard. Milbury once singled out Kasparaitis as a "fierce competitor," and, only a day before the trade, he assured the defenseman that he would remain an Islander as long as Milbury was general manager.[80] Kasparaitis was packing for the Islanders' upcoming West Coast trip when he received a surprise phone call from Milbury informing him of the deal. "I was like, 'What do you mean, I got traded? You told me that I was here until you're here.' So basically, that was kind of a shock to me."[81]

After ending his relationship with Kasparaitis poorly, Milbury got off to a bad start with Smolinski. Since Smolinski was holding out in Pittsburgh, Milbury had to sign him as part of the trade, and the sides promptly agreed to a one-year deal believed to be about $1 million.[82] When Smolinski joined the team, Milbury made clear that the salary he just dished out, high by Islanders standards, came with high expectations. Vukota remembered a stunned Smolinski walking into the Islanders' locker room for the first time after a conversation with Milbury. "He goes, 'Can you believe that guy? He just told me, "Don't embarrass me. I gave you a lot of money."' So here's a ten-year veteran. He's never been spoken to that way. You're taught as a player to separate the business from the game." After being blindsided by Milbury, Smolinski was also taken aback when he saw his fisherman jersey for the first time. "It was a joke," he said. "You come into the room and you see this logo, and you're kind of chuckling. You try and grow a beard to see who can look like the fisherman throughout the year. You have to make light of it."[83]

The good-natured Smolinski quickly overcame any shock over his new uniform. In his debut as an Islander he contributed the tying goal to help the Islanders earn a point against the Mighty Ducks.[84] With a proven scorer in the fold, the team sprang to life. In Smolinski's first eleven games with his new club, the Islanders had their most impressive tear of the fisherman era, securing six victories and two ties to raise their record to 10-11-8 by December 12.[85] The rejuvenated offense scored thirty-five goals behind the first line of King, Green, and Pálffy and the second line of Niklas Andersson, Smolinski, and Marty McInnis, remaining potent even after Milbury juggled the players around.[86] Tommy Salo was sensational in net, earning his first two career shutouts and the best third-period save percentage in the league.[87] Five-foot-nine Claude Lapointe, hustling on the third line, delivered a series of bone-crunching hits, including one with such force that a pane of glass in the right corner exploded.[88] The stretch culminated with an 8–2 drubbing of the Coyotes and a delicious win over the Rangers at Madison Square Garden. When former Islanders star Clark Gillies returned to Nassau Coliseum to watch his retired number 9 raised to the rafters, he shared his enthusiasm with the energetic crowd. "This team is playing great hockey," Gillies said, "and getting better and better every day."[89]

It was good enough to catapult the Islanders, dismissed over the summer as cellar dwellers, into an early-season playoff spot.

As the Islanders ascended the standings, their fans were just as excited about the pending sale of the franchise. On November 26 John Spano resurfaced at a news conference at Nassau Coliseum to formally announce his agreement to buy a 90 percent interest in the team. Spano fortified his status as a fan favorite by describing how he would pump money into the team and the arena without meddling with Milbury's hockey decisions. "The goal of this new ownership group will be to build the next generation of champions," Spano said. "Every decision we make will be based on one question: What is best for hockey?"[90] In a photo op for the gaggle of reporters, Spano stood alongside Nassau County executive Thomas Gulotta, the area's highest-ranking official, while they held up matching number-96 jerseys to commemorate the year of the purchase. Some observers took Gulotta's presence as a hopeful sign that the county might chip in public funding to help renovate or replace the Coliseum. Then, in what seemed like a peace offering, Gulotta handed Spano a county flag.[91]

The fan base was overjoyed. The *7th Man* gleefully suggested that the Islanders should adopt "Happy Days Are Here Again" as their theme song and suggested another Cup was in the offing with an all-caps, front-page headline that pleaded, "HEY! STANLEY!!! YOU CAN COME HOME!" Long Islanders inundated Spano with letters and calls of support. On Thanksgiving Eve Spano took out full-page newspaper ads expressing gratitude to the fans. "I will do everything I can," Spano wrote, "to return a winner to you."[92] Spano also met with the leaders of the Save the Islanders Coalition, who voluntarily changed the group's name to Support the Islanders Coalition now that Spano was assuming control.[93] "It relieves a lot of pressure on the fans," said one of the group's cofounders, Art Feeney. "The fans are happy."[94] Hopes were raised so high that almost any outcome shy of a second dynasty would be disappointing.

In hindsight the rush to crown Spano as the savior of the franchise—by fans, the press, and the outgoing ownership—blinded them to red flags. The Islanders unveiled Spano as their new owner before the sale was even approved by the NHL Board of Governors, a step that was initially scheduled for December but then suspiciously postponed until January.[95] After Spano was formally introduced by the team, the press felt free to jump the gun, too. The front page of *Newsday* blared, "Done Deals." The *Daily News* headline read, "New Era Begins for Isles." In the *New York Times*, columnist Dave Anderson included Spano among the sports figures he wanted to thank on Thanksgiving, for buying the Islanders and promising to keep them on Long Island. The press ignored questions about Spano's net worth, wrongly assuming that he must have been thoroughly vetted by the Islanders and the NHL. *Newsday* greeted him as "rich Uncle Pennybags on the Monopoly board." The *Times* assured its readers that Spano was paying $165 million for the team and added, with no evidence, "and there's more where that came from." In one common contradiction, *Newsday* blamed the team's descent on outgoing owner John Pickett running the team from Florida, labeling him absentee, but explained away the impact of Spano holding the reins from even farther away in Dallas. Reacting to the media coverage, the Islanders' Rich Pilon said, "It can't be any worse than Pickett."[96]

In just a few months' time Spano supplanted Milbury as the most high-profile Islander, appearing on more front pages and television segments than the ESPN analyst-turned-coach and any of the players. He was also the most popular. Fans chanted his name and waved "Spano for President" signs, contributing to a newfound electric atmosphere at the Coliseum. The Islanders took notice. Even before Spano took control the team tried to translate the enthusiasm over his coming into ticket sales. The day after Spano's introductory news conference, the Islanders ran an ad in *Newsday* that prodded fans to "celebrate our new ownership with great seats starting at $15." Another spot in December alluded to the passion that Spano had generated in the arena: "You can feel it! There's a new energy and excitement at Nassau Coliseum." Curiously, one ad took the unusual step of naming the prospective owner. On December 18 the team promoted an upcoming game beneath a bold pull quote from Spano: "JOIN US FOR A NIGHT TO REMEMBER." The ad consisted of an eleven-sentence statement in which Spano thanked fans for their warm welcome and said he felt "extremely privileged to be part of a team so rich in tradition."[97]

Alongside Spano's statement in the *Newsday* ad was the image of an unnamed Islanders player in full stride. It was Žiggy Pálffy, the team's leading scorer. Looking back, the Islanders' unwillingness to promote Pálffy as the face of the franchise is puzzling. During the two seasons when the Islanders wore the fisherman jerseys, Pálffy was the best player on the roster, potting ninety-one goals to rank him among the league leaders. The team's second-best scorer, Travis Green, had forty-eight, many of them assisted by Pálffy. "Žiggy was a budding superstar in the league," said Green, who had the two most productive seasons of his career playing with Pálffy. "Highly skilled. Great hockey sense. Could see the ice very well. Had a bullet of a shot."[98] In the 1995–96 season the dynamic right wing scored 19 percent of the Islanders' goals, the second-highest percentage among the NHL's top scorers. As 1996 turned into 1997, Pálffy had 23 percent of his team's tallies.[99] Not only could he score, but he also possessed the qualities that teams usually look for when choosing players to market. The happy-go-lucky Pálffy was young and handsome, with an infectious smile and a flowing mullet that left strands of brown hair peeking out from the back of his helmet. Some spectators could be seen wearing Pálffy wigs at Nassau Coliseum.[100] Most important from a marketing perspective, Pálffy was exciting to watch. "Žiggy Pálffy was always fun to see," said goalie Tommy Söderström. "He could do whatever he wanted with the puck."[101]

The Islanders recognized Pálffy's talent. He was named the Islander of the Year for the 1995–96 season, and a glowing article in the *Blade* applauded him for working to overcome his perceived defensive liabilities and taking private English classes to better communicate with coaches and teammates. In summing up his breakout season, the article noted, "Very few would have expected his star to rise so quickly." Despite acknowledging his ascension, the Islanders decided against marketing their best player. Although Milbury had designated Pálffy an alternate captain, management was concerned about putting too much pressure on him to become a leader. "He was not the type of player who can put a team on their back and lead a team deep into the playoffs," said Brett Pickett, the son of the Islanders owner. "It just wasn't who he was." Pálffy also went through fits of indifference on the ice that troubled his coaches more than they should have. "Some nights, if he decided that he wasn't gonna play to his potential, there's nothing you could do about it," said assistant coach Guy Charron. "You had to deal with it, but it was frustrating for a coach because you knew how good this kid could be." The concerns about Pálffy played out in the newspapers. In the twenty-three-month period when the fisherman served as the Islanders' primary logo, from June 1995 through April 1997, the team published nearly one hundred ads in *Newsday* revolving around photographs of players such as Darius Kasparaitis, Brett Lindros, and Mathieu Schneider. Pálffy was the centerpiece just once, in October 1996, even though he outscored and outlasted Kasparaitis, Lindros, and Schneider on Long Island.[102]

By not pushing Pálffy in advertisements, the Islanders missed an opportunity to associate the fisherman jerseys with one of the most exciting players in professional hockey. With almost zero promotion, Pálffy had become the talk of the NHL. The Islanders' opponents usually sought him as an intermission guest on their telecasts. An NHL International broadcast crew insisted on speaking with him. ESPN anchorman Keith Olbermann obsessed over him on *SportsCenter*.[103] Although the Islanders rarely employed Pálffy as a promotional tool, the NHL did. *Rinkside*, the league's magazine for season-ticket holders, dedicated five pages to a glowing profile of Pálffy titled "Enchanting Isle," complete with a full-page action photograph showing Pálffy following through on a slap shot. The mainstream media gave him ink, too. In December 1996 the *New York Times* singled out Pálffy for a rare profile on an Islanders player, calling him the "most promising talent" on a team "with little identity or recent success."[104]

The praise did not impact the Islanders' marketing approach. As Pálffy kept racking up points, the Islanders continued to promote themselves as John Spano's team. It proved to be a catastrophic decision.

In the second half of December, Pálffy and the Islanders followed their rise in the standings with a plunge. After the Bryan Smolinski trade lifted the team to a 6-3-2 run and into playoff position, the Islanders dropped twelve of their next sixteen games, including a six-game losing streak. The old signs of organizational strife reappeared. When Todd Bertuzzi was demoted to the minors on December 12 the young forward was so angry that he demanded a trade before backing down.[105] After a loss an impatient Milbury threatened more changes. "I can assure you, people will pay a price," he told *Newsday*. "Not everybody. I can't send them all down. I can't trade them all. But that kind of loss cannot be tolerated."[106] As it turned out Milbury's next target was not on the ice but in the front office. The day after Christmas, he fired assistant general manager Darcy Regier, who had been in the organization since 1978 but clashed with Milbury over how he criticized his players in the media.[107] With Regier out of the picture, Milbury kept ridiculing the roster that he himself had assembled, telling reporters that Berard "has you reaching for the Pepto Bismol on occasion," Bertuzzi was "immature emotionally," and Smolinski's pace was "not always what it should be."[108] By the All-Star Break in January, the Islanders were 13-22-9. A shoulder strain kept their franchise player, Žiggy Pálffy, from performing in the sport's greatest showcase.[109]

As the Islanders sank in the standings, the season-long celebration of the team's twenty-fifth anniversary inevitably encouraged discussion about how far the franchise had fallen. As a tribute to their history the Islanders chronicled the dynasty years not only in the *Never Say Die* videotape but also in a book titled *Pride and Passion*. In addition, the team scheduled a series of anniversary promotions culminating during Presidents' Day weekend with the return of the championship players on February 15 and the display of the Stanley Cup on February 17.[110] Each autograph signing by a player from the 1980s team and nostalgia piece in the *Blade* was gobbled up by fans eager to relive the glory years. Unfortunately, that also meant the current Islanders were often compared against their predecessors. When the Islanders rebranded, management talked about unburdening a roster of young, fragile players on a rebuilding team from the impractical expectations associated with the classic logo and encouraging them to forge their own identity. Now the franchise itself was encouraging comparisons between the players of the early 1980s and the mid-1990s. The last chapter of *Pride and Passion* tasked the current Islanders management with finding "their Butch Gorings, Wayne Merricks, and Duane Sutters." Fichaud was likened to "another cocky netminder by the name of Bill Smith."[111] In one interview Bertuzzi expressed frustration with his frequent comparisons to Clark Gillies. "I'm here to make my own mark, not to keep a legend's name going," Bertuzzi said. "Right from day one, it's been 'Bert and Gillies.' That's the way it's been. People are still going to want another Gillies."[112] The Islanders had enough trouble trying to escape last place, let alone match the credentials of Hockey Hall of Famers.

The team was also in tumult off the ice. Before one game, Rob Di Fiore, dressed up as Nyisles, was about to enter the bowl at Nassau Coliseum when he felt a burning sensation inside the costume. The warmth was emanating from an overheating battery that he wore in a fanny pack to charge the goal light atop Nyisles's helmet. Di Fiore managed to quickly shed the costume without injury, but the incident made him reconsider what he once thought to be a dream job.[113] Islanders winger Paul Kruse, who arrived in a trade with Calgary in November, had been telling Di Fiore that the man who played the Flames mascot had a lucrative contract.[114] Di Fiore had no contract at all. Concerned about his safety, and hearing about the perks afforded to other mascots, Di Fiore confronted his bosses. He said he asked for a contract from Tim Beach, the Islanders' director of game events.[115] Beach contended that Di Fiore demanded not only a contract but also his own office and access to a masseuse and a chiropractor.[116] The team, unwilling to make such concessions to a part-time employee, fired him. The role of Nyisles passed to Rich Walker, who used to accompany Di Fiore around the arena. "I'm still in shock," Di Fiore told a reporter at the time. "I feel like a piece of me died. This isn't about a mascot. It's about a person."[117]

It was also about money. Claiming the Islanders still owed him $2,200 from appearances across Long Island, Di Fiore took the team to small-claims court. He was awarded just $150, the amount he used to earn for working a single game. "I was crying," Di Fiore said. "Like, are you kidding me?"[118] In a final indignation Di Fiore had still not received the money six months later. He wrote an angry letter to Milbury, and the money arrived soon after. The dispute with Di Fiore was not the only legal mess pitting the Islanders against a former employee. The team's longtime physician, fired in the off-season, was also suing for $19,800 that the team allegedly refused to pay because it blamed him for the concussions that caused Brett Lindros's early retirement.[119] Reports of the proceedings made the Islanders seem petty and cheap.

Behind the bench, Milbury was burning out. On January 10 he was ejected from a game against the Penguins for cursing and taunting the referee to "have another doughnut."[120] After a loss to St. Louis on January 20 Milbury took the unconventional step of ordering his exhausted players back on the ice for forty-three minutes of drills as punishment for allowing four goals in the third period.[121] Some

St. Louis players watched the spectacle and sympathized with the Islanders. "They're banging on the glass at Milbury, giving him the finger, telling him that's embarrassing and that's a joke," Paul Kruse said of the visiting Blues. "It was nice to see their guys sticking up for us even though they just destroyed us."[122] The Islanders did not feel a similar camaraderie with their coach. Scott Lachance called the postgame skate "embarrassing," and Derek King acknowledged that Milbury's tactics "could backfire."[123] While some Islanders were underperforming, Milbury, whose only previous coaching experience was with a talented Bruins team, was mistaking the general lack of skill on the roster for a lack of effort. Three days later Milbury traveled to Dallas to discuss his role on the team with John Spano.[124] In what both sides called a "mutual decision," Milbury announced that he would focus on his GM duties and hand over the coaching job to his assistant Rick Bowness.[125]

Bowness was a predictable replacement. After an undistinguished playing career in the NHL, Bowness coached in Winnipeg, Ottawa, and Boston, where he worked under Milbury and took the injury-plagued Bruins to the conference finals in 1992. He was more conventional than Milbury but just as passionate, once touching off a controversy in Boston by instructing two of his veteran players to stay in the dressing room if they were not going to play with pride.[126] Islanders players welcomed the change. "He's a phenomenal coach and a phenomenal person, handled things a little bit differently," Dan Plante recalled.[127] Before his debut on January 24 Bowness laid out a daunting goal for a team with weak offense and suspect goaltending: "We want to make the playoffs."[128] The team played better under Bowness, although initially not good enough to make a postseason push. In their first twenty-four games under the new coach the Islanders won ten and lost thirteen with one tie. The mediocre stretch put them at 24-36-10 on March 16, six points out of the final playoff spot with only twelve games remaining.[129]

Already a punch line around the league because of the fisherman jerseys, the Islanders became fodder for jokes again when a game versus the Devils produced an awkward moment. On a critical power play,

Green made a deft pass to Pálffy, zooming down the right side of the slot, and Pálffy put the puck in the net to cut New Jersey's lead to 3-2. Then, to the surprise of everyone in the arena, Pálffy skated behind the net to Green, puckered his lips, and moved in.[130] "I was kind of hooting and hollering," Green recalled, "and Žiggy, being the European he was, decided he was gonna give me a big kiss." It was no peck on the cheek, either: the players kissed on the lips with their mouths open. The intimate goal celebration perplexed the Islanders broadcasters. "And, uh, did we just see a kiss?" asked play-by-play announcer Howie Rose. Color analyst Ed Westfall chimed in, "Uh oh. How far can you go with this, boys?" Word of the smooch carried through the NHL. On *Hockey Night in Canada* commentator Don Cherry needled Pálffy, who was wearing a visor. "I know those guys who wear visors are sweeties," Cherry said, "but that's a little too much." The *Ottawa Sun* wondered whether fans would toss Hershey Kisses onto the ice to celebrate Pálffy's goals and joked about the players landing an endorsement deal for "T and Z's Lip Balm."[131] The rebuilding Islanders, desperate to be taken seriously, were garnering widespread media attention only as a source of comic relief.

With the trade deadline nearing on March 18, the media speculated whether Milbury would buy talent to bolster the playoff run or sell off key players to build for the future. He ended up doing both. In a cost-cutting move, Milbury acquired a fifth-round draft pick from Hartford in exchange for Derek King, an enigmatic winger who ranked among the team's all-time leaders in goals and assists but was unpopular with fans. Given King's pending free agency, the shrewd trade guaranteed the Islanders a future prospect while still allowing the possibility of re-signing King in the off-season. Milbury's second deal of the day was more significant in the short term. Craving a playmaker to center Pálffy's line, the general manager shipped Marty McInnis, a junior goalie, and a draft pick to Calgary in order to obtain Robert Reichel. At age twenty-five, Reichel was the best player in either trade. He had back-to-back forty-goal seasons with the Flames in 1992-93 and 1993-94 before a contract dispute and decreased ice time soured him on Calgary.[132] The trade was the fresh start that Reichel needed. He knew assistant coach Guy Charron from their time together with the Flames and played with Pálffy at a tournament in Czechoslovakia a few years prior. "The Islanders are good for me," he told the *Blade*, "and I think I will be good for them."[133]

Trading for Reichel signaled Milbury's resolve, despite a tight budget, to complete the fisherman era in the postseason. With Reichel centering Pálffy and Smolinski on a newfangled top line, the Islanders finally had the scoring punch they needed. Twenty-five seconds into his first shift as an Islander on March 19, Reichel assisted on a Pálffy goal. He finished his debut with a goal and two assists in a 7–4 victory that moved the Islanders within four points of the final playoff berth.[134] "I was very happy to step in that game and have success," Reichel said. "After that first game, I was very confident to be part of the organization." In a subsequent home-and-home against Boston, Reichel had two goals and three assists in the first game and added four assists in the second. His arrival ignited his linemates. In Reichel's first five games, Pálffy scored seven goals and four assists and Smolinski had three goals and five assists as the Islanders went undefeated.[135] "He raised my game to a height that I could strive to," Smolinski said. "I loved playing with those two guys. They were awesome competitors." The second line, with Green centering Niklas Andersson and a recharged Bertuzzi, was also producing, and Salo was brilliant in goal. Entering the final month of the season, the Islanders were just a point out of the playoffs. Bowness was asked how many people gave the team a chance to make the postseason back in October. "None," he replied. "Zero."[136]

As soon as the Islanders began to silence their skeptics, however, the team fell apart. In the most critical stretch of the season the young Islanders tensed up. They lost face-offs. They allowed odd-man rushes. They stopped scoring, and they could not clear the crease. Their last seven games included only one win against five losses and a tie. "We're done," Bertuzzi declared after the Islanders were mathematically eliminated from playoff contention. "It's a tough pill for everyone to swallow."[137] The Islanders closed out their home schedule against Hartford on April 11, which was designated Fan Appreciation Night at Nassau Coliseum. The crowd of 15,382 surely appreciated the 6–4 victory, as well as the rare sight of the classic logo on the jerseys.[138]

On April 12 the Islanders skated in the fisherman jerseys for the final time against the Capitals in Washington. Fittingly, as they had ninety times over the past two seasons, they lost that game, too.[139] It took little time for the organization to move past the logo that had identified the team for the past twenty-three months. After the season ended the Islanders took out ads in *Newsday* for a sale at the team store. The spots reminded fans, "Our new team jerseys, featuring the original Islanders logo, make a great gift for Mother's or Father's Day."[140]

Although the Islanders failed to reach the playoffs, John Spano's much-hyped purchase of the team, combined with a seven-win improvement over 1995–96, made the final season of the fisherman jerseys feel like a turning point. Berard, who led first-year players with forty-eight points, was selected the NHL's rookie of the year.[141] Pálffy, quickly establishing himself as a star, scored forty-eight goals, the fifth most in the league, and received some votes for the NHL's most valuable player award. Average home attendance went up 10 percent.[142] If Spano pumped the sort of money into the team that he promised he would, the fan base might actually look back on the fisherman era fondly, as a period when their team found its savior.

7

FROM SAVIOR TO DEVIL

By the spring of 1997, almost everyone around the Islanders—the fans, the media, and even the players—accepted John Spano as the owner. By outward appearances he was running the team. The Islanders introduced him at a press conference in November, the NHL Board of Governors approved the sale in February, and Spano was appearing regularly in the owner's box at Nassau Coliseum. The press reported that Spano was negotiating a new cable television contract for the Islanders, mulling over trades with Milbury, and presenting concepts for a new arena to Nassau County officials.[1] Legally, however, Spano did not own the franchise yet. The Islanders remained under the control of John Pickett pending the closing of his $165 million deal with Spano, which was scheduled for April 7.[2]

As the closing approached, suspicions about Spano were growing. Spano twice dined with Tom Croke of the Support the Islanders Coalition, who thought the prospective owner's behavior was strange. "It was the most uncomfortable two dinners I'd ever had in my life," Croke said. "No matter what type of subject I brought up, hockey, nonhockey, could not get a word out of this guy. He just clammed up." At other times Spano canceled meetings, explaining that his wife had breast cancer and he wanted to be by her side when she underwent chemotherapy. It was a lie.[3]

During one get-together with Spano, Croke offered his skills as a computer consultant to evaluate the Islanders' technological infrastructure. The men agreed to a salary of $120,000, and Croke shut down his successful consulting firm. He came to work in the Islanders offices in Nassau Coliseum, only to find that Spano had not told anyone to expect his arrival. "No one had any idea what I was doing there,"

Croke said. "He hadn't told anybody. They were all taken aback. They immediately got their attorney involved to get me out of the building."[4] After a few months passed, Croke returned to seek compensation for the breach of his oral contract. He was confronted by Milbury, who was incensed that Spano agreed to hire Croke, a relentless critic of ownership. Milbury said that he grabbed Croke by the collar and led him out the door.[5] According to Croke, Milbury briefly put his hand on Croke's forearm but let go once Croke told him to do so.[6] Whatever happened between them, the men agreed on one point: Spano was acting strangely.

Meanwhile, Spano's tendency to boast about his wealth made others wonder whether he was actually as rich as he said he was. Islanders goaltender Éric Fichaud remembered the prospective owner bragging to anyone who would listen that he had the money to sign the Red Wings' all-star center Sergei Fedorov, a restricted free agent.[7] In an interview with *Newsday* Spano mentioned that he spent $140,000 a month on fuel for private jets to fly him between Dallas and Long Island.[8] Spano bragged more to *Sports Illustrated*, saying that he "owned every great car that was ever made" and had "the houses and everything else."[9] During a meeting with Croke, Spano said that he had donated $1 million to an influential New York senator. Since the campaign contribution limit was only a few thousand dollars, Croke knew that Spano was either lying or breaking the law.[10] Even more troubling, Spano, who was married, spent many nights at the Garden City Hotel, one of the most exclusive lodging places on Long Island, drinking and partying with attractive women. Milbury recalled the owner summoning him for a meeting there. After the two men talked hockey for a while, Spano changed the subject. "He says, 'They'll be here in a little while,'" Milbury remembered. "I said, 'John, who? What are you talking about?' He said, 'The girls.' He said, 'The girls. First they'll do each other, and then they'll do us.'"[11]

Milbury didn't know then, but Spano was resorting to alcohol and sex to cope with the stress of leading a double life. To the public, Spano was a successful businessman with a net worth of $250 million. It was an illusion. In reality, Spano had assets totaling only $1.2 million, not even enough to pay the highest-salaried player on the Islanders, let alone run the team.[12] To nobody's knowledge but his own, Spano was perpetrating one of the greatest scams in the history of professional sports, and he did not know how much longer he could pull it off.

Despite what Spano told people, his background was unremarkable. Raised in an upper-middle-class family of barbers and merchants, he went to a parochial high school in Ohio, not a prep school, as he claimed, and his first job as a sales associate in Pittsburgh paid him $20,000, a salary so meager that he lived with his boss for a while. Next, Spano moved to Dallas to work for an auto loan company, only to lose his job when the company folded. In 1990 he used money that he said he inherited from his grandfather—although that story, too, was disputed—to start an equipment-leasing business named the Bison Group, which attained moderate success but nothing as grand as he made it out to be. Despite his insistence, he did not own any jets or a home in the Hamptons. The limousines that escorted him around Long Island and the money he dished out freely for stays at exclusive hotels were funded by team accounts.[13]

With little wealth of his own, Spano depended on his connections to convince the NHL that he could afford a team. The Bison Group was valued at just $3 million and employed only twenty-two people, not the six thousand that Spano counted in a tall tale to the Islanders.[14] Through his business transactions Spano became friendly with much richer businessmen, and they mingled at a local country club. Because he was hanging out with high rollers, people figured he was one. He never had any staff members accompanying him, because he couldn't afford any; observers simply concluded that he was hands-on. NHL commissioner Gary Bettman introduced Spano to Pickett, who was eager to sell to someone who would be visible on Long Island and keep the team there. Bettman, assuming the Islanders would vet Spano, spent a few hundred dollars on an investigation into Spano that apparently showed nothing amiss.[15] Pickett trusted Spano because Bettman vouched for him as "the type of person we want as an owner."[16] A real estate firm owned by former Dallas Cowboys quarterback Roger

Staubach loaned money to Spano, figuring he had been checked out by the banks.[17] Along the way, no one bothered to seriously inspect his bank accounts or his background, or to investigate why his attempt to buy the Dallas Stars two years earlier fell through.

Islanders players had a chance to peek behind the curtain of Spano's concocted lifestyle on April 1, when the team came to town to play the Dallas Stars and Spano invited them for dinner at his house.[18] Spano lived with his wife Shelby in University Park, a tony north Dallas suburb. Spano said their Tudor home was worth $3 million that he paid in full—another lie, since he was actually paying off a $1.8 million mortgage and owed $85,000 in property taxes. On the night the Islanders came over, the Spanos put on a show, bringing in a ten-piece band to serenade the players as they dined on Mexican food.[19] Most of the team was impressed. Bryan Smolinski wasn't. "I'm thinking, For a guy that's got over $200 million, I was expecting a little more. I'm like, 'This is bullshit.' I said, 'This is not happening.' He didn't have really any cars. He didn't really have anything. He just had a real nice house, probably no different than what I'm living in now. Probably less. And I'm thinking, Man, isn't this awkward? And everyone's trying to find the light. They're like, 'Man, this is pretty sweet.' I'm like, 'No, it's not. This sucks.'"[20]

Only a week after dining with the players, Spano faced the deadline to close the deal. In an anxious effort to drum up $165 million in a matter of weeks, Spano amazingly managed to persuade Fleet Bank to give him an $80 million loan, using the team, its assets, and the cable television rights as collateral. Next, he negotiated to pay off the remaining $85 million in five annual installments of $16.8 million. That meant he had to scrounge up just the first payment, $16.8 million, in order to close the purchase on April 7.[21] Spano had a few possible options to secure quick cash. He sought investors to pay up front for the new arena he envisioned for the Islanders, and he pursued a loan from Cablevision, which was negotiating for the Islanders' television rights.[22] Neither effort came through by the closing date. Short $16.8 million, Spano devised one final scheme, concocting a letter that appeared to show confirmation from a London bank that it would wire

$16.8 million to Pickett. He handed off the letter to his lawyers, who did not recognize it as a forgery and assured Pickett that the money was on its way. Pickett, eager to finish the transaction, closed the deal. Spano officially became the Islanders owner.[23]

As the weeks wore on, Spano never made the $16.8 million payment he owed Pickett. He once delivered a personal check for the amount but stopped payment the next day, before Pickett could deposit it. On another occasion he wrote a check drawn on what he described as his most profitable company, and it bounced. Spano stayed up late at night, wondering how he could buy more time. He eventually decided to play around with zeros. First, Spano offered to wire $5 million to Pickett in good faith, only to send $5,000. Then he said that he had sent $17 million, when he had actually wired $1,700. Frustrated over Spano's inability to pay, Pickett sought an arbitration proceeding, asking the NHL to return the Islanders to him. In a letter asking for the proceeding, Pickett's lawyer listed the many absurd excuses that Spano had used— meddling by the NHL and his own attorneys, the faulty work ethic of bankers, an incompetent associate at a London law firm, the inability of banks to process routine wire transfers, the lack of integrity of the federal wire system, errors by the Internal Revenue Service, "ravenous" South Africans, a bomb threat by the Irish Republican Army that held up the London Underground, and acts of God. Finally, Pickett's lawyer noted that Spano lied about an offshore trust with more than $100 million in assets. "If this trust does not exist," the letter wondered, "is there any substance at all to Mr. Spano?"[24] It was a good question.

Even as he was trying to buy more time, Spano kept up his appearance as the Islanders owner. When he met with broadcaster Stan Fischler in May, Spano asked for a curious favor: the supposed multimillion-aire wanted Fischler to use his connections to get him free Rangers playoff tickets. Fischler was stunned. "I'm thinking to myself, He's asking me? This guy owns the team! I said, 'You know what's the best thing to do? Call up Neil Smith, the [Rangers] GM. I'm sure he'll be able to take care of you.' After I left, I said, 'What the hell is this?'" While telling the story years later, Fischler said that Spano was not the sugar daddy he made himself out to be. Spotting some cheap sugar packets on a table, Fischler picked them up and said, "That's the kind of sugar he was."[25]

Although people in the know suspected Spano could not afford to buy the Islanders, the fan base remained unaware about any snags in the deal for almost three months after the closing. The first red flag popped up at a meeting of the NHL Board of Governors on June 25, when the Islanders were represented by their general counsel and an alternate governor, marking the first time since February that Spano did not attend. A subsequent story in *Newsday* revealed Spano's missed payment to Pickett and NHL commissioner Gary Bettman ordering Spano not to touch team assets. Playing off a famous line from the movie *Slap Shot*—in which a hockey player asks management, "Who own da Chiefs?"—the article wondered, "Who owns the Islanders?" Pickett said he did not know, but he took issue with the characterization of the breakdown in the sale as a dispute between himself and Spano. "The term 'dispute' is really a poor choice of words," he insisted. "There is no dispute. He owes me money and hasn't paid it."[26]

By early July, Spano was unsure who owned the team anymore. "Am I still the owner of the Islanders?" he asked a reporter. "Right now, I'm in limbo." His money problems opened up the entire organization to questions about its finances. *Newsday* reported, only half-jokingly, that the Islanders were managing to pay their utility bills at Nassau Coliseum and had not sold off their furniture or the pictures of championship teams. "Everything was so positive here," Nystrom told the newspaper. "Now we don't know."[27]

The matter was settled soon after. On July 11 the NHL announced that Spano agreed to relinquish his ownership of the Islanders in exchange for a guarantee that Pickett would not sue him. Spano released a statement saying the decision was "right for my loved ones," even though it meant "giving up my first love, hockey."[28] Ten days later, authorities came to Dallas to arrest Spano, only to learn he had absconded to the Cayman Islands. There was brief speculation that he might never return.[29] Spano did fly back to New York, on the advice of his attorney, and he was arraigned on charges of bank and wire fraud in a courtroom just blocks from Nassau Coliseum.[30] After a prosecutor dramatically accused Spano of weaving "a tangled web of lies and broken promises," Spano changed his mind about pleading not guilty and cut a deal.[31] From there his life quickly unraveled. His wife divorced him and sold the Dallas house where they once hosted the Islanders players. He moved to Philadelphia, where he developed a drug addiction and tried to pay his rent with a bad credit card, bounced checks, and wire transfers, so his bail was revoked and he was sent to a correctional facility. In 2000 he was sentenced to seventy-one months in prison for the charges stemming from the aborted Islanders purchase.[32] After his release in 2004 he returned to Ohio to start another company, where he again committed fraud. He was sentenced to an additional four years.[33]

As the scandal unfolded Milbury worried that Spano's misdeeds would overshadow the Islanders' progress in the fisherman era. "We're all a little edgy about how this might affect our fans," Milbury said. "It would be a shame if the way we finished the season and the way we positioned ourselves is being lost in this."[34] His fears were well founded. More than any other figure, Spano had become the face of the Islanders in the midst of a daring rebrand. Now he was headed to prison. "My reputation went from savior to devil," Spano admitted.[35] Everything that he had promised, from the acquisition of superstar players to the construction of a new arena that would keep the team on Long Island, was off the table. The franchise would revert to the absentee owner who had overseen its decline, a man that *Newsday* described as "roughly as popular as the ill-conceived fisherman." A headline in the *7th Man* was even harsher toward Pickett: "Spano's Scheme Collapses, So the Ogre Returns!" The newsletter also called him the NHL's version of Dracula, "back to resume sucking the franchise dry."[36]

The dramatic turn of events was bound to affect how the jerseys would be remembered. Long Islanders had pinned their hopes on Spano, and reading their excited reactions years later, with the knowledge that Spano was a fraud all along, is heartbreaking. "Things are getting good again," Louis Eterginoso, a season-ticket holder since the Islanders' inaugural season, told the *Blade* in April 1997, when Spano missed his first $17 million payment. "It starts at the top and this John Spano looks like he's going to be a tremendous owner." In June, as Spano was forging documents and making excuses for his inability to pay, the *7th Man* rejoiced, "A new day is finally dawning! Be a part of it! John Spano is committed to winning!"[37] The 1996–97 season had ended with electricity in the Nassau Coliseum stands, too. Attendance averaged only 10,774 fans in the first ten home games, but after Spano's introduction, the number soared to 13,100 for the final thirty-one dates.[38] Once the deal foundered, fans were devastated. One man told a television news crew that he wanted Spano to get thirty years in prison for "the grief he's put me through personally."[39] The *7th Man* made an argument, hard to dispute, that the Islanders had the "most abused fans in sports."[40]

After years out of public view Spano reemerged in 2013, agreeing to an on-camera interview for an ESPN documentary about his purchase of the Islanders. His interviewer was the film's director, actor Kevin Connolly, best known for starring in the HBO series *Entourage*. Connolly, who grew up on Long Island rooting for the Islanders of the 1980s, interspersed clips from the Spano interview with archival footage and interviews with the likes of Milbury, Gary Bettman, and the Islanders' attorneys. Connolly was gentle in his questions for Spano, perhaps out of gratitude for his cooperation, and the documentary framed his crimes in a lighthearted and at times complimentary manner, the story of a man who cleverly overcame his inadequate finances to live out every fan's dream of owning a favorite sports team. "They painted Spano out to be this folk hero," said Tim Beach, the Islanders' director of game events. "No. He was a crook. He was a crook back then, and he's a crook now." In the film Spano acknowledged the scam was "100 percent my fault," and he choked up describing how his family, who put up their homes to make his $3 million bond, were "caught up in my mistakes and got hurt." However, his final statement was more wistful than repentant. "It was everything I hoped it would be, and actually it was more. Consequences, like we said, weren't tremendous, but it was a fulfillment of a dream, even if it was a short period of time. I mean, for four months, I owned the New York Islanders." In a subsequent interview with the *New York Times*, Spano clarified,

"I don't want anybody to think I don't have remorse or regret. I do."[41] As with many aspects of Spano, his true feelings about the scam may never be known.

In the wake of the bungled sale, the NHL reevaluated its vetting process for prospective owners.[42] "We have to go back and assess the procedures so it never happens again," Bill Daly, the NHL's senior vice president for legal affairs, told *Sports Illustrated*.[43] No more hearts of hockey fans would be broken by a con artist.

After the Spano deal fell apart Pickett made clear his intentions to find a new buyer. Ironically, Spano's furious attempt to find enough money to close the sale actually raised the value of the franchise. By extending the team's cable television deal to 2031, Spano ensured the Islanders would receive $400 million over the next thirty-four years.[44] Pickett's asking price went from $165 million with Spano to $200 million from any future suitors. He trusted the negotiations to his son Brett, who had remained on Long Island after his father left. Surprisingly, the public relations debacle with Spano, rather than scaring away potential suitors, awakened curiosity in owning the Islanders. There was interest from a group led by former Islanders star Clark Gillies and another that included Bob Gutkowski, a former president of Madison Square Garden, and Nelson Doubleday and Fred Wilpon, co-owners of the New York Mets.[45] Even Yankees owner George Steinbrenner, who pumped millions into his baseball team in the Bronx, put in a call to the Picketts.[46]

In September the Islanders were sold for the second time in five months, this time to buyers who actually had the money to pay for the team. For $195 million the team went to a company headed by Steven Gluckstern, the chairman of a large broker-market reinsurer and a co-owner of the Phoenix Coyotes, who sold his stake in the Coyotes to make the deal. The group also included New York real estate developers Howard Milstein and Stephen Ross.[47] Unlike Spano, the men came with solid financial pedigrees and experience in the sports business. Milstein was involved in serious attempts to start leagues to compete against Major League Baseball and the National Football

League, while Gluckstern presided over the relocation of the Winnipeg Jets to Arizona in 1996–97, when the Coyotes had a winning record and made the playoffs in their inaugural season.[48] The men clearly had more interest in redeveloping the area around Nassau Coliseum than pumping money into the Islanders, but they also wanted to build a contending team, since 80 percent of the profit margin in the league came from playoff revenues.[49] Gluckstern promised to be a hands-on owner. "Owning a sports team for me was a fantasy from when I was a young boy," he shared in an interview years later. "There's something powerful about being able to live out your own dreams."[50]

For the Pickett family, relinquishing ownership of the Islanders was bittersweet. John Pickett had had a stake in the team since its first game in 1972, and for the past seventeen years he had been either the majority or sole owner. Over that time his relatives all became fans. "It was incredibly hard," said Brett Pickett. "We kept the skybox, so we kept coming to the games, but it's very hard to let go. It was part of my life my entire life." Yet the family patriarch, who admitted his absentee ownership hurt the franchise, was glad to have found a buyer with capital to spend on players and a new arena. On the day the deal was announced John Pickett put out a statement praising Gluckstern's experience as a businessman and NHL team owner.[51] "They were winners," Brett Pickett remembered. "These are guys who are used to winning, and they knew that the logo needed to be the heritage logo."[52]

With a deep appreciation for sports branding and a flair for showmanship, Gluckstern figured to be an entertaining owner as the Islanders moved past the fisherman era in the 1997–98 season. He was raised in a family of intellectuals: his mother had a doctor of education degree in counseling psychology, and his father headed the Physics Department and served as provost at Amherst, the flagship campus of the University of Massachusetts. Showing as much ambition as his parents, Gluckstern earned a master's in business administration from Stanford and a doctorate in education from Amherst, and his colorful path to the owner's box included seven years as a teacher and school administrator.[53] "He is a great businessman," the Coyotes president said at the time, "but I think he is a marketer at heart." In Phoenix,

Gluckstern faced the challenge of selling hockey in persistently warm weather. He sold the Coyotes as sports entertainment, hiring bands to perform outside the arena before all home games, installing a jumbo video screen, and regularly setting off fireworks. Gluckstern inserted himself into the promotions, too. During the Coyotes' playoff run, the team encouraged fans to "white out" the arena by dressing in all white to throw off the opponents. Gluckstern showed up at his rinkside seats in a white tuxedo.[54]

Gluckstern's eccentricity carried over to Nassau Coliseum. At his introductory press conference Gluckstern admitted growing up in southern Connecticut as a Rangers fan in the days before the Islanders existed. He joked to reporters, "My kids and I got together last night and burned all our Rangers paraphernalia." It was Gluckstern's first crack at charming fans who had learned to become suspicious of whoever occupied the owner's box. Unlike Phoenix, where Gluckstern had to drum up interest in a new hockey market, Long Island presented the challenge of trying to win back disenchanted fans who viewed the fisherman jerseys as a turn from tradition. He became the hands-on owner that Pickett wasn't, leaving his fingerprints on new marketing efforts. "Owners have to care about their teams for teams to be successful," he professed years later, "and they show that in different ways."[55]

The closing of the sale to Gluckstern's group in February 1998 marked a key moment in the Islanders' branding campaign. Although the fisherman jerseys had already been cast away, the owners responsible for the failed rebranding—including the introduction of Nyisles, the trade for Kirk Muller, the hiring of Mike Milbury, and the unveiling of the new logo—remained in charge when the 1997–98 season began. The passing of the torch to Gluckstern and Milstein allowed the Islanders to move past the fisherman era in a way that Pickett and the Gang of Four could not. Two of the executives most associated with the rebrand, Pat Calabria and Tim Beach, left the team. At Nassau Coliseum, the announcement of the sale, and ownership's commitment to bring "a fifth Stanley Cup" to Long Island, led the crowd to erupt with applause.[56] In one of the most noticeable changes from the Pickett regime, the Islanders began running a series of offbeat newspaper ads that acknowledged the organization's shortcomings. A large spot in the *New York Times* announced Gluckstern's acquisition of not only the Islanders but also "millions of long-suffering fans who have endured a serious depression and are owed a vigorous recovery." Another ad in *Newsday* honored the dictionary definition of an Islanders fan—someone who "never, ever gives up hope in the club," despite management turnover, long lines for the Nassau Coliseum bathrooms, rude comments from Rangers fans, and "silly logo changes." The ad closed with the original logo and a pledge from Gluckstern and Milstein to reward the loyalty of the fan base.[57]

Gluckstern also preyed on fans' hunger for another championship. One ad in *Newsday* pictured the four Stanley Cup banners in the Nassau Coliseum rafters next to a blank spot where a fifth banner could be raised. The space read, "Coming Soon." The same image was plastered on a billboard on Hempstead Turnpike, where the Islanders' dynasty teams paraded in the early 1980s. Gluckstern thought that promising a fifth title would associate the Islanders with winning again. "Remember this was a losing franchise," he said. "In many ways, people think of it as a cursed franchise. One can argue it's still cursed."[58] The front office viewed the tactics with more skepticism. Despite the optimism brought by the sale of the team, the 1997–98 Islanders were hardly championship caliber. The team wouldn't even qualify for the playoffs or finish with a winning record that season. There was no reason to believe a team that had just traded away its promising young captain, Bryan McCabe, would contend in the near future, either.[59] At best the pledge that a fifth Stanley Cup was "coming soon" was premature; at worst, it was baseless. Beach was aghast when ownership pitched the idea of raising a "Coming Soon" banner to the rafters. His resistance precipitated a falling-out with Gluckstern and his departure from the team. "They were asking me to do stuff that you just, as a fan, would never want to be part of," Beach remembered. "Raising a Stanley Cup banner that says, 'Coming Soon'? I said, 'We would become the mockery of the league.' And they never did it, so if that was worth getting fired over, it was."[60] Beach left to work for the Mighty Ducks, the team whose strong uniform sales had encouraged the Islanders to switch jerseys a few seasons earlier.

The new ownership closed the fisherman era with two symbolic gestures in one week in March 1998. The first came on Tuesday, March 3, which was designated True Islander Fan Night. The promotion was designed to repair the strained relationship between the team and its alumni brought on by changing the classic logo. Before the Islanders played the Philadelphia Flyers, the franchise they defeated to win their first Stanley Cup in 1980, a pregame ceremony honored the players from the championship teams. With Bruce Springsteen's "Glory Days" blaring over the public address system, nineteen former players took the ice, including Mike Bossy, the franchise leader in goals, and Bob Nystrom, who scored in overtime to clinch the title. A surprise appearance was made by Bryan Trottier, the team's all-time leading scorer, who had filed for bankruptcy and reportedly refused to appear at previous Islanders events unless he was compensated.[61] (Gluckstern and Milstein apparently got Trottier to come by paying him to autograph pucks that were mailed to season-ticket holders as gifts.)[62] The Islanders also made an effort to merge the past with the future. In an emotional moment, former Islanders captain Denis Potvin, the personification of the Stanley Cup teams, handed over the captain's jersey to Trevor Linden, recently acquired in a trade with Vancouver.[63] Whereas the fisherman jerseys had been unveiled to grant the team a new identity, True Islander Fan Night was about tying the team to its heritage. "This doesn't mean you live in the past," Bossy said. "It means you embrace what the team did back in those days."[64]

As part of the festivities the team gave an unusual assignment to fourth-line enforcer Steve Webb, who made his NHL debut that season. Seeking a flashy end to the fisherman era, the team told Webb to skate to center ice in his fisherman jersey and dramatically rip it off to reveal a jersey with the original logo. "Actually, I was a little nervous not really knowing what I was supposed to do," Webb recalled. "Skate to center ice, rip it off, and then what? I didn't really have a script or anything so I didn't really know what to expect." He followed orders, and the arena erupted with cheering and applause.[65]

Opinions on the display varied. Some, including Tom Croke of the Support the Islanders Coalition, thought it was an effective way of admitting the fisherman jerseys were a mistake and moving on. "I had friends of mine who wanted to see the thing burned," Croke said. "They wanted to see all the Islanders take off their fisherman jerseys, throw it in one of those fifty-five-gallon drums, and burn it." Others viewed the destruction of the jersey as an unnecessary gimmick that only called more attention to the disastrous rebrand and disparaged the well-intentioned people behind it. Learning of the spectacle decades later, designer Pat McDarby, who worked on the new logo for SME, expressed surprise and anger. "Don't make a media circus out of it," he said. "You're taking everybody who was involved in that thing and embarrassing them."[66]

On Saturday, March 7, the Gluckstern group took another swipe at the fisherman jerseys. The Islanders offered an unusual invitation for fans to bring any merchandise with the fisherman logo to Nassau Coliseum and trade it in for a T-shirt with the original crest. "Our mission," said a top Islanders executive, "is to restore dignity to Islanders fans and to fishermen everywhere by ending this doomed association."[67] Fans arrived to the game versus the Colorado Avalanche with 1,295 jerseys, shirts, and caps to exchange. Every item was donated to the American Red Cross of Gloucester, Massachusetts, the site of the corporate headquarters of Gorton's frozen fish.[68] Gluckstern, ever the showman, dressed up for the occasion to greet fans on the arena concourse. The eccentric Islanders owner, who already had a salt-and-pepper beard that evoked the fisherman's, wore a large yellow overcoat to complete the look. "There was a lot of laughter and cheering and fun," Gluckstern remembered. "People were engaged again, saying, 'Okay, here's an owner that's willing to go and have fun and make fun and be part of trying to get some excitement.'" Brett Pickett thought the outfit was effective. "It was a fun way to call attention to it, so I was delighted that that happened." Others frowned upon the costume. Islanders broadcaster Howie Rose thought Gluckstern wanted to be perceived as caring about the fans without spending any money on players. "I just thought that it was a gratuitous show of interest in the team at least on the surface when not very below the surface it was a rather obvious ploy for a little attention."[69]

Even as the Islanders disavowed the fisherman logo, the team retained the man most associated with the rebrand. In fact, Mike Milbury's powers within the franchise were increasing under the new ownership, to the dismay of the fan base. On March 11, with the Islanders coming off an encouraging 6-4-2 streak, Milbury fired Rick Bowness as coach and reinserted himself behind the bench, saying he thought the team needed a "boost."[70] Outsiders were skeptical that Milbury, after clashing with his players during his first stint as coach, would somehow inspire them in his second. The 7th Man railed, "Why now, Mike? Even fans who wanted Bowness out are disgusted that Milbury has jumped back in."[71] He coached nineteen games to close out another losing season, then returned to coach forty-five more in 1998–99 before hiring a replacement.[72] In parts of four seasons coaching on Long Island, Milbury finished with twice as many losses as wins and no playoff berths.

Interestingly, many of the players whom Milbury coached with the Islanders went on to coach professionally themselves. When those players-turned-coaches were asked whether they incorporated elements of Milbury's coaching style into their own, some of them laughed at the thought. Dean Chynoweth, who became an assistant coach with the Islanders for three seasons from 2009 to 2012, said that Milbury's misguided attempts to inspire the team led him to "do things which in today's game would never happen." When Milbury informed Chynoweth that he had been traded in 1995, the coach took the unusual step of asking a player for advice on how to run the team that just discarded him. Chynoweth told Milbury that he was misreading some of the players. "I said, 'You're a smart guy. You'll figure it out,'" Chynoweth recalled.[73] Milbury never did.

Still, former Islanders players largely spoke diplomatically about Milbury. They said they respected Milbury's will to win, if not his methods. Chris Taylor, an assistant coach for the highest minor league affiliate of the Buffalo Sabres, said that playing under Milbury taught him to treat players as he wanted to be treated—apparently better than Milbury treated the Islanders.[74] Chris Luongo, an assistant coach with a program that develops amateur players in the United States for international competition, said that he places expectations on players and puts demands on them, as Milbury did.[75] Even Travis Green, who was traded and characterized as a "gutless puke" by Milbury, stayed positive.[76] "Mike had a lot of passion, a lot of fire in him," Green said in 2015, when he was coaching the highest minor league affiliate of the Vancouver Canucks, on his way to a promotion to the Canucks' head-coaching job. "If you have passion and you have fire, you know that at least a person's trying to do the right things."[77]

Like Milbury, Nyisles also lingered at Nassau Coliseum after the fisherman logo was abandoned. The new ownership, which had so flamboyantly moved away from the fisherman jerseys, spared the mascot to avoid a total remake of the franchise in a short time period. "I don't think we were wild about it, but you also don't want to change everything overnight," Gluckstern said. "It's sort of identified there. It was part of a transition." Time has clouded exactly when the Islanders dispensed with Nyisles, but primary sources establish that he made his last appearance sometime between the spring of 1998 and the fall of 2001, when the Islanders introduced his replacement, Sparky the Dragon.[78] There is no record of the Islanders ever producing merchandise featuring Nyisles, and only a handful of photos of the mascot have surfaced online. Rob Di Fiore, who played Nyisles, cracked the oversize head on a turnstile and left it behind in small-claims court when he sued the Islanders. He did keep the other elements of the outfit, though: a jersey, shorts, and suspenders from the original costume, worn during the shortened 1994-95 season; the jersey with the fisherman logo, worn in 1995-96 and 1996-97; two hockey bags; a pair of skates; and the fanny pack that held the battery to charge the light atop the mascot's head.[79]

While the new ownership group disavowed the fisherman logo, they never spent the money necessary to rehabilitate the Islanders from the disastrous rebrand. As dynasty goaltender Billy Smith said on True Islander Fan Night, "It's not the shirt that's going to win you the Stanley Cup. It's what you put under the jersey."[80] Gluckstern and Milstein were not inclined to open their wallets for high-caliber players, though. They predicated any improvements to the roster on obtaining development rights from Nassau County to erect a new arena and build a hotel, stores, and restaurants on the surrounding property.[81] With the negotiations between the team and the county stalling, ownership neglected the Islanders.[82] "They kept the team for a while, but they didn't spend a nickel on it. I mean, not a nickel," said Islanders broadcaster Howie Rose. At one point Rose and broadcast colleague Joe Micheletti gently tried to persuade David Seldin, the team president under Gluckstern and Milstein, that ownership might make a profit on the franchise if they put some money into it. Seldin balked.[83] He complained that the Islanders were losing $11 million a year already and said that no more money would be spent until a new arena was built.[84] Rose figured the owners had underestimated the difficulty of securing the development rights, effectively leading them to purchase the team only to watch it rot when the pipe dream of a smooth redevelopment did not materialize. "They were just misinformed or misguided or both and, like a lot of people in that situation, guilty of some hubris. And boy, they paid the price. But more to the point, and more importantly, and more unfortunately, so did Islander fans."[85]

Unwilling to spend on elite players, the Islanders had little chance to compete in the postlockout NHL. In three seasons under Gluckstern and Milstein from 1997–98 to 1999–2000, the Islanders went 78-138-30, with two last-place finishes and zero playoff berths. The rebranding of the Islanders might have been remembered as an unfortunate but brief chapter in the franchise's history if Gluckstern and Milstein led a renaissance in its immediate aftermath. Instead, the fisherman era was seen as the root of an extended period of losing and humiliation. "When I look through that era that I was there, the one thing that was not stable with the Islanders was ownership," said Rich Pilon, who played with the Islanders for twelve seasons—and under four ownership groups—from 1988 to 1999. "That team didn't have the stability up top from ownership and money, whatever you want to call it, to put the team in the right direction and keep it there. There was just too much change."[86]

Nearly a quarter century after its inauguration, the failed rebranding of the Islanders presents enduring lessons for the sports industry. The first is that a team should not embark on any sort of rebrand, especially one as drastic as replacing its primary logo, without a period of reflection on the costs and benefits of change as well as research to gauge the opinions of its fan base. The Islanders' indefensible neglect of standard information-gathering tools, such as focus groups, interviews, and surveys, led the organization to underestimate fans' affinity for the original logo and downplay the similarity between the new logo and the Gorton's fisherman. In their haste for a quick payday, the Islanders' brain trust did not distinguish between selling clothing to consumers who want to update their wardrobe with the latest fashions every season and selling new jerseys to fans with strong emotional attachments to the logo their favorite team had worn for its entire twenty-three-year existence. Even the most basic research would have demonstrated that fans did not associate the original logo with losing to the Rangers in the 1994 playoffs, as Islanders ownership assumed. For most fans the logo conjured fond memories of the franchise's heyday in the early 1980s, which in turn evoked their own personal feelings of joy from rooting for championship teams that represented the area where they grew up. Sports marketers must appreciate the profound affection that fans feel for the logos of teams they have devoted countless hours, and many dollars, to following.

The second most important lesson from the fisherman logo story involves the redeeming impact of winning. Among the many factors that harmed the rebrand, none were more damaging than the abandonment of the classic logo, which distanced the Islanders from the rich tradition that fans held dear, and the humiliating resemblance to a frozen seafood mascot, which spawned negative media coverage. The early mockery of the rebrand placed the Islanders in a defensive position heading into the inaugural season of the fisherman jerseys. However, as fans made clear in period interviews, the Islanders had a chance to recover on the ice. No matter the aesthetic shortcomings of a uniform, its ultimate success rests in the performance of the team that wears it. The Islanders rebranded at a time when the team was struggling, and the new logo became associated with losing. Due to the superstitious nature of sports, fans blamed the poor performance on the fisherman. The best time to unveil new jerseys is when a team is on the verge of success, as Wayne Gretzky's Los Angeles Kings were in 1988. Although no team can guarantee a winning season, the Kings had reason to expect deep playoff runs with Gretzky on board, while the Islanders had little hope that their roster of untested rookies and disgruntled veterans would bring a championship to Long Island. The silver-and-black uniforms came to identify the Kings during an upswing, and fans had little reason to miss the purple and gold worn in leaner times. Alternately, the Islanders' last-place finishes in 1995–96 and 1996–97 made fans long for a return to the logo of their Stanley Cup years.

Another lesson from the fisherman logo story is that rebranding does not concern uniforms alone. A jersey is just one element of a brand. Teams must view the rebranding process as a holistic change within the organization, encompassing everything the team presents to the public as part of its identity, including its history, players, former players, coaches, owners, mascot, and venue. In planning a rebrand, franchises should determine which brand elements are most valued by their fans and retain them, and identify which aspects are less popular and refresh them. The Islanders' greatest assets in the fisherman era were the dynasty players whom fans held in high regard, but the team underutilized them as ambassadors for the new brand. In fact, the Islanders alienated their alumni by changing jerseys without conferring with most of them and replacing a coach who had played alongside them with a coach who played against and disparaged them.

Rebrands have a greater chance of success when high-profile former players endorse them, allaying any concern among the fans that their heroes of yesteryear are being pushed aside and aren't on board with the changes.

The last major lesson concerns the designation of a standard-bearer for a new brand. While teams generally select players to appear in advertisements, the Islanders promoted the fisherman brand primarily through their coach Mike Milbury and later their owner John Spano, whose promise to pump money into the franchise excited the fan base. In both cases the team ignored red flags. The volatile Milbury had only two seasons of coaching experience and a reputation for strange behavior, while Spano's attempts to buy two other NHL franchises had fallen through and his net worth had not been properly vetted. Milbury's dubious motivational techniques and Spano's exposure as a con artist further damaged the fisherman brand. The team would have been much better off rebranding around an exciting player such as Žiggy Pálffy. Before a rebrand, sports marketers should coordinate with a team's general manager to designate a handful of principal players to represent the new image, preferably ones with pleasant personalities, long-term contracts, and records of recent success or reasonable expectations of immediate performance. To ensure continuity the organization should avoid trading those players in the first few years after the rebrand is enacted.

The disastrous reception for the fisherman uniforms demonstrated the worth of the NHL's third-jersey program. Inaugurated in 1996, the program allows teams to test new uniforms for a limited number of games and benefit from almost guaranteed bumps in revenue without catching criticism for completely abandoning their traditional sweaters.[1] Had the Islanders continued wearing their original logo in most games and used the new logo on a third jersey, the fisherman would not have become such a lightning rod. "That was the lesson that I think people learned: sometimes, be careful. Don't alienate your core base," said Fred Scalera, the former vice president of licensing for NHL Enterprises. "I guess what we all found out was that in the Islanders' case, we alienated their core base of fans and they lashed out."[2]

In the aftermath of the fisherman jerseys, many sports franchises have elected to alternate between two logos in the course of a single season. The strategy could grow in popularity in coming years due to heightened concern over the sensitivity of team logos and monikers. In particular, a handful of professional sports teams, including the NFL's Kansas City Chiefs and Washington Redskins, MLB's Atlanta Braves and Cleveland Indians, and NHL's Chicago Blackhawks, have come under attack for clinging to imagery that critics deem derogatory toward Native Americans. These clubs would be foolish to abandon the logos that have identified their franchises for decades and remove them from all uniforms and advertisements, as the Islanders did with their original logo. Instead, at least one franchise has chosen to downplay its classic crest but still retain it in some form. In 2016 the Indians moved their controversial Chief Wahoo logo, a red-faced, toothy caricature of a Native American, from their caps to their shoulder patches. The change allowed the Indians to appear sensitive to criticism from fans and media, and gradually phase out Chief Wahoo by the 2019 season, while temporarily retaining the logo that had appeared on the team's top-selling cap the previous season.[3]

There is no accounting for taste when ranking the worst NHL uniforms of all time. The Gorton's look-alike logo, dubious waves, and disjointed nameplates have placed the fisherman jersey high on almost every critic's list. Still, professional hockey has produced plenty of clunkers that challenge the fisherman for worst-dressed status. There's the barber-pole jerseys of the 1912–13 Montreal Canadiens, with dizzying stripes of red, white, and blue, and the Flying V uniforms unveiled by the Vancouver Canucks in 1978, with a deep *V* running from collar to crotch in a bizarre color scheme of yellow, orange, and black.[4] The revolution in uniform design in the mid-1990s also spawned the Mighty Ducks' Wild Wing jerseys, with a cartoon duck in a goaltender's mask bursting through a sheet of ice, and the Los Angeles Kings' "Burger King" sweaters, featuring a king's head similar to the mascot for the fast-food chain.[5] In 1996 the St. Louis Blues commissioned outfits so unsightly, with an overabundance of trumpets and musical notes, that their coach reportedly refused to let his players wear them.[6]

What separates the fisherman from other widely criticized NHL designs, however, is the number of games in which it was worn. The Islanders wore the fisherman jersey for every game in the 1995–96 season and the vast majority of games in 1996–97. For the past two decades the most maligned NHL uniforms, including the Ducks' Wild Wing and the Kings' Burger King sweaters, were seen in a much smaller number of games, and discarded with much greater ease than the fisherman, as part of the third-jersey program.

Even if the fisherman jerseys do not stand alone as the worst hockey uniforms ever, the Islanders' rebranding in the mid-1990s stakes a strong claim as the worst sports-branding effort of all time. In public memory the rebrand is associated with not only the questionable aesthetics of the jerseys but also three last-place seasons from 1994–95 to 1996–97 that were marked by one humiliation after another. In the span of just twenty-eight months the Islanders witnessed more embarrassment than most teams endure over twenty-eight years. There were the Gorton's comparisons and the "We want fish sticks!" chants, leading to mockery in international media and fans turning against the team by starting newsletters and protesting in the parking lot. There was the trading of a fan favorite for a player who refused to report and tanked, leading to the firing of a general manager and the rise of a replacement who clashed with his players and the alumni of a dynasty team. The mascot drew comparisons to fire hydrants and mountain men, and the man in the costume ended up taking the team to court. The arena deteriorated into the worst in the league. Control shifted from an absentee owner to a con artist to two men more concerned with real estate than real improvement. All the bad times were associated with the fisherman.

Stunningly, the men associated with the rebrand fell into even greater disrepute over the years. John Spano, after serving time for charges relating to the botched Islanders sale, was sent back behind bars twice more. He spent four years in prison for theft and forgery from 2005 to 2009, reentered society and appeared in the ESPN documentary in 2013, and then was sentenced to another ten years in 2015 on more forgery charges.[7] The group that engineered the rebranding campaign also ran afoul of the law. In 2009 Paul Greenwood and Stephen Walsh, two members of the Gang of Four, were charged with using their commodities-trading firm to steal from investors in order to buy cars, horse farms, and a collection of stuffed animals.[8] Greenwood was sentenced to a decade in prison, while Walsh, the strongest advocate of the fisherman jersey, got twenty years.[9] A subsequent co-owner, Sanjay Kumar, was sentenced to twelve years in prison in 2006 after pleading guilty to charges of conspiracy, fraud, and obstruction of justice stemming from his tenure as a chief executive officer at a large software company.[10] At one point the sentences of Spano, Greenwood, Walsh, and Kumar meant that members from three of the past four Islanders ownerships had served time, a trail tracing back to the fisherman era and inevitably affecting how fans remember the rebrand. "We lead the league in convicted felons," cracked Tom Croke of the defunct Support the Islanders Coalition.[11]

The misadventures of Mike Milbury also added to the infamy of the fisherman jerseys. Milbury, who was brought into the Islanders organization as part of the rebrand, remained the general manager until June 8, 2006, and stayed on as senior vice president until May 29, 2007, outliving the fisherman jerseys by a decade.[12] By the time he left the franchise the man who was chosen as the public face of the Islanders in the fisherman era had become a public enemy. He presided over seven losing seasons. He fired seven coaches. He traded away all the best players from the mid-1990s teams, including Bryan Berard, Todd Bertuzzi, Travis Green, Scott Lachance, Bryan McCabe, Žiggy Pálffy, Robert Reichel, Tommy Salo, Mathieu Schneider, and Bryan Smolinski, only to watch them flourish with other franchises. One newspaper nominated Milbury for a lifetime achievement award for bad trades.[13] It is even more difficult for Islanders fans to forget about Milbury's failings since he remains in the public eye as a television analyst for NBC.

Similarly, the players who wore fisherman jerseys are hard for Islanders fans to embrace. In a cruel twist the only mass-produced figurine ever made of an Islanders player in a fisherman jersey was a four-inch-tall Starting Lineup statuette of Kirk Muller, whose refusal to report to the team placed him on par with Milbury among the most despised figures in club history. Fittingly, the Muller figurines, which still float around for sale online, were packaged with a card showing him in the jersey of the Montreal Canadiens, the franchise he never wanted to leave.[14] The most productive Islander to wear the fisherman jersey was Žiggy Pálffy, but Milbury traded him in 1999 to Los Angeles, where he racked up even more points than he had on Long Island. Among the other well-known players to wear fisherman jerseys, Wendel Clark and Robert Reichel were traded before they could cement their legacies on Long Island. Several prominent players of the period diluted their goodwill among Islanders fans by suiting up for the hated Rangers, including rookie of the year Bryan Berard, captain Pat Flatley, highly touted defenseman Bryan McCabe, goalie Jamie McLennan, all-star Mathieu Schneider, and fan favorites Darius Kasparaitis and Rich Pilon. Éric Fichaud and Tommy Söderström never developed into the goalies of the future. Other Islanders went on to greater success elsewhere—Todd Bertuzzi in Vancouver, Tommy Salo in Edmonton, Bryan Smolinski in Los Angeles, and Martin Straka in Pittsburgh. In 2004 Bertuzzi drew a twenty-game suspension, one of the longest in NHL history, for seriously injuring a player by sucker-punching him from behind and driving his face into the ice. It was the type of violent behavior clearly rooted in his upbringing with the Islanders.

In 2000 the Islanders were purchased by a group led by Charles Wang, the chairman of Computer Associates.[15] Under Wang's ownership merchandise with the fisherman logo returned to the concession stands at Nassau Coliseum, and the team ran a one-night promotion in 2015 in which Islanders players skated in warm-ups in jerseys bearing the fisherman. After Wang moved the Islanders to the Barclays Center in Brooklyn for the 2015–2016 season, the team unveiled its most original uniform in twenty years, a third jersey with the NY from the original logo and a black-and-white color scheme.

To match the Islanders' black-and-white uniforms, goaltender Jaroslav Halak commissioned a new mask in the same colors, but with the fisherman logo above the center of the cage. In his first game in the mask the usually reliable Halak gave up three goals on only eleven shots and was pulled after one period.[16] Islanders fans on social media blamed his headwear.[17] A month later Halak donned the mask again and had another awful game, allowing three goals on the first eight shots he saw.[18] As superstitious fans debated the curse of the fisherman, Halak stopped wearing the mask. However, the Islanders went ahead with plans to give away ten thousand miniature replicas of the helmet at a game in March 2016. On Instagram, fans responded to a photograph of the mask with mockery. One commented, "Why is the old fisherman logo at the top??? Terrible."[19] On the night that his helmet was handed out, Halak performed well until late in the third period, when he stretched to make a routine save, grabbed his leg in pain, and skated toward the dressing room.[20] The next day the Islanders announced that their top goaltender had suffered a groin injury and would miss the next six to eight weeks, effectively ending his season and dimming the team's hopes of a deep playoff run.[21] The string of unlucky events supported the idea of a fisherman logo curse. As one sports radio host posted on Twitter, "There's a special kind of bad karma to get a long term injury on a night tied to a promotion."[22]

Further damaging the reputation of the fisherman logo are the Rangers fans who have kept needling the Islanders over the Gorton's similarity for the past twenty years. Islanders statistician Eric Hornick, who has worked for the team since 1982, has heard the taunts many times in recent seasons. "To this day when the Islanders go into the Garden and things are not going well, you'll hear Rangers fans chanting, 'We want fish sticks!'"[23]

Despite the controversy over the Islanders rebrand, the fisherman jersey holds special significance for the men who wore it. At the time the players were interviewed for this book in 2015, almost every one still had the uniform they wore two decades earlier. Asked why they would keep an article of clothing they disliked, many players cited playing a plurality of their NHL games—or, in some cases, their first or last shifts in the league—with the fisherman on their chests. Others said the jersey was proof they reached the highest level of professional hockey. In a typical response, Mathieu Schneider said, "Playing in this league is a privilege no matter what you say about any given jersey."

Dan Plante, who spent his entire four-year career with the Islanders, said the jersey reminded him of his journey from small-town Wisconsin, where he grew up and used to compete in lumberjack contests, to the world's biggest market. "I was a northern Wisconsin hillbilly and got to go to New York," he said. "It was quite a different way of life. I've got nothing but great memories about Long Island and the area and the franchise, for sure." An exception to the rule was Chris Taylor, who said the fisherman was the only jersey he ever gave away. "I don't think I liked the design. I didn't think it had the Islander tradition." Darius Kasparaitis, who also gave his away at some point, was looking to buy a replacement online, so he could wear it in pickup games and "get abused by my friends." The fisherman was the last NHL jersey ever worn by Bob Halkidis, but he doesn't have one either, because he spent almost the entire season in the minor leagues.[24]

Several players said the penny-pinching Islanders charged them to take their sweaters home. Paul Kruse may have paid more than any of his teammates. A gritty fourth-liner, Kruse once received a $1,000 fine for breaking a new rule against fighting before puck drop. He heard that most teams were reimbursing players, so he asked Mike Milbury about covering the cost. Not surprisingly, Milbury balked. "I said, 'Well, what about my jerseys? Can I have both my jerseys?'" Kruse remembered. "And he thought about it for a minute. He was riding the bike. And he goes, 'Yeah, you can have 'em.' So essentially those two jerseys cost me $1,000." Actually, the price Kruse paid may have been a steal. Nostalgia has built up so much over the years that online sellers have asked for as much as $1,000 for a single fisherman jersey that was not even worn in a game. For most players the sentimental value of the uniform exceeds whatever they could make on eBay. Jason Herter, a career minor leaguer, played his only NHL game in a fisherman jersey and returned to the minors without it. A few years later he contacted the Islanders about getting the uniform back. Milbury mailed it free of charge.[25]

Other players disobeyed the Islanders in order to retain their fisherman gear. When Bryan Smolinski was traded in 1999, he took his hockey bag, emblazoned with the fisherman logo, to Los Angeles. One day the Kings equipment manager told Smolinski that the Islanders wanted the bag back, even though the team had reverted back to the classic crest. "I'm like, 'Well, you can go tell them to screw themselves. I'm not giving it back. It's not even the logo!'" Smolinski said. "Why did they want the bag back? I think they wanted to use the bag."[26]

The game-worn fisherman jerseys were scattered around the world, wherever the players put them. They were hanging on the wall of Brent Severyn's athletic performance center in Plano, Texas, and sitting in Robert Reichel's basement in the Czech Republic. Tommy Söderström's was somewhere in his attic. Travis Green left his with his parents. In Sweden the thirteen-year-old son of Niklas Andersson had a poster in his room that showed his father in the fisherman sweater. Dad kept the uniform itself in his garage. Rich Pilon, meanwhile, said he kept his jersey in the bedroom closet, ready to go whenever a special moment struck. "My wife liked it," he explained. "Sometimes when we go to bed at night, she wants me to wear it." Then he burst into laughter and said he was only joking.[27]

In interviews for this book, the men involved in rebranding the Islanders expressed frustration over the tendency to oversimplify and mischaracterize what went wrong, and they seemed eager to explain the rationale behind their widely criticized decisions. They were disappointed over the outcome of the rebranding, but also at peace. Ed O'Hara, whose design firm created Nyisles and the fisherman jerseys, admitted the team erred in changing its identity, and he acknowledged that better research by his company, SME, would have caught the logo's similarity to the Gorton's character before it was released. "Look, 100 percent, it was a mistake," he said. O'Hara chalked up the missteps as a learning experience that taught SME to seek feedback from fans, sponsors, and news media before introducing a new brand. Far from losing business over the disastrous Islanders rebrand, SME became a leading sports-branding firm, developing brands for the World Series, the NBA Finals, the Kentucky Derby, the Indianapolis 500, and Madison Square Garden, as well as many collegiate and professional teams. Despite O'Hara's success, though, some people still associate him with the fisherman jerseys. "We've done twenty uniforms in the NHL. We've done fifteen in the NBA. And this is the one that people keep talking about. We've had a lot of notoriety on all our other work, but this one always comes up. And I always say, 'You know, Babe Ruth struck out two thousand times.'"[28] The reference was fitting. Among its many contracts, SME became the agency of record for Ruth's former team, and perhaps the most recognizable brand in professional sports, the New York Yankees.

The fisherman jerseys did not hinder the careers of any Islanders executives. Pat Calabria, the team's vice president of communications and point person on the rebrand, went on to become a vice president at a state university in Farmingdale, Long Island. Looking back, he pointed out that the people tasked with rolling out the jerseys had no control over the losing on the ice, which probably hurt the rebrand more than anything else. "Was it the right decision or the wrong decision? I think you could debate that," he said. "What I will say is, if it was the right decision, it was made at the wrong time."[29]

Tim Beach, the Islanders' director of game events in the fisherman era, ended up running game entertainment for the NFL's Arizona Cardinals. Asked for his reflections on the Islanders' rebranding, Beach referred to the sitcom *WKRP in Cincinnati*, about a radio station with low ratings. In one 1978 episode a well-intentioned promotion on Thanksgiving goes horribly wrong when turkeys are thrown out of a helicopter and plunge to their deaths. Beach said the punch line, uttered by the station's general manager, reminded him of the Islanders' missteps in rolling out the fisherman logo. "A lot of times when there's a bad idea that goes wrong in my life, I'll look at someone and I'll say, 'As God as my witness, I thought turkeys could fly.'"[30]

On February 20, 2014, author Nicholas Hirshon conducted an hour-long interview with graphic designer Pat McDarby, whose sketches inspired the Islanders' mascot during the fisherman era. A year later McDarby died on March 14, 2015, at age fifty-seven. This interview is included as an appendix because of McDarby's high profile in the sports-branding business and his passing just one year after the discussion with the author, making this the final extensive interview he appears to have granted. His obituary in the *New York Times* credited him with designing more than two hundred logos in collegiate and professional sports, including designs for the NHL's New York Rangers, the NBA's New Jersey Nets, the Indianapolis 500, various Major League Soccer events, and what is now World Wrestling Entertainment. In the verbatim transcript of the interview that appears below, McDarby describes his role in the Islanders' rebranding process and expresses frustration about the modern sports-branding industry.

HIRSHON: How did you come to work for Ed O'Hara and SME, or were you a private contractor at that point, or how was that working?

MCDARBY: I had known Ed when he worked at Colgate, and I had done some freelance work for them at that time. I had lost contact with him for a little while. And one day he calls me up, and he says, 'Why don't you come in and see if you can do some work for us?' I was a finished illustrator. I did some designs at that time, but it was mostly illustration. He knew I had hands and I could sketch and do that kind of stuff, so he brought me in. They had just finished the Panthers off, the Florida Panthers, that was their first big job. And all of a sudden, it spread like wildfire. He had me work on the Maryland Terrapins. That was my first job with them, and that turned out great, and they chose my design. And from there on, I was full-time freelance with them for four years, doing designs like the Rangers and Madison Square Garden. And then we did the Islanders, which was a very interesting project.

HIRSHON: Right. And you would have been working for them then those, I think you said, four years for freelance. That would have been in the mid-'90s?

MCDARBY: It was from '96 to 2000. I did over two hundred projects with them.

HIRSHON: With SME?

MCDARBY: What's that?

HIRSHON: With SME?

MCDARBY: That's Sean Michael Edwards. That's the name of the partners who owned it.

HIRSHON: Okay. Do you remember the first time he contacted you about the Islanders project specifically?

MCDARBY: I was there. I was working pretty much full-time. I did full-time freelance for them. The Islander project came in, and we did our first round of sketches. It was mostly lighthouses. That was our initial approach, which I think should have been the logo. It was a beautiful, beautiful logo. It had hope, the light and the dark. The Islanders were trying to come out of that. They were in a bad couple of seasons they had there, so they needed some hope for the future. So we proposed to come out with the lighthouse on the front, but somebody over there had got stuck on the fisherman. [He laughs.] Some of the fishermen really came out good. They were very heroic, almost like a Neptune god. We did some of that, too. We did some Neptune approaches and stuff like that. There was a whole bucking wave–type design approach. That's what we called buckets. There are different approaches we take on the logo. The fisherman, I thought, was pretty good. But then for some reason they got more cartoony with it in the future revisions. When I worked on the face, they wanted more attitude, and it got looking more like Popeye, and I was like, Eh. It was actually my least favorite of the designs I've done for them. And it came to fruition, because they had riots in the street over the damn thing. [He laughs.] People protesting over a logo that we did was pretty funny and embarrassing.

HIRSHON: When you were first approached about the project, were you told to work with a maritime theme?

MCDARBY: They had buckets. What would depict the Islanders? First we did what's been called evolutionary logos that were just based off what they already had. We just dimensionalized it, made some of the outlines bolder and the type a little modern. There was a bunch of approaches like that. Then you had, What else is Islanders? Lighthouse. Lighthouse is perfect. You have the radiating light, and we were going with this whole wave theme. The three-color wave thing on the bottom. So we had that approach. And then the heroic fisherman. Those are the three that I remember that we went through.

HIRSHON: And you really thought that the lighthouse would be a better design?

MCDARBY: Absolutely.

HIRSHON: Why is that?

MCDARBY: I think we all did. Well, symbolically it's just stronger, and it just meant more than a fisherman, you know?

HIRSHON: Although it seems like you thought that the fisherman could work, just not with the angle they eventually took with the cartoonish quality.

MCDARBY: It got too cartoony. Yeah. The one thing with SME at that time, they used to sell this whole in-your-face approach. That was kind of big. We always had one approach that was in your face, and that was the in-your-face approach. The lighthouse was not an in-your-face type of icon. So they wanted this in-your-face fisherman with a hockey stick.

HIRSHON: There were also different permutations of the fisherman himself, right?

MCDARBY: Yes.

HIRSHON: So what were some of the other ideas? I know you said at some points he was looking more heroic or like a god or something or like Neptune from the sea.

MCDARBY: You were looking up at him. I think some of the hockey sticks had a trident on the other end. I think it actually was like Neptune, if I remember correctly. Then it definitely morphed into the Gorton's fisherman. We had concerns too that we might have some legal problems with Gorton's. [He laughs.] But they approved the sketches, and that's how we went forward. Like I said, the ones we did, it was definitely more looking up at a heroic angle, in kind of a Rockefeller Center, Deco-type style. And it worked. It worked. It was New York. I liked a lot of those sketches.

HIRSHON: But eventually you thought that he got too much of an attitude also? Because I know he has the grimace on his face. People have brought that up.

MCDARBY: That's the whole thing. They kept adding that. They kept adding the in-your-face attitude, and that's what SME was all about at that time. That's what made them sell, that whole style.

HIRSHON: All right. Were there other aspects of the way he was dressed or anything else that kind of changed over time?

MCDARBY: No. We might have had nets hanging off the stick and stuff like that, just little things, but he was pretty much in a slicker. The type of slicker was changing from time to time. It was more about making it correct. Your sketch is usually not that right. Something's come out of your head, and then you research it and you find out what it really looks like. That's all I can remember as far as that's concerned.

HIRSHON: All right. 'Cause part of the confusion that I'm having here is since you were involved in both projects, both the mascot and then the logo, I know they happened at different times, 'cause it seems like the mascot was introduced in the '94-'95 season, and then the logo didn't come until '95-'96.

MCDARBY: The mascot was definitely part of the final logo. We had the final logo first. It just wasn't announced. I think his name was Salty or something like that. We developed that first 'cause it was a quick thing to do. They wanted to get some news out about what was gonna happen. They put that out. There's some funny stories with that too, with the mascot. One of the meetings I had, I was actually thinking about creating fish sticks, like a hockey stick with a fish on the end of it. [He laughs.] I used to do stuff that like that, and they used to laugh at me. The other one was a hockey puck in the middle of a fish, and how are the pucking fish? [He laughs.]

HIRSHON: So this would have all been part of the mascot design or the logo?

MCDARBY: It was just ideas. We were just coming up with merchandising ideas and the mascot. It's a whole marketing program that you come up with. Of course, that stuff was just lighthearted. It wasn't really serious.

HIRSHON: Gotcha. Yeah, because with the article from the *Times* from 1995, it's from January, and they do have a photo of the mascot skating around, but they also have these three sketches at the top, and I couldn't tell if they're sketches that you actually came up with or if they're just things they're throwing out there.

MCDARBY: Those are mine. Those are mine.

HIRSHON: Those are yours. Okay. Because it looks like in some of them he's—there's various ages. One of them kind of looks more like Santa Claus to me all the way at the end.

MCDARBY: [He laughs.] Yeah.

HIRSHON: Yeah. And I guess the one in the middle is kind of the one they adopted. I don't know how well you remember it, but he has the light on top of his head and the helmet.

MCDARBY: Yeah. When he scored, the light would go off.

HIRSHON: Right. The goal light. Yeah. And then there's others that kind of look, I don't know, more like a Popeye kind of an image, or something else.

MCDARBY: Well, one of those sketches was somebody else's. We usually had two to three guys working on it. Yeah, one was kind of real Santa Clausy. I think mine, he had crabs hanging onto his beard and stuff like that.

HIRSHON: Yeah. I'm looking at that one. That seems to be the one that they went with, although I guess they didn't have the crabs.

MCDARBY: [He laughs.] No crabs, though.

HIRSHON: No crabs, but otherwise it looked pretty similar.

MCDARBY: [He laughs.] Yeah.

HIRSHON: So what did you say? You originally nicknamed the mascot something?

MCDARBY: I think it was Salty.

HIRSHON: Salty, like the salt of the earth?

MCDARBY: Yeah. You know, saltwater.

HIRSHON: Oh, okay. Because I've heard the second season he got the name Nyisles. You know, NY Isles. And I know that was on the back of his jersey.

MCDARBY: Oh, yes. That's what it was. That's what it ended up being. Right.

HIRSHON: The Salty thing was just something that you guys in meetings were saying, or was he actually officially named . . .

MCDARBY: When you're labeling things, you go, 'Oh, what could his name be? Salty.' One of my favorite ones, we did—there was a roller-blade team out on Long Island, and they had a shark. The Jawz. It was the Long Island Jawz.

HIRSHON: Yeah, the Long Island Jawz. Yup.

MCDARBY: And I think their mascot was Chum. [He laughs.]

HIRSHON: Did you do that for them too?

MCDARBY: Yes. I did that for them.

HIRSHON: Oh, great. So the idea behind the mascot, was a lot of this marketing? I understand at that time they were trying to appeal to kids. Was that ever coming into it?

MCDARBY: Yeah. It was a more family-driven marketing plan, and that's probably why they went with the fisherman too, to try to appeal to the kids. I loved the color palette. I thought the color palette was fantastic.

HIRSHON: What did you like about it?

MCDARBY: The teal was a different color. Otherwise you're using New York colors like they always do. Teal just added that whole water approach to it, which I liked.

HIRSHON: Okay. Because part of the concern that Ed brought up is that teal was very popular at that time because of the Charlotte Hornets.

MCDARBY: Yes. Yes, it was. We did the Jaguars too. They happened to be part of the SME palette.

HIRSHON: Right. But he said he was concerned that maybe teal was already on the way out, that it had already been tried and done at that point.

MCDARBY: It might have been. Well, it wasn't in hockey, though. It was in football. They had it for the Panthers, and they had it for the Jaguars. He might have been afraid that we might have been using it too much, and it was a hot color at the time.

HIRSHON: So when you're coming up with these original designs, was there any thought ever given to other kinds of sea creatures like crabs and lobsters and all that kind of stuff?

MCDARBY: In the initial, when you're creating the buckets, everything gets thrown out there. It can be everything from a shark to a striped bass or a bluefish. Anything that would say New York Islanders. Even the map. But then they narrow it down before you start sketching. They narrow it down to maybe three or four buckets, and then you do ideas for each of those, and then you present them.

HIRSHON: Okay. So by the time you were brought into the process, you were told specifically fisherman or bayman idea?

MCDARBY: Yes. Fisherman, lighthouse, an evolutionary approach, which is just dimensionalizing the type, making it nice, better, stronger.

HIRSHON: Were you sitting in on the meetings at Nassau Coliseum where officials from the NHL and the Islanders were there?

MCDARBY: No, I wasn't there. I was in the office. They always had Ed and either one salesman would go there and do the face-to-face presentations with them. Now the actual guy whose logo was chosen was a guy named Andrew Blanco.

HIRSHON: Okay.

MCDARBY: He was the guy who did the actual drawing for the fisherman.

HIRSHON: For the fisherman logo that ended up being picked?

MCDARBY: Yes.

HIRSHON: And his last name is Blanco, B-L-A-N-C-O?

MCDARBY: Yes. And he's now a musician down in Venezuela called King Chango.

HIRSHON: Huh. Had he worked on other projects there?

MCDARBY: You mean Andrew? Yeah. Andrew's a very good designer.

HIRSHON: That begs the question: What do you think went wrong if anything with the logo? Was it just that the team wasn't that good? Why was it so poorly received?

MCDARBY: No. No. It's always difficult to mess with tradition. You never know what's gonna happen. The Islanders had a dynasty for a lot of years and then they started going bad, and when the team didn't do well, the logo affected it. But I'll tell you what I think made the logo just go really bad is when they played the Rangers, all the fans would be yelling, "We want fish sticks!"

HIRSHON: Right.

MCDARBY: And as a player, you don't want to be bombarded with stuff like that. It was a poor choice. And he definitely looked too much like the Gorton's fisherman, you know?

HIRSHON: Was that a conscious thing that you were talking about in meetings, or did that not come up until afterwards, the comparison to Gorton's?

MCDARBY: That didn't come up until later. I definitely thought that we were treading on thin ice with that, mind the pun there. [He laughs.]

HIRSHON: About the comparison to Gorton's fisherman?

MCDARBY: Yeah. Yeah.

HIRSHON: So it was kind of a risk that you guys knew about, but you just decided we're gonna take it?

MCDARBY: Yeah. Yeah. It was an in-your-face fisherman. And that's what they approved. I can't take blame for that. I can't give blame to Ed or Andrew, because that's where we were directed. I had hundreds of sketches they could have chose from, and that's what they chose.

HIRSHON: But it was pretty much Andrew working alone on this one logo that ended up being picked.

MCDARBY: Yeah. Yeah. But like I said, we all did sketches. They end up in the buckets, and they chose that one.

HIRSHON: Gotcha.

MCDARBY: But originally, his original sketch was more heroic and, like I said, more Art Deco-looking. It had a pretty cool style. Now I doubt you could ever get a hold of those sketches, because SME threw a lot of that stuff away.

HIRSHON: Right. Ed said that he did have some papers, and he thought he had some original sketches that he offered to try to fish out for me.

MCDARBY: They used to have these gray books with everything in them. If he held onto them, he would have them.

HIRSHON: You don't happen to have anything from that period, do you?

MCDARBY: I'd have to look. I doubt it. They kept all the original artwork. I'd have copies and stuff like that, if I still have it. But I probably couldn't give it to you, because it's supposedly property of SME, and only they can give that out.

HIRSHON: I understand that. At some point, I guess, if you do come across it, I could run it past Ed, or you could do it, because he said to me about his own papers that, well, the only one who would have any rights to it would be SME, and "I'm granting you permission, so it's not a problem." So I think that he understands that aspect of it.

MCDARBY: Right. You'd have to get it from NHL too, though.

HIRSHON: He was under the impression that the NHL wouldn't be involved in this part of it, because these are designs that were never officially commissioned by the NHL, even though the team was commissioning them in some sense.

MCDARBY: Then it's just SME. And you'd have to get permission from them.

HIRSHON: Right. That's what he was saying. And that's why he was saying, "I'll give you permission," and all of that.

MCDARBY: Yeah. Okay. So hopefully he still has the original sketches. If he does, it'll explain pretty much what I'm telling you. You'll see the different buckets of ideas that we had approached.

HIRSHON: And I also noticed that Nyisles, the mascot himself, seemed to change over the different seasons. This photo that's in the *New York Times* shows him as being very overweight, this roly-poly kind of figure.

MCDARBY: He's round. He's barrel-chested.

HIRSHON: Yeah. And then later on, the next season, it seems like he's slimmed down significantly.

MCDARBY: Yes.

HIRSHON: He worked out all summer or something. And he all of a sudden has much more of a hockey player kind of build. So was that a conscious decision too?

MCDARBY: Yes. Yes. You throw the first thing out there, then you get responses from it. "Ah, he's too fat. He looks slow." So they made him more athletic the next year. But he probably also had a hard time walking down the aisles too. [He laughs.]

HIRSHON: Yeah. I saw there were some quotes in that story from the guy who was apparently wearing the outfit, at least in the early days, and talking about the attitude that they wanted. I guess everything you were saying. He's supposed to have this New York attitude, in-your-face, obnoxious even, and maybe that went a little too far.

MCDARBY: Tough.

HIRSHON: Yeah, tough. It seems like here what you've brought up, there's kind of this conflict here. On the one hand, you want him to be something where kids are gobbling up the merchandise and they want to hug the mascot and get their photo, but on the other hand, you want him to have this New York toughness and obnoxiousness. That doesn't seem to go hand in hand with each other.

MCDARBY: No. It's a very tough sell.

HIRSHON: Yeah.

MCDARBY: A very tough sell. But the death of the logo was because it looked too much like the Gorton's fisherman. If there wasn't a Gorton's fisherman logo out there, no one would have had anything to say. They wouldn't be yelling, "We want fish sticks!" That to me is what really killed it. I think design-wise it was a pretty decent logo. Not one of my favorites, but it was okay. I designed the Liberty logo for SME, the New York Rangers. Now that's more my style. It's more classic. The lighthouse is more classic, more hockey. And it would have endured a lot longer. I mean, what complaints could you have against that? The lighthouse was the secondary logo.

HIRSHON: Mmm-hmm.

MCDARBY: I don't know if you know that. It was on the shoulder.

HIRSHON: On the shoulder. Yeah. So you actually designed the lighthouse that's on the shoulder?

MCDARBY: No. No. Andrew did that one too.

HIRSHON: Oh, he did that one too. But you did other versions of different lighthouses?

MCDARBY: Yes.

HIRSHON: Do you know what the inspiration was for the lighthouse? Was there a particular one that they were going for?

MCDARBY: A lighthouse is a lighthouse. We just researched a lighthouse. I think the best part of the design was how he interpreted the rays of light. That was really well done. It was just a really nice, nice logo. If Ed has still the mock-ups of how that looked on the front, you'll see it was a really good logo. Frankly, they should still do it.

HIRSHON: Yeah. I think at this point they're so afraid, and you've seen it over the years now. The Islanders are afraid to change their jersey in any way beyond just the background color.

MCDARBY: It's one of the worst logos in hockey.

HIRSHON: It's what?

MCDARBY: It's one of the worst logos in hockey.

HIRSHON: The current one that they have?

MCDARBY: Yeah. It's an old 1980s-looking logo. The type is bad. The NY is bad. A lot of people have this emotional attachment to it only because how great the team was. That's the only thing. But if you look at it from a design standpoint, that logo just is amateurish.

HIRSHON: What about it doesn't work?

MCDARBY: The map of the state behind the type. The type is just kind of clunky and not even. It's typographically not well done. There's no dimension to it. I just don't like it.

HIRSHON: Okay. The other issue that some people have brought up besides the Gorton's fisherman, like you've said, just the attachment to the old logo. And if they had never won in that old jersey, if this had been the first-ever logo . . .

MCDARBY: They would have had no attachment to it. If that team stunk from its inception, they'd have no attachment to it.

HIRSHON: Yeah. Exactly.

MCDARBY: They have all these retro jerseys now. And what is that all about? It's about the same thing. It's about the heyday, the glory days of your team, if there was an Original Six or whatever. People gravitate to that when they were great.

HIRSHON: Right.

MCDARBY: It has nothing to do with how well it's designed.

HIRSHON: And when you were talking about the logo or the mascot, Ed was saying that often they didn't like to talk about it in terms of fishermen, maybe to avoid the Gorton's fisherman, but they used to use the term *bayman*. Do you remember that?

MCDARBY: What was the term?

HIRSHON: *Bayman*.

MCDARBY: Bayman. The bayman. Yeah.

HIRSHON: Yeah? That's what you guys would say sometimes?

MCDARBY: [He laughs.] What is he? He's a fisherman.

HIRSHON: Right. I guess it's sort of a euphemism.

MCDARBY: If it was a bayman, well, maybe he thought that he wouldn't look like the Gorton's fisherman because they had clam guys out there. The baymen were more clam guys. They were clammers. I actually kind of think we had some secondary logos with clamming boats on them. That's a vague recollection, though.

HIRSHON: Well, that would make some sense, because Ed was saying the reason why they used baymen was because Billy Joel had just come out with that song 'Downeaster *Alexa*.'

MCDARBY: Yes. Yes. Right.

HIRSHON: And that they wanted to kind of evoke that image of the bayman. And even when they unveiled the logo officially, they actually brought in these guys from a baymen's association to stand alongside the logo and talk about Long Island heritage.

MCDARBY: Oh, okay.

HIRSHON: Were you involved in any of that, like the official rolling out, going to games?

MCDARBY: No. I'm a pair of hands. That's basically it. I came in and sketched it.

HIRSHON: And as this logo is being unveiled and then it's being panned, what was the feeling in the company? Was it embarrassing to be part of this?

MCDARBY: The next year. They thought it was great when they first came out with it. And it did pretty good with the sales, too, if I remember correctly. It was something new. It was something fresh. People, they bought it up. But once they started getting panned and made fun of, the people who were Islander fanatics, they wanted their old logo back. You're always gonna come up against that kind of thing with change.

HIRSHON: But in all the logos you've ever worked on, was this up there among the most vilified or controversial or however you want to frame it?

MCDARBY: It's the most controversial.

HIRSHON: How about in all of sports? Because I'm sure you have an appreciation for other logos beyond what SME has done or what you did. Looking at the totality of sports logos, where do you think it ranks in that controversial aspect?

MCDARBY: It's gotta be up there. I don't know of any other logo that had people picketing it and hating it. You're talking one or two. I'm trying to think of some of the other ones that got panned. Nothing that we've done at SME. I mean, everything was pretty successful. Out of SME that was the most embarrassing one. But again, you're directed. I can't blame SME for anything that was done. They had over a hundred choices. They could have chosen anything else. You wonder how it gets to that point sometimes. Is it design by committee? A lot of people talking? But SME did have that. They were selling that in-your-face stuff at that time. Of all the sketches that we did, the fisherman was the only real article that we had to put that in-your-face attitude on.

HIRSHON: Mmm-hmm. And as you recall, the time that you really realized this logo was gonna be doomed was when the Rangers fans started chanting against it, "We want fish sticks!"?

MCDARBY: Yes. Yeah. "We want fish sticks!" Yeah.

HIRSHON: Yeah.

MCDARBY: I was in the audience when they first played the Rangers.

I was at the game, and I was just hiding my head. [He laughs.] And I'm a Ranger fan, unfortunately. [He laughs.]

HIRSHON: So this was at the Garden, you're talking about?

MCDARBY: I was at the Garden. They gave me tickets to go see the game the first time the Islanders were on the ice with the new logo on.

HIRSHON: This was the very first time they wore the logo, or just the first time versus the Rangers?

MCDARBY: No. No. The first time at the Rangers.

HIRSHON: Okay.

MCDARBY: They had their unveiling at the Coliseum.

HIRSHON: Right.

MCDARBY: I didn't go to that one.

HIRSHON: Yeah. I saw some old clips too from the *Times* and other papers about people throwing, of course, fish sticks on the ice but also just fish itself. Supposedly that happened at the Garden.

MCDARBY: Yeah. Yeah. It was just too much fuel for your opposition where it became embarrassing. And you don't need that from your logo.

HIRSHON: Right. They were doing that to themselves enough on the ice.

MCDARBY: What's that?

HIRSHON: They were doing that enough to themselves on the ice with just being a poor team.

MCDARBY: Yeah. They were a poor team. Yeah. If they won the Stanley Cup that year, people wouldn't have said anything. That's just the way it is, though.

HIRSHON: Well, is there any other aspect of either the mascot or the logo that I haven't touched on you want to go into?

MCDARBY: No. That's pretty much as much as I can remember, too. It's been a long time.

HIRSHON: Right. I know it's a while ago.

MCDARBY: Well, I grew up in the Bronx, and I've done, like I said, over a hundred team identities and stuff, and my friends, guys in the Bronx, are cruel as it is. I have this one friend. He always introduces me, "Hey, here's the guy that did the Islander logo!" [He laughs.] I say, "Hey dude, that's not the only logo I did!" [He laughs.] They don't let you get a big head up in the Bronx. They like to bring you down. [He laughs.]

HIRSHON: Well, which other logos are you proud of? Of course, we're talking about this one that's not necessarily the best work.

MCDARBY: The Liberty logo was my favorite. And the Madison Square Garden identity, but that's not a team. That was a venue.

HIRSHON: Which logo did you do for the Garden?

MCDARBY: I did the whole identity logo. And MSG Network. And if you ever see the Garden bags, the plastic bag, the illustration on the front of them is mine.

HIRSHON: Ah. That's all yours.

MCDARBY: Yeah.

HIRSHON: I know there is some sort of a Madison Square Garden logo, I haven't seen it in a while, but there was something that has the side of the building on it. That's yours, I guess?

MCDARBY: Yes. It's the building. It's looking up at the Garden. You see the Chrysler Building and the Empire State Building in the background.

HIRSHON: Okay.

MCDARBY: And it's all purples and blues.

HIRSHON: This kind of begs the question: Did you want to ruin the Islanders 'cause you're a Rangers fan?

MCDARBY: No. No. I have no control over that.

HIRSHON: Right. Right.

MCDARBY: No. I have a lot of pride in what I do, and I think everybody at SME did too. That's your business. You try to do the best job you can for all your clients. 'Cause you do a bad job and you're out. And that's a very narrow business. That's a very small niche to be in. And SME was the best at the time.

HIRSHON: And have you continued to do the logos? I saw on your website you still have a bunch of stuff up there.

MCDARBY: I just—I don't know if you know the UFL [United Football League]?

HIRSHON: Uh huh. Yup.

MCDARBY: I did all the logos for that league.

HIRSHON: Oh, wow.

MCDARBY: And at the turn of the millennium, I did Major League Soccer. Without SME. I left SME in 2000.

HIRSHON: Okay. When you're doing Major League Soccer, was that all of their teams or the logo for—

MCDARBY: No. It was the league logo and all-star logo and the Connecticut logo and their whole identity package. They have conference logos—West Conference, East Conference. Did all those.

HIRSHON: Gotcha. So besides the sources that I've already mentioned to you—obviously I've spoken to Ed, and I'm gonna try to reach Andrew and some other people—but is there any other person you think would be good to talk to, or a place to go to, an archive where some of this might be still in existence?

MCDARBY: Um, well, who was the—I'm trying to think who was the owner of the Islanders at that time, because he had a big part in the whole thing.

HIRSHON: The main owner was John Pickett, who apparently was an absentee owner, but the remaining 10 percent were a few other guys. I think they called them a Gang of Three or Gang of Four. Robert Rosenthal was probably the one that you may remember.

MCDARBY: I don't remember him. But there was definitely somebody over there pulling—making the decisions. Like I said, I never met with those guys. I just got reports back and I got job descriptions of what we had to do, and that's where I would go work from.

HIRSHON: Gotcha.

MCDARBY: But there was somebody definitely at the ownership over there making these decisions. If I remember Ed, he didn't want that. I don't know if he told you that that he didn't want that.

HIRSHON: Yeah. That's what he told me. Yeah.

MCDARBY: Yeah. He didn't want that logo. He was definitely trying to sell the lighthouse.

HIRSHON: But apparently he said, like you're saying, that the owners were very gung-ho about the fisherman, perhaps with the prospect of sales and with the mascot.

MCDARBY: It is more family friendly. A lighthouse—how do you connect with an inanimate object? But symbolically, I think it's a better thing, but you're not gonna sell it to kids. You can't worry about selling to kids. You sell it to your fans.

HIRSHON: Mmm-hmm. I guess that speaks to the 1990s in general. Ed was also saying with the Mighty Ducks, that had just come out, and everybody was thinking about, How can we get more cartoonish and get to that Disney kind of level?

MCDARBY: And actually, one of SME's largest coups, one of their best designs from that time, was the Raptors. It was a cartoon dinosaur. They didn't have a team yet, and they were selling millions of dollars' worth of fashion. If you look at the Islander logo and the Raptors logo, it has a similar feel to it. They're trying to build on that success, I guess.

HIRSHON: And I think that was Ed's point. Maybe it worked for the Raptors a few years earlier, but by the time the Islanders were using it—

MCDARBY: Yes. And it was a great success. The other thing with the Raptors was the fashion colors. SME started using the fashion forecasts to choose the color palettes. It matched with the Nike sneaker of the time. I think they did that with the Islanders, too.

HIRSHON: I know that the Islanders never came out with any sort of merchandise besides selling the fisherman logo on pucks and on the jerseys obviously, but apparently they never came out with dolls and other sorts of things that they were at first thinking about that would have maybe been more lucrative.

MCDARBY: I think that they might have been waiting to see if it had any impetus as far as it being a good thing. I don't think they would get into merchandising in the first year. When they'd seen it going south, they just probably said, "No, let's not go forward with this."

HIRSHON: I guess that was a good decision.

MCDARBY: Yes. It was.

HIRSHON: 'Cause you'd have millions of these fisherman dolls in some basement in Nassau Coliseum.

MCDARBY: With the fish.

HIRSHON: Yeah. Exactly. Sleeping with the fishes.

MCDARBY: [He laughs.]

HIRSHON: All right. I think that's pretty much what I wanted to cover. Thank you very much for your time. And of course, this is all very flexible and I'm still working through some of these things, so if you don't mind, I may be in touch again and I'll certainly keep you abreast of what I'm doing.

MCDARBY: If I find anything, I'll email you to let you know what I got.

HIRSHON: Yeah. That would be great. And if you want me to run it past Ed again, or if you want to do that to make sure that it's okay.

MCDARBY: Well, Ed and I are not on good terms, though. [He laughs.]

HIRSHON: Oh, okay.

MCDARBY: He probably didn't even mention my name.

HIRSHON: Oh, no. He actually didn't. But I didn't know if that was because he didn't want—at one point, he said during the conversation that he didn't want to get too involved with naming people as if he was blaming people. So I think that that was part of it. But anyway, I saw your name luckily when I was going through that one story, so I'm glad that that exists.

MCDARBY: Yeah. We've had our falling-out, but I have no animosity towards Ed. It was a great time in my life, and it was some of the best work I've ever done. Let it lie.

HIRSHON: I appreciate the opportunity also to put it in context, because that's what—I think it's easy for people to say, "Oh, yeah, it's one of the worst logos of all time," but not appreciate what was going on at that time with these logos geared toward kids.

MCDARBY: There was definitely purpose for everything that we did with it. Design-wise, it's a nice logo, but the content is what killed it. You know what I'm saying? We massaged that logo till it looked really nice. The color palette's nice. It's a nice circular logo. From a design standpoint, it's a good logo, but from a content, it's a bad logo.

HIRSHON: In 1995, before the Islanders could even officially unveil the logo, there was a story in the *Daily News* that pans the logo and first makes the comparison to the Gorton's fisherman in public.

MCDARBY: Really?

HIRSHON: And the headline of the story was "New Isles Logo Will Make You Sea Sick."

MCDARBY: [He laughs.] Oh my God.

HIRSHON: And they did a photo illustration of Denis Potvin, who was the captain of the Cup teams, and they show the new logo on his jersey.

MCDARBY: Oh, boy.

HIRSHON: The author is really harsh on the Islanders and has this whole thing about the Islanders. "All they have left is their storied history 'cause they're such a bad team now, but now they're even gonna move away from their history and they're gonna make the dynasty team obsolete." He really runs hard on them.

MCDARBY: He probably was a diehard Islander fan from that era and doesn't like change. And anytime you do this kind of thing, third jerseys, everything, actually, when they asked me to work on the Liberty logo, I was like, "No way." I said, "You can't change the Rangers logo." And then when they told me, "Oh, it's a third jersey," I said, "Oh, okay. That's all right. As long as they're not wearing it all the time." You're taking away a tradition, people's—their experiences with their fathers and their sons. That's just an image that's ingrained in their DNA. And then you're changing that. That's always gonna go up against—you're asking for trouble.

HIRSHON: Yeah. Something that Ed had brought up also was that the NHL introduced the third jerseys a few years after the fisherman. If this had maybe been an Islanders third jersey, it wouldn't have been as poorly received as this idea that you're moving away from the dynasty teams, like forget the old Islanders logo that people had this attachment to.

MCDARBY: Exactly. And actually that's what they started to do. I think that was probably a knee-jerk reaction to the Islanders logo. People said, "Well, okay. We're gonna keep the traditional logos. Maybe we'll update the color palette. But we'll use this only on days that Fox Sports is televising the games." You know? But it's still a way for them to sell more merchandise.

HIRSHON: The one point I made to Ed, or everyone who I speak to, because I spoke to a guy from the Islanders too, is that I've been to a lot of Islanders games over the years, and even recently people still wear the fisherman jersey. You see it all the time in the stands. So as much as people might want to say they don't like it, like you said, the sales—

MCDARBY: It's a nice-looking logo. It is. Like I said, kids would gravitate more to it. We've done that too. We've done youth logos. And that's what it is. It's a youth logo.

HIRSHON: Yeah. So I know that it still has that appeal to a lot of people and some sort of emotional attachment even though the team wasn't good then. But I think it still represents, for a certain generation of fans—it's kind of like my dad was the dynasty years and then I was the fisherman years.

MCDARBY: Right.

HIRSHON: So that's probably still going on a little bit.

MCDARBY: It's the only Islander jersey they have, so when they go to a game, they're gonna put it on. [He laughs.]

HIRSHON: Well, I think there's that too, especially when you shell out 140 bucks for a jersey, you're not gonna necessarily get rid of it.

MCDARBY: That's right.

HIRSHON: I heard this story that I've gotta confirm, but apparently when the Islanders finally moved away from the fisherman, they actually sent Steve Webb out onto the ice, who was one of their enforcers at the time, and they had him tear off the jersey at the end of the game, like actually rip it to shreds.

MCDARBY: Oh really? "This is it. It's over with." They made a media circus out of it, huh?

HIRSHON: Yeah. Which I thought was kind of like, Why are you bothering? It's probably best for PR to just quietly let this go away, but to actually send your goon out onto the ice and say, "Okay. Rip it to shreds. It'll get cheap laughs and cheap applause."

MCDARBY: But to me, that means your front office failed. That's what you're telling me. Right? The people who chose this logo are your management, and apparently they don't know what the hell they're doing. That's all you're saying. You're right. You're right. Just make it go away. Don't make a media circus out of it. [He laughs.] You're taking everybody who was involved in that thing and embarrassing them.

HIRSHON: And there was another story from that time too, where right before they got rid of the jersey, apparently they held this event at the Coliseum where if you brought in your fisherman jersey, you could exchange it for the old Islanders logo jersey, and they donated the fisherman jersey to a town in Massachusetts where the Gorton's seafood brand is based.

MCDARBY: [He laughs.] I've never heard that. That's great.

HIRSHON: It was to the American Red Cross in that town where Gorton's is based. Again, it's kind of funny to look back, but it's also like, Are you drawing more attention to something that obviously didn't succeed? Why don't you just wear it during the time the NHL tells you to wear it and then let go of it and do it quietly?

MCDARBY: Exactly. Bury it in the backyard.

HIRSHON: Yeah. But they called a lot of attention to it. I don't know. The whole era, they handled things in a very unique way when a lot of other teams, I think, would have gone through a much different process of whether they adopted the logo, and then once they realized it was a failure how they could have gone about it instead of this very public way.

MCDARBY: There's something odd about the way it went, too. I think somebody was very adamant for that logo, because normally SME would do test markets. They'd go out with the sketches and see what the people on the island would like. We definitely used to use that information. Now I don't remember that ever happening with the Islanders. I think somebody was adamant to have this fisherman in their own way. They were set on it, and they weren't changing on that.

HIRSHON: And I asked Ed about that. Did you do focus groups or surveys or some kind of outreach?

MCDARBY: Yeah. We used to do that with all our logos.

HIRSHON: And he said that in this case the Islanders said, "We want to do that on our side," and they ran their own—or said they ran their own—internal investigation, and they were content. At that point, that's sort of on the Islanders for either making up the fact they did this or whoever they interviewed may have said that they liked it. I'm not sure.

MCDARBY: Well, I mean, focus groups are ridiculous for the first thing, 'cause you could skew it any way. If you just show it to a kid, if they say, "This is who you want to market to," of course the kid's gonna pick the fisherman because most kids don't know who the Gorton's fisherman is either, you know?

HIRSHON: And they just liked the animate object.

MCDARBY: Yeah. They're like, "Oh, that's a tough fisherman. That's cool."

HIRSHON: Yeah. So I don't know how that all went down, but that is an interesting dynamic, and I'm gonna try to reach out to some of the Islanders' owners at that time. Apparently, they're still on Long Island. So that's part of this process, too. As I'm finding names in stories like yours, I'm just trying to contact people, and some people aren't around or they may not want to talk about this.

MCDARBY: When you finish this report, I'd love to take a look at what these other people have to say. It's very interesting to me.

HIRSHON: The *Daily News* article really interests me 'cause I feel like that got out ahead of them, and even though a lot of people may have liked the jersey, once they heard that "Oh, this is a jersey you shouldn't like," because the *Daily News* ridiculed it—

MCDARBY: They already had a preconception to dislike it.

HIRSHON: Exactly. Yeah.

MCDARBY: That's the power of the media, you know. Where with the Rangers, when we came out with the Liberty logo, it was so well received, something like $8 million in the first week that they sold in merchandise. It was ridiculous. It was a ridiculous number. It all comes down to good marketing.

HIRSHON: I was reading something about this fisherman logo where the Islanders had been twenty-sixth in jersey sales out of thirty teams, or whatever there was at that time, and they went up to seventeen.

MCDARBY: They made money.

HIRSHON: So it's not like it was a financial failure. I think it did make them money. It was just more of a cultural lashing.

MCDARBY: The problem is, in the end, who loses out are the manufacturers. They've got all this merchandise, and after the first initial push, they have all this stuff that they've made, and no one buys it because of the backlash. Those are the people who lose out. The team doesn't lose out as much as the manufacturers do.

[Two minutes were excluded from transcription when Hirshon responded to McDarby's inquiries about the nature of this research.]

HIRSHON: I'll definitely keep you in the loop as things proceed.

MCDARBY: I don't do much sports anyway. I work for Toys 'R' Us now, toy logos. But I did love doing sports stuff. I'm a very big sports person. I'm trying to get back into it, but it's so hard to get involved, just getting in touch with the league people. And most of them have in-house design personnel. There are very few good logos coming out lately from my standards. I think the best logo that came out in the last ten years is probably the Texans.

HIRSHON: Oh, yeah. The Texans logo. It's a very classic kind of design, simple.

MCDARBY: And some of the worst are like the Ravens. Those are the worst logos in sports.

HIRSHON: It seems like the general movement at this time is more towards retro logos, and they're just going back to the logos the teams wore in the '70s and '60s and '50s.

MCDARBY: Exactly. Because the team had a heyday when they were successful. That's the emotional response that they want and tying back into that.

HIRSHON: Even with the Islanders now, they're saying that one of the things the fans are clamoring for is the old, old logo when they first were there in the '70s, which I guess was a little bit different.

MCDARBY: Oh, God. So bad. So bad. I mean the Capitals did it, too. They went back to their old logo. I don't get it. They're from the time, and they look it. But at least update them, refresh them. You can do that, too.

HIRSHON: I guess it's just cheaper, right, if you go back to the logo you've already copyrighted, that you already used years ago.

MCDARBY: Oh, sure. Yeah. It's a simple fix. But to me, the whole reason SME even became a company is because these new jerseys and these new identities made money. It was a new jersey to buy. It's new merchandise to buy. And it was fresh, and it was new. And that's what all these teams jumped on board to do because they saw the numbers. But in the Islanders' case, that's why they jumped on board, to make money, but they didn't think about the content. A lot of times, evolutionary logos, we just take the logo that they all remember and freshen it up, give it some dimension, give it some Mylar threading that made it pop, you know? And we could have done that, too.

HIRSHON: Yeah. And in the years since, it seems like that's what they've done, taken that same logo and just changed some of the colors in it, had different sorts of camouflage on it, or make it white instead of orange.

MCDARBY: When they came out with just the NY with the hockey stick, that was okay. That was just pulled off the old logo. But they didn't do anything to it. They didn't do enough to it to make it fresh, you know?

HIRSHON: Yeah, personally, I wasn't a big fan of that, either. I felt if you're going for the maritime, this is the whole problem that Long Island has with its image and what represents Long Island. To just have the NY seems to disconnect from the whole idea that we're the suburban team against the big-city Rangers, and that's why we have a map of Long Island or a fisherman or something that represents us.

MCDARBY: Right. Something that separates you from the city of New York.

HIRSHON: And when you just take off the NY, it's sort of like we're going away from that. But they are moving to Brooklyn, so that's, I guess, part of the idea. We're gonna start forgoing the maritime, and we're big city too now.

MCDARBY: I'm gonna try to get involved in that. I'm gonna call the NHL and see if I can get involved in that, the redesign of the Islanders.

HIRSHON: Yeah. I'm wondering what they're gonna do 'cause they keep saying they're gonna keep the old logo, but they also talked about a third jersey that'll look kind of like the Nets jerseys with some sort of black-and-white scheme. A lot of people are really worried in the face of the fisherman. They're kind of worried what they're gonna do. Can you still have Long Island on the jersey if you're not playing in Nassau or Suffolk County?

MCDARBY: It's crazy to me that you would keep that name. If you're in Brooklyn, call it the Brooklyn—something from Brooklyn—the Brooklyn Bridges or whatever. I'm from Brooklyn. Why would I watch the Islanders? I live in Brooklyn. You're not recognizing your core audience. It doesn't make sense.

HIRSHON: They made the argument that Brooklyn is technically on Long Island, but as you know, from a cultural standpoint, it's a ways away. It's a world of difference between people in Brooklyn and how they live and their kind of urban style with the subway and everything, and then you have Long Island with the—

MCDARBY: Brooklyn wanted to dissociate themselves from New York altogether. They want to become a state of their own. That's the mentality of Brooklyn. You're putting the Islanders in Brooklyn. I don't know. Doesn't make much sense.

HIRSHON: I hear you. Well, that'll be fun if you get involved in that. It'll be kind of coming full circle for you, I suppose.

MCDARBY: Yeah. I'll have some retribution. Do a really great logo for them. [He laughs.]

HIRSHON: Exactly. They could use it. They haven't had an original idea in a while, so that would be fun.

MCDARBY: Yeah. Yeah. I take a lot of pride in my work. When something goes bad like that, you feel really bad. You do, you know? 'Cause you put your best efforts out there, and when it's just strategy that goes bad, there's nothing you can do about it, you know?

HIRSHON: Right. For what it's worth, I've seen a lot of people posting old photos of them with Nyisles in the Coliseum parking lot or at the game, so people still appreciate your designs. It's still out there.

MCDARBY: That's cool.

INTRODUCTION

1. Allan Kreda, "Islanders Struggling to Adjust without an Injured Top Wing," *New York Times*, February 4, 2015, B14; Justin Tasch, "Isles Admit Kyle Has Eye Injury," *New York Daily News*, February 4, 2015, 58.
2. "Florida Panthers at New York Islanders," WRHU (Hempstead NY), February 3, 2015.
3. Adam Gretz, "The Islanders Are Bringing the 'Fisherman' Logo Back for One Night," January 9, 2015, http://www.cbssports.com/nhl/eye -on-hockey/24949447/the-islanders-are-bringing-the-fisherman-logo -back-for-one-night; Sean Leahy, "Islanders to Bring Back Infamous Fisherman Logo One Last Time," October 6, 2014, http://sports.yahoo .com/blogs/nhl-puck-daddy/islanders-to-wear-modernized-version-of -infamous-fisherman-jerseys-one-last-time-011508289.html; "The 20 Worst NHL Jerseys of All Time," March 5, 2015, http://www.si.com/nhl /photos/2015/03/05/20-worst-nhl-jerseys-all-time/1; Gabe Zaldivar, "New Big Ten Logo and the Worst Logos in Sports History," December 13, 2010, http://bleacherreport.com/articles/542429-new-big-ten-logo -and-the-worst-logos-in-sports-history/page/22.
4. "Florida Panthers at New York Islanders."
5. Daniel Fraudman, Twitter post, February 3, 2015, 2:12 p.m., "The fisherman jersey was greedlanternjet levels of dumb. #isles #islestwitter," https://twitter.com/DFraudmanOnNYI/status/562690165983178752; Mark Nagi, Twitter post, February 3, 2015, 10:39 a.m., "Still hideous. MT @NYIslanders: Tonight is the night the #Fisherman returns. The #Isles wearing for warmups only.," https://twitter.com/MarkNagi/status /562636482390028288; John Crozier, Twitter post, February 3, 2015, 6:45 p.m., "Ahoy, Captain '@NYIslanders: Here it is! @91Tavares models tonight's #Fisherman warmup jerseys on the ice. #Isles,'" https://

twitter.com/_The_Croz/status/562758869236330497; Steve Lloyd, Twitter post, February 3, 2015, 9:14 a.m., "Yarr! MT @NYIslanders: Tonight is the night the #Fisherman returns. The #Isles are throwing it back. (warmups only)," https://twitter.com/TSNSteveLloyd/status /562615127359623168; Frankie Folsom, Twitter post, February 3, 2015, 12:53 p.m., "Attention Millennial asswipes. Stop saying the #Isles #Fisherman sweaters are dope. They're a disgrace.," https://twitter.com /jimmyfrance75/status/562670192141271043; Yung Flanagan, Twitter post, February 3, 2015, 9:11 a.m., "MY EYES RT @NYIslanders: Tonight is the night the #Fisherman returns. The #Isles are throwing it back to the 90's," tweet deleted; Chris Howrad, Twitter post, February 3, 2015, 9:57 a.m., "People are treating the 'Fisherman' logo likes it's a swastika. #Isles," https://twitter.com/Chrishowrad/status/562625818954719232.

6. Miloch, "Introduction to Branding," 7.

7. Keller, "Conceptualizing, Measuring, and Managing."

8. Aaker, *Managing Brand Equity*, 14.

9. Bauer, Stokburger-Sauer, and Exler, "Brand Image and Fan Loyalty"; Gladden, "Brand Equity," 7–9.

10. Miloch, "Introduction to Branding," 3–12.

11. Gladden, "Brand Equity," 3.

12. Pitts and Stotlar, *Fundamentals of Sport Marketing*, 267.

13. Schaaf, *Sports Marketing*.

14. Kochman, "Major League Baseball"; Stevens, Loudon, and McConkey, "Sport Marketing"; Smith, "Meltdown in Marketing."

15. Botte and Hahn, *Fish Sticks*; "Big Shot," *30 for 30*, first broadcast October 22, 2013, by ESPN, directed by Kevin Connolly.

16. Margalit Fox, "Patrick McDarby, 57, Sport Logo Designer," *New York Times*, March 19, 2015, A25.

1. BIRTH OF A BRAND

1. "Gretzky Trade Press Conference Video," http://video.kings.nhl.com /videocenter/console?id=20199&catid=733.

2. Fred Scalera, telephone interview with the author, September 18, 2015.

3. Austin Murphy, "A King in Edmonton," *Sports Illustrated*, October 31, 1988, 40–47.

4. Bernie Wilson, "The Great One Has Been Just That for Kings," *Los Angeles Times*, January 22, 1989, 24.

5. Tracy Dodds, "Time to Thaw?," *Los Angeles Times*, October 19, 1988, 4.

6. Miller, *Tales from the Los Angeles Kings Locker Room*, 125.

7. Scalera, telephone interview.

8. Steve Zipay, "Colors of Money: Great Logo Is Priority No. 1 for a New Team," *Newsday*, August 18, 1993, 140.

9. Richard Sandomir, "Skate Like a Duck, Quack Like a Duck, Market Like Disney," *New York Times*, August 30, 1993, C2.

10. Batchelor and Formentin, "Re-branding the NHL."

11. Scalera, telephone interview.

12. Mullin, Hardy, and Sutton, *Sport Marketing*, 204–5.

13. Gretz, "The Islanders Are Bringing the 'Fisherman' Logo Back for One Night"; Leahy, "Islanders to Bring Back Infamous Fisherman Logo One Last Time"; "The 20 Worst NHL Jerseys of All Time"; Zaldivar, "New Big Ten Logo and the Worst Logos in Sports History."

14. Steve Zipay, "No Go on New Logo," *Newsday*, April 21, 1996, B12, B21.

15. Botte and Hahn, *Fish Sticks*, 5.

16. Steve Somers, telephone interview with the author, December 10, 2013.

17. Somers is seen making this statement about twenty minutes into *Oh Baby! MSG Network Presents the Stanley Cup Season of the 1993–1994 New York Rangers*, produced by Joe Whelan (ABC Video, 1994).

18. "1994 NHL Playoffs Summary," Sports Reference, http://www.hockey-reference.com/playoffs/NHL_1994.html.

19. Stan Fischler, interview with the author, July 31, 2015.

20. Tim Beach, telephone interview with the author, September 14, 2015.

21. Brett Pickett, telephone interview with the author, November 11, 2015.

22. Eric Mirlis, telephone interview with the author, October 12, 2015.

23. Beach, telephone interview.

24. Botte and Hahn, *Fish Sticks*, 7–9, 16–18.

25. Joe Lapointe, "Arbour's Resignation Seems to Be at Hand," *New York Times*, April 25, 1994, C2.

26. Pat Calabria, telephone interview with the author, February 17, 2014.

27. Chris King, telephone interview with the author, September 9, 2015.

28. Joe Lapointe, "A River Runs Through Him: Rangers Overwhelm Hextall and Isles," *New York Times*, April 18, 1994, C1; Robin Finn, "Islanders Get a Goal; Rangers Get 3d Victory," *New York Times*, April 22, 1994, B9; Joe Lapointe, "Rangers Face New Goalie, but Little Else Changes," *New York Times*, April 19, 1994, B9; Robin Finn, "Rangers Sweep as

Islanders Can't Even Find Any Moral Victories," *New York Times*, April 25, 1994, C1.

29. Howie Rose, telephone interview with the author, September 28, 2015.

30. Andreff and Szymanski, *Handbook on the Economics of Sport*, 638.

31. Zipay, "Colors of Money."

32. Beach, telephone interview.

33. Scalera, telephone interview.

34. Calabria, telephone interview.

35. Scalera, telephone interview.

36. Peter Marks, "Distilling That Perfect Islander Image," *New York Times*, January 22, 1995, 25; Zipay, "Colors of Money."

37. Zipay, "Colors of Money."

38. Ed O'Hara, telephone interview with the author, February 14, 2014.

39. Mark Herrmann, "Isles' New Look Ready," *Newsday*, June 22, 1995, A67.

40. Herrmann, "Isles' New Look Ready"; O'Hara, telephone interview.

41. Beach, telephone interview; Calabria, telephone interview; O'Hara, telephone interview; Scalera, telephone interview.

42. Scalera, telephone interview.

43. Marks, "Distilling That Perfect Islander Image."

44. Marks, "Distilling That Perfect Islander Image."

45. Hirshon, *Images of America*, 69.

46. Barry Landers, telephone interview with the author, November 3, 2015.

47. Mitchell Freedman, "Museum Sought at Big Duck's Flanders Site," *Newsday*, January 11, 2013; Landers, telephone interview.

48. Joe Gergen, "The Ducks Live On," *Newsday*, March 2, 1997, B10.

49. Scalera, telephone interview.

50. Diane Ketcham, "About Long Island: The Baymen's Friend," *New York Times*, September 9, 1990, LI1.

51. Matthiessen, *Men's Lives*, 4; Stephen Holden, "Billy Joel: 'Storm Front,'" *New York Times*, October 29, 1989, H34; Matthiessen, *Men's Lives*, 5.

52. For Joel's Long Island roots, see John J. O'Connor, "Billy Joel in Taped Concert on HBO," *New York Times*, July 22, 1983, C24. For Joel's numerous concerts at Nassau Coliseum, see John J. O'Connor and Stephen Holden, "The Pop Life: Billy Joel on the Dark Side," *New York Times*, December 29, 1982, C18. For the song's sympathetic tone toward the Long Island baymen, see Holden, "Billy Joel: 'Storm Front.'"

53. O'Hara, telephone interview.

54. "Baymen and Friends," *East Hampton Star*, September 27, 1990; Tom Clavin, "Exit the Bayman," *New York Times*, September 26, 2004, LI1, LI10.
55. Scalera, telephone interview.
56. Calabria, telephone interview; O'Hara, telephone interview.
57. O'Hara, telephone interview.
58. O'Hara, telephone interview; Beach, telephone interview.
59. Fox, "Patrick McDarby, 57, Sport Logo Designer."
60. Pat McDarby, telephone interview with the author, February 20, 2014.
61. Marks, "Distilling That Perfect Islander Image."
62. Marks, "Distilling That Perfect Islander Image."
63. Marek Fuchs, "Inside the Mascot Suit, a Buddy with a Past," *New York Times*, May 20, 2001, WE1.
64. Rob Di Fiore, telephone interview with the author, October 19, 2015.
65. Di Fiore, telephone interview.
66. Joe Lapointe, "Management and Labor Shed Some Light," *New York Times*, August 31, 1994, B13.
67. Joe Lapointe, "It's Contagious: Clock Ticks on New Labor Crisis," *New York Times*, September 26, 1994, C3.
68. Jeff Williams, "Isles Get a Shock," *Newsday*, January 11, 1995, A72.
69. Joe Lapointe, "Pact Reached for Salvaging Hockey Season," *New York Times*, January 12, 1995, A1.
70. Arnold Abrams and Tom Demoretcky, "Hockey Fans Out of Penalty Box," *Newsday*, January 12, 1995, A3.
71. Gary Babyatzky, "The Fans Are Back," *Newsday*, January 20, 1995, A39; "With Half as Many Games, Each One Counts Twice as Much," *Newsday*, January 14, 1995, A29.

2. A FROZEN-DINNER FRANCHISE

1. Abrams and Demoretcky, "Hockey Fans Out of Penalty Box."
2. Jeff Williams, "Mullen's Career at End," *Newsday*, January 13, 1995, A77.
3. Jason Diamos, "Can Henning Bring Magic Back to Burbs?," *Newsday*, January 21, 1995, A33.
4. Jeff Williams, "No Time to Lose," *Newsday*, January 20, 1995, A74.
5. Peter Charbonneau, "The New Faces of '95," *Blade*, January 21-28, 1995, 2.
6. Steve Jacobson, "Isles Fans Will Love Lindros," *Newsday*, January 22, 1995, S4; "I've Waited Eighteen Years to Play Professional Hockey," *Newsday*, January 20, 1995, A63.

7. Cal Fussman, "For the Love of Hockey," *Newsday*, January 23, 1995, B4.

8. Mark Herrmann, "For Openers, It's One Night to Remember," *Newsday*, January 22, 1995, S2; "What's New: Facts and Figures about the Shortened Season," *Newsday*, January 15, 1995, S11.

9. Jeff Williams, "It's Ziggy to the Rescue," *Newsday*, January 22, 1995, S3.

10. Marks, "Distilling That Perfect Islander Image."

11. Di Fiore, telephone interview.

12. Jason Diamos, "Isles' Debut a Success on Palffy's 2 Goals," *New York Times*, January 22, 1995, S8.

13. Williams, "It's Ziggy to the Rescue."

14. Jason Diamos, "Islanders Discover That Pretty Doesn't Count," *New York Times*, January 23, 1995, C2; Jeff Williams, "A Goal for Dad," *Newsday*, January 23, 1995, A46.

15. Jeff Williams, "A Family Affair," *Newsday*, January 24, 1995, A58.

16. Williams, "A Family Affair."

17. Eric Mirlis, "Nobody's Little Brother," *Blade*, February 9–11, 1995, 10–11; "Henning Tackles the Fans' Full-Court Press," *Blade*, February 9–11, 1995, 38–39.

18. Jeff Williams, "Hextall's Return to the Coliseum Not Likely to Evoke Many Tears," *Newsday*, January 24, 1995, A58.

19. Jeff Williams, "Auspicious Start," *Newsday*, January 25, 1995, A68.

20. Jim Smith, "Eric Nets 2 Goals, Brett Gets Victory," *Newsday*, January 25, 1995, A69.

21. "Lindros Signs: Isles Make a Statement," *Islander Insider*, February 1995, 1.

22. Smith, "Eric Nets 2 Goals, Brett Gets Victory."

23. Jeff Williams, "Rockhead Hockey," *Newsday*, January 29, 1995, S15.

24. Mark Herrmann, "Isles Shuffle Lines, Take King Off Bench," *Newsday*, January 31, 1995, A53.

25. Jeff Williams, "Shakeup Wakes Up Islanders," *Newsday*, February 1, 1995, A67.

26. Mark Herrmann, "It's Isles' Time," *Newsday*, February 3, 1995, A82.

27. Herrmann, "It's Isles' Time."

28. McDarby, telephone interview; Jacobson, "Isles Fans Will Love Lindros"; "You Can't Body Slam the Enemy," *Blade*, February 9–11, 1995, 4.

29. Diane Ketcham, "Long Island Journal," *New York Times*, April 2, 1995, LI3.

30. Ilana Gazes Kariamis, telephone interview with the author, October

15, 2015; Jeff Williams, "Lively Weekend: Islanders Survive Sluggish Offense against Devils," *Newsday*, February 19, 1995, 5.

31. "Rare Footage of Original Islanders Mascot Nyisles," YouTube, from the Montreal Canadiens–New York Islanders game televised by SportsChannel on February 28, 1995, posted by "stevienics1991," November 25, 2015, https://www.youtube.com/watch?v=AaOIXUwCiDQ&list= PLpssn6pzwVxZub7rXO5Lv7dq2yx-MQjvA&index=27.

32. Jason Kay, "NHL Entertainment Not Limited to Ice," *Hockey News*, March 24, 1995, 47; Rose, telephone interview.

33. "Family Fun Day," *Newsday*, October 21, 1996, A55; Ketcham, "Long Island Journal"; Williams, "Lively Weekend."

34. Jeff Williams, "Mahoney [*sic*] Rips Lack of Effort," *Newsday*, February 10, 1995, A84; Jim Smith, "Cash-Poor Isles May Deal Thomas," *Newsday*, February 2, 1995, A74; Jim Smith, "Islanders: We Can and Will Pay the Price," *Newsday*, February 3, 1995, A82.

35. Jeff Williams, "In Your Face," *Newsday*, February 21, 1995, A54.

36. Jeff Williams, "Isles for the Defense," *Newsday*, March 1, 1995, A70.

37. Jeff Williams, "Isles Find Solid Play in Tommy," *Newsday*, February 27, 1995, A42.

38. Mark Herrmann, "Darius' Season Is Over," *Newsday*, February 26, 1995, S5.

39. Jeff Williams, "Middle of Nowhere," *Newsday*, February 15, 1995, A62.

40. Mark Herrmann, "Lindros: Learning the Waiting Game," *Newsday*, February 25, 1995, A32.

41. Steve Zipay, "A Slip Is Showing in NHL," *Newsday*, February 19, 1995, S21.

42. Feeney provided the inaugural issue of the newsletter to the author. It was undated but, based on the content, appears to have been printed in January 1995.

43. Art Feeney, telephone interview with the author, October 3, 2015; *Islander Insider*, January 1995.

44. Jeff Williams, "Not Islanders' Night," *Newsday*, March 10, 1995, A86.

45. Jeff Williams, "Thomas Irked by Isles' Offer," *Newsday*, March 5, 1995, S8.

46. Jeff Williams, "Always Ready to Aid the Needy," *Newsday*, March 6, 1995, A42.

47. Jeff Williams, "Isles Drop 5th Game in a Row," *Newsday*, March 19, 1995, S11.

48. Jim Smith, "Don's Fan Club," *Newsday*, March 22, 1995, A65.

49. "Voices from the Stands . . . ," *Islander Insider*, March 15, 1995, 4.

50. Ketcham, "Long Island Journal."

51. Ketcham, "Long Island Journal."

52. Calabria, telephone interview.

53. Jeff Williams, "Tommy Terrific," *Newsday*, March 24, 1995, A102.

54. Rich Walker, telephone interview with the author, October 16, 2015.

55. Di Fiore, telephone interview; "Ice Chips," *Islander Insider*, April 1, 1995, 3.

56. Jeff Williams, "Desperate Straits," *Newsday*, March 31, 1995, A102.

57. Jeff Williams, "Cellar, Not Stellar," *Newsday*, March 29, 1995, A66.

58. Jim Smith, "Nordiques Moving?," *Newsday*, March 30, 1995, A85.

59. Mark Herrmann, "Mr. Islander," *Newsday*, March 29, 1995, A64.

60. Jason Diamos, "Islanders Recall the Glory Days, Then Return to Reality," *New York Times*, April 2, 1995, S4; Jeff Williams, "Enough to Make Him Cry," *Newsday*, April 2, 1995, S13; Jeff Williams, "Nystrom Day Doesn't Pay for Isles," *Newsday*, April 2, 1995, S13.

61. Diamos, "Islanders Recall the Glory Days, Then Return to Reality."

62. Jim Smith, "Adieu, Pierre," *Newsday*, April 6, 1995, A94.

63. Jeff Williams and Jim Smith, "So Long, Benoit," *Newsday*, April 7, 1995, A94.

64. Peter Botte, "Hogue Dealt to Leafs as Isles Clean House," *New York Post*, April 7, 1995, 104.

65. Joe Haberstroh, "Turgeon Trade Evokes Mixed Feelings," *Newsday*, April 6, 1995, A95.

66. Jeff Williams, "The Perils of Pierre," *Newsday*, April 2, 1995, S26-S27.

67. Jim Smith, "Give Deal a Chance," *Newsday*, April 6, 1995, A95, A93; Peter Botte, "Turgeon-to-Habs Begins Isles' Purge," *New York Post*, April 6, 1995, 70.

68. Smith, "Give Deal a Chance."

69. Smith, "Give Deal a Chance."

70. *Islander Insider*, April 20, 1995.

71. Botte, "Turgeon-to-Habs Begins Isles' Purge."

72. Associated Press, "Trade Pays Off Quickly as the Canadiens Win," *Newsday*, April 6, 1995, A94.

73. Jay Greenberg, "Turgeon Had to Go," *New York Post*, April 7, 1995, 105.

74. Smith, "Give Deal a Chance."

75. Mathieu Schneider, telephone interview with the author, October 30, 2015.

76. Botte, "Turgeon-to-Habs Begins Isles' Purge."

77. *Islander Insider*, April 20, 1995.

78. Fischler, interview.

79. Jim Smith, "Trade Upsets Muller," *Newsday*, April 8, 1995, A39.

80. Schneider, telephone interview.

81. Chris Botta, "A Defenseman Who Never Rests," *Blade*, April 16–22, 1995, 3.

82. Joe Lapointe, "Muller Keeps Islanders Waiting for Now," *New York Times*, April 8, 1995, 37; Colin Stephenson, "Kirk Tells Isles: Beam Me Up Later," *New York Daily News*, April 8, 1995, S35; Peter Botte, "Distraught Muller May Retire Rather than Report," *New York Post*, April 8, 1995, 47; Jim Smith, "Sharp Soderstrom Unable to Prevent Tie," *Newsday*, April 9, 1995, S3.

83. Calabria, telephone interview; Lapointe, "Muller Keeps Islanders Waiting for Now"; Landers, telephone interview.

84. Colin Stephenson, "Muller: Lots of Catching Up," *New York Daily News*, April 10, 1995, S54; Peter Botte, "Muller Time Finally Comes for Islanders," *New York Post*, April 10, 1995, 61.

85. "Rinkrats," *Ottawa Citizen*, April 10, 1995, D3.

86. Jeff Williams, "New Look Is No Help," *Newsday*, April 12, 1995, A68.

87. McDarby, telephone interview; Calabria, telephone interview; McDarby, telephone interview.

88. McDarby, telephone interview; Shaun Assael et al., "Covering the Bases," *Wall Street Journal*, September 16, 2006, http://www.wsj.com /articles/sb115813082638561774.

89. Scalera, telephone interview.

90. Jim Baumbach, "Pickett: Islanders Not Affected by Charges Facing Ex-Execs," *Newsday*, February 27, 2009; Botte and Hahn, *Fish Sticks*, 19.

91. Beach, telephone interview; Bob Van Voris, "Walsh Ordered to Prison for $554 Million WG Trading Fraud," November 19, 2014, http://www .bloomberg.com/news/articles/2014-11-20/walsh-ordered-to-prison -for-554-million-wg-trading-fraud.

92. Calabria, telephone interview.

93. Pickett, telephone interview.

94. Bob Nystrom, telephone interview with the author, November 25, 2015.

95. Fire Island Lighthouse Preservation Society, http://www.fireislandlight house.com/history.html; "Big Shot."

96. Neil Best, "What a Mess!," *Newsday*, April 17, 1995, A44; Jim Smith, "Isles Blown Away," *Newsday*, April 15, 1995, A26; Jeff Williams, "At Last, Lead Is Held," *Newsday*, April 19, 1995, A68; Jeff Williams, "Net Improvement," *Newsday*, April 13, 1995, A86.

97. Peter Botte, "Hot Tommy Right Choice for Isles," *New York Post*, April 13, 1995, 112; Peter Botte, "Smooth Sailin' for Isles' 'Hobey,'" *New York Post*, April 14, 1995, 83; Jeff Williams, "Isles Get Rookie Assist," *Newsday*, April 14, 1995, A76.

98. Steve Zipay, "Potvin Brings His Views to TV," *Newsday*, April 14, 1995, A76, A74.

99. Campbell, *1995*, 52–78.

100. John T. McQuiston, "Families of the Dead and the Survivors Cheer the Verdict," *New York Times*, February 18, 1995, 1, 26; Peter Marks, "L.I.R.R. Murderer Argues for Reversal," *New York Times*, March 21, 1995, B5; John T. McQuiston, "Rail Gunman to Spend Life behind Bars," *New York Times*, March 23, 1995, B1, B8.

101. "Uniform Update," *Schenectady Daily Gazette*, April 15, 1995, C1; Colin Stephenson, "Isles' New Logo Would Be Sea Sick: Uniforms Only Portray Tradition Gone Fishin'," *New York Daily News*, April 20, 1995, 84.

102. Stephenson, "Isles' New Logo Would Be Sea Sick."

103. Mirlis, telephone interview; O'Hara, telephone interview.

104. Jim Smith, "Isles Look to the Future," *Newsday*, April 20, 1995, A72; Larry Brooks, "Muller's No Islander," *New York Post*, April 20, 1995, 80, 58; Jeff Williams, "Flyers End Jinx, Clinch Playoff Spot," *Newsday*, April 21, 1995, A92; Chris Botta, telephone interview with the author, February 21, 2014.

105. Calabria, telephone interview; Patrick Calabria, email to the author, October 14, 2014; Pember and Calvert, *Mass Media Law*, 78–79; Calabria, email to the author.

106. These trademark forms can be found online through the Trademark Electronic Search System of the United States Patent and Trademark Office, http://www.uspto.gov/trademark. Fletcher submitted separate paperwork to trademark the logo for sales of clothing and for "entertainment services," the use of the logo on players' uniforms, and to promote the team. The clothing filing can be found under serial number 74647149 and registration number 2201625, while the entertainment services filing carries serial number 74646848 and registration number 2276216.

107. Anthony Fletcher, telephone interview with the author, March 3, 2015. Also, see the application for the clothing trademark in the Trademark Electronic Search System.

108. Bob McKenzie, "Punishment Better Suited to NHL Crimes," *Toronto Star*, April 23, 1995, F3.

109. Chris Botta, "The Great Logo Debate of 1995," *Blade*, April 24–May 2, 1995, n.p.

110. "Canucks Bunch of Softies in Own Zone, Coach Says," *Toronto Star*, April 28, 1995, C2; *Islander Insider*, April 20, 1995.

111. Jeff Williams, "Isles Out of the Hunt," *Newsday*, April 23, 1995, 17.

112. Jeff Williams, "Ferraro's Play Could Pay Off," *Newsday*, May 3, 1995, A65.

113. Jeff Williams, "Quick Exit for Henning," *Newsday*, May 4, 1995, A106.

114. Frank Brown, "Forget Lorne, Fire Logo," *New York Daily News*, May 4, 1995, 88.

3. THE BAYMEN AND THE BRUIN

1. Jeff Williams, "Quick Exit for Henning"; Steve Zipay, "Roughing Up Maloney," *Newsday*, May 5, 1995, A79; Steve Zipay, "Jiggs Out as Isles' Broadcaster," *Newsday*, May 27, 1995, A49.

2. Mark Herrmann, "Team Makes Moves with No Destinations," *Newsday*, May 4, 1995, A107.

3. Herrmann, "Team Makes Moves with No Destinations."

4. Botta, "Great Logo Debate of 1995."

5. Botta, "Great Logo Debate of 1995"; *Islander Insider*, April 20, 1995.

6. Botta, "Great Logo Debate of 1995"; Rich Pilon, telephone interview with the author, September 4, 2015.

7. Botta, "Great Logo Debate of 1995"; Nystrom, telephone interview.

8. Éric Fichaud, telephone interview with the author, September 4, 2015; Nystrom, telephone interview.

9. Botta, "Great Logo Debate of 1995."

10. Colin Stephenson, "Islanders Picture Old Logo," *New York Daily News*, May 26, 1995, 77.

11. Russell Drumm, "A Bunt Full of Bass for the Camera Only," *East Hampton Star*, April 12, 1990, 120; Linda Sherry, "New Ballad by Billy Joel Voices Baymen's Plight," *Southampton Press*, April 12, 1990, page number unknown.

12. "Baymen and Friends"; Drumm, "A Bunt Full of Bass for the Camera Only"; Dele Olojede, "Piano Man Plays Benefit for Baymen," *Newsday*, September 5, 1990, 8; Susan Pollack, "A Fishing Community Struggles to

Survive," *National Fisherman*, August 1990, 12–15; Sherry, "New Ballad by Billy Joel Voices Baymen's Plight."

13. Arnold Leo, telephone interview with the author, September 21, 2015; Leo to Calabria, April 20, 22, 24, 1995, box 6, folder 135, East Hampton Town Baymen's Association Archive.

14. Leo, telephone interview; Leo to Calabria, April 22, 1995; Leo, telephone interview.

15. Dan King, telephone interview with the author, September 25, 2015; Leo, telephone interview; King, telephone interview.

16. Calabria, telephone interview; Brad Loewen, telephone interview with the author, September 25, 2015.

17. Ketcham, "About Long Island"; Bill Bleyer, "Billy Joel's Romance with the Sea," *Newsday*, December 26, 1995, B4–B5; Calabria, telephone interview.

18. Media advisory, June 21, 1995, box 6, folder 135, East Hampton Town Baymen's Association Archive.

19. "Get Close to the Islanders without Getting Checked," *Newsday*, June 21, 1995, A57.

20. Len Hochberg, "From 'Mickey Mouse' to the Big Cheese: Devils in Cup Finals after Years of Failure," *Washington Post*, June 15, 1995, B4.

21. Mark Herrmann, "Isles' New Look Ready," *Newsday*, June 22, 1995, A67.

22. King, telephone interview; Jason Molinet, "New Design Has Young Fans Excited," *Newsday*, June 23, 1995, A89; Zipay, "No Go on New Logo."

23. Mark Herrmann, "The Logo Is Local," *Newsday*, June 23, 1995, A88.

24. Herrmann, "The Logo Is Local."

25. King, telephone interview.

26. Herrmann, "The Logo Is Local."

27. Herrmann, "The Logo Is Local."

28. Michael K. Ozanian et al., "Suite Deals," *Financial World* (May 9, 1995): 42–52; Stephenson, "Isles' New Logo Would Be Sea Sick"; Steve Zipay, "Switching Styles in Vogue," *Newsday*, June 23, 1995, A89.

29. Ozanian et al., "Suite Deals."

30. Warren Strugatch, "A Potential Barrier to Coliseum Plans," *New York Times*, November 7, 2004, L13.

31. Pickett, telephone interview.

32. Molinet, "New Design Has Young Fans Excited."

33. Herrmann, "The Logo Is Local"; Molinet, "New Design Has Young Fans Excited"; Leo, telephone interview.

34. Herrmann, "The Logo Is Local."

35. Darius Kasparaitis, telephone interview with the author, November 16, 2015.

36. Travis Green, telephone interview with the author, November 13, 2015.

37. Herrmann, "The Logo Is Local"; Pilon, telephone interview.

38. Jason Diamos, "Muller May Not Stay for New Look," *New York Times*, June 23, 1995, B15; Peter Botte, "Muller May Wear Islanders' New Colors for Real," *New York Post*, June 23, 1995, 80.

39. Molinet, "New Design Has Young Fans Excited."

40. "ESPN Shows Off Isles 'New' Uniforms," YouTube, from Game Three of the 1995 Stanley Cup Finals, televised by ESPN on June 22, 1995, posted by "McKay4429061," January 9, 2008, http://www.youtube.com/watch?v=W-JL3N9KqDE; Mirlis, telephone interview.

41. Len Berman, email to the author, August 17, 2015.

42. "News at 10," WPIX, June 22, 1995, WPIX Archives.

43. Eric Fichaud, telephone interview with the author, September 4, 2015.

44. Botte, "Muller May Wear Islanders' New Colors for Real"; "Fisherman's Friends," *New York Daily News*, June 23, 1995, 80; "What Do You Think?," *Newsday*, June 23, 1995, A88.

45. Steve Zipay, "If Daly Leaves, Will Riley Go to Turner?," *Newsday*, June 23, 1995, A72, A68.

46. Mark Herrmann, "Muller Looking to Extend His Stay," *Newsday*, June 23, 1995, A89.

47. Jeff Williams, "Islanders in a Strong Bargaining Position," *Newsday*, June 1, 1995, A88; Jeff Williams, "Isles Pitch to Hay," *Newsday*, June 27, 1995, A50.

48. Adrian Dater, "Islanders Eye Goring for Job," *Denver Post*, May 13, 1995, C9; Jim Smith, "Isles, Sutter Talking," *Newsday*, May 26, 1995, A84; Jeff Williams, "Isles Eye Milbury, Melrose, Sutter," *Newsday*, May 21, 1995, S10.

49. Williams, "Isles Eye Milbury, Melrose, Sutter."

50. "Milbury Quits Eagles before Starting," *New York Times*, June 3, 1994, 10; Jim Smith, "Isles Need Milbury," *Newsday*, May 12, 1995, A80.

51. Jim Naughton, "Bruins Win, Then Battle with Fans at Garden," *New York Times*, December 24, 1979, A1; Dave Seminara, "Over the Glass and into Lore," *New York Times*, December 23, 2009, B11.

52. Dave Luecking, "NHL Might Alter All-Star Process," *St. Louis Post-Dispatch*, January 20, 1991, 6F; Jim Proudfoot, "How a Goon Gets to Be an NHL All-Star," *Toronto Star*, January 9, 1991, E3.

53. Smith, "Isles Need Milbury."

54. Jason Diamos, "New Coach Emphasizes Break with Isles' Past," *New York Times*, July 6, 1995, B15; Jim Smith, "Milbury Is Isles' Guy," *Newsday*, July 2, 1995, 2-3; Jim Smith, "New Islander Coach," *Newsday*, July 2, 1995, A3; Jeff Williams, "Isles Have Their Man," *Newsday*, July 5, 1995, A70.

55. Diamos, "New Coach Emphasizes Break with Isles' Past"; Jeff Williams, "Milbury Demands Total Effort," *Newsday*, July 6, 1995, A79, A57; Jeff Williams, "Taking Charge," *Newsday*, July 6, 1995, A78.

56. Diamos, "New Coach Emphasizes Break with Isles' Past."

57. Diamos, "New Coach Emphasizes Break with Isles' Past"; Mark Herrmann, "Isles Know They Need Talent, Too," *Newsday*, July 6, 1995, A79.

58. *Never Say Die: The Story of the New York Islanders*, produced by Darryl Lepik and Marc Forest (NHL Enterprises, 1996).

59. Mick Vukota, telephone interview with the author, October 25, 2015; "IT'S MILBURY!!!!," *Islander Insider*, July 15, 1995; Mark Herrmann, "The Windup," *Newsday*, April 7, 1996, B16.

60. Frank Brown, "Mike Bails Out Isles' Ship," *New York Daily News*, July 6, 1995, 60; Herrmann, "Isles Know They Need Talent, Too."

4. NEW TEAM, DASHED DREAM

1. Nicholas Hirshon, "Inside the NHL: Bon Voyage, Captain Gorton," *Hockey News*, November 7, 2006, 10.

2. Diamos, "New Coach Emphasizes Break with Isles' Past."

3. Jeff Williams, "Ferraro's Play Could Pay Off," *Newsday*, May 3, 1995, A65.

4. Colin Stephenson, "Rangers Circle Isles' Ferraro," *New York Daily News*, July 19, 1995, 54.

5. Jeff Williams, "Thomas Irked by Isles' Offer," *Newsday*, March 5, 1995, S8.

6. Jim Smith, "A Matter of Pact," *Newsday*, September 28, 1995, A96; Jim Smith, "Thomas' Promises," *Newsday*, September 19, 1995, A54; Jeff Williams, "Isles, Kasparaitis Far Apart in Talks," *Newsday*, August 3, 1995, A76.

7. Mark Herrmann, "Is Fichaud a Savior?," *Newsday*, July 18, 1995, A46.

8. Joe Lapointe, "It's Sign One, Draft One for the Busy Islanders," *New York Times*, July 9, 1995, S2; Smith, "Thomas' Promises."

9. Doug McConachie, "Ehman Left His Mark on Hockey," *Regina Leader-Post*, March 24, 2006, C6.

10. "Isles Shuffle the Deck," *Islander Insider*, February 1995; Herrmann, "Isles Know They Need Talent, Too."

11. Jeff Williams, "Bertuzzi, Isles Still Facing Off," *Newsday*, July 7, 1995, A56.

12. "Todd Bertuzzi Has the Goods," *Blade*, October 14–20, 1995, n.p.

13. Jim Smith, "Bertuzzi Issues Isles Deadline," *Newsday*, March 29, 1995, A66.

14. Mark Herrmann, "Bertuzzi Deal at 11th-Hour," *Newsday*, July 9, 1995, 19.

15. Guy Charron, telephone interview with the author, November 7, 2015.

16. Charron, telephone interview; Bob Froese, telephone interview with the author, September 14, 2015.

17. Mark Herrmann, "Farm-Raised Talent," *Newsday*, July 9, 1995, S19.

18. Herrmann, "Farm-Raised Talent"; Mirlis, telephone interview.

19. Chris Luongo, telephone interview with the author, November 24, 2015.

20. Steve Zipay, "Holy Matteau! Rose Joins Isles," *Newsday*, August 25, 1995, A98.

21. Zipay, "Holy Matteau!"; "Rating the Talkies," *Islander Insider*, February 1995; Rose, telephone interview.

22. Howie Rose, "A Rose by Any Other Name . . . ," *Blade*, October 14–20, 1995, n.p.

23. Fischler, telephone interview; "Islanders Name Killian," *New York Times*, October 14, 1992, B14; Feeney, telephone interview.

24. "The Islanders' Idea of Summer Vacation," *Newsday*, August 10, 1995, A66; "Be Part of the Salute to Honor Long Island's Firefighters and Emergency Volunteers," *Newsday*, September 13, 1995, A53.

25. "Order Season Tickets This Week," *Newsday*, August 20, 1995, S21; "This Is Our New Coach," *Newsday*, September 3, 1995, 20; "This Is Brett Lindros," *Newsday*, September 17, 1995, S22; "This Is Matt Schneider," *Newsday*, October 3, 1995, A39; "This Is Our New Uniform," *Newsday*, September 4, 1995, A33.

26. Mark Herrmann, "Islanders Facing Tough Road Ahead," *Newsday*, September 10, 1995, S16.

27. Chris Botta, "Greener Pastures," *Blade*, October 14–20, 1995, n.p.; Green, telephone interview.

28. Botta, Mirlis, and Serby, *New York Islanders*; Art Feeney, "Isles Make Play-Offs!," *Islander Insider*, September 15, 1995.

29. Williams, "Isles, Kasparaitis Far Apart in Talks"; Dean Chynoweth, telephone interview with the author, November 27, 2015; Niklas Andersson,

telephone interview with the author, September 5, 2015; Dan Plante, telephone interview with the author, November 6, 2015.

30. Danton Cole, telephone interview with the author, September 16, 2015.

31. Herrmann, "Islanders Facing Tough Road Ahead"; Jim Smith, "Islanders Preview," *Newsday*, October 1, 1995, S29; Jeff Williams, "Islanders Sign McKenzie," *Newsday*, August 1, 1995, A50; *Islander Insider*, September 15, 1995.

32. Jim Smith, "Don's Focus: Team, Not Pact," *Newsday*, September 27, 1995, A62.

33. Smith, "Don's Focus: Team, Not Pact"; Jim Smith, "Isles Deal for Semak, Sign Vaske," *Newsday*, September 15, 1995, A96.

34. Peter Botte, "Kasparaitis Makes Good on Threat to Bolt Isles," *New York Post*, October 14, 1995, 34.

35. Joe Lapointe, "Pucks about to Drop Again," *New York Times*, September 10, 1995, B5.

36. Jim Smith, "Bertuzzi Is Impressing," *Newsday*, September 30, 1995, A39.

37. Colin Stephenson, "Cole Has Isles Role," *New York Daily News*, September 27, 1995, 58.

38. Jim Smith, "Johansson Is Something Special," *Newsday*, September 14, 1995, A86.

39. Larry Sicinski, "New Look for Islanders," *Hamilton Spectator*, September 13, 1995, D3.

40. Jason Diamos, "Isles Keep Options Open on Redden, Top Prospect," *New York Times*, September 28, 1995, B19.

41. Smith, "Bertuzzi Is Impressing."

42. Jason Diamos, "Make No Mistake about It, Milbury Is in Charge of Isles," *New York Times*, September 12, 1995, B13.

43. Colin Stephenson, "Islanders Getting Milbury's Message," *New York Daily News*, September 12, 1995, S53.

44. "Pre-season Highlights," *Toronto Star*, September 23, 1995, E3.

45. Vukota, telephone interview.

46. Jim Smith, "Net Gain for Isles' Fichaud," *Newsday*, September 20, 1995, A67.

47. Colin Stephenson, "Isles Wait on Future," *New York Daily News*, September 26, 1995, 55.

48. Cammy Clark, "Palffy Shapes Up with Hat Trick," *Newsday*, September 24, 1995, S18.

49. Charron, telephone interview; Vukota, telephone interview.

50. Charron, telephone interview.

51. "Palffy Forgets Pout and Powers the Isles," *New York Times*, October 3, 1995, B12.

52. "Rangers Islanders Line Brawl Oct 2, 1995," YouTube video, from the New York Rangers–New York Islanders game televised by MSG on October 2, 1995, posted by "bdmbrokers," May 12, 2013, https://www.youtube.com/watch?v=-nOc-Ybe6ns.

53. Vukota, telephone interview.

54. Vukota, telephone interview.

55. Jim Smith, "Islanders Find Help in Sweeney," *Newsday*, October 3, 1995, A51.

56. Jim Smith, "Trading Places Times 3," *Newsday*, October 4, 1995, A62; Colin Stephenson, "With Wendel, Isles Instant 'Contenders,'" *New York Daily News*, October 5, 1995, 122.

57. Milan Tichy, telephone interview with the author, September 2, 1995; Cole, telephone interview; Jim Smith, "Clark Just Too Brittle for Islanders," *Newsday*, October 5, 1995, A79; Stephenson, "With Wendel, Isles Instant 'Contenders.'"

58. Smith, "Clark Just Too Brittle for Islanders."

59. Charron, telephone interview; Mirlis, telephone interview.

60. Michael Farber, "High Flyers," *Sports Illustrated*, October 9, 1995, 88–97; Dave Luecking, "Eastern Conference Preview," *St. Louis Post-Dispatch*, October 6, 1995, 7D; Smith, "Islanders Preview"; Joe Lapointe, "'95–'96 NHL: Eastern Conference Outlook," *New York Times*, October 1, 1995, B9.

61. Alan Hahn, "Recalling the Spirit of '75," *Blade*, October 14–20, 1995, 6–7.

62. Green, telephone interview; Andersson, telephone interview; Jim Smith, "New Coach Glad to See Kasparaitis," *Newsday*, October 10, 1995, A48; Kasparaitis, telephone interview.

63. Colin Stephenson, "Championship Hopes? For the Isles, None Atoll," *New York Daily News*, October 8, 1995, 87.

64. Jason Diamos, "Milbury Returns to Boston, but with Isles," *New York Times*, October 7, 1995, 33.

65. Jim Smith, "Opening Tale of 2 Isles," *Newsday*, October 7, 1995, A45.

66. Peter Botte, "Milbury to Unveil New Fleet of Isles," *New York Post*, October 7, 1995, 40.

67. Smith, "Opening Tale of 2 Isles."

68. "October 7, 1995 New York Islanders @ Boston," YouTube video, from the New York Islanders–Boston Bruins game televised by WSBK Boston and SportsChannel New York on October 7, 1995, posted by "Stevienics19913," September 12, 2014, https://www.youtube.com/watch?v=khO_mW8XqUQ.

69. Charron, telephone interview.

70. "October 7, 1995 New York Islanders @ Boston."

71. Jason Diamos, "New Top Line Shows Promise for Islanders," *New York Times*, October 8, 1995, S10; Colin Stephenson, "Milbury Savors Boston Tie Party," *New York Daily News*, October 8, 1995, 73; Jim Smith, "Handsome Tie," *Newsday*, October 8, 1995, S9.

72. "October 7, 1995 New York Islanders @ Boston."

73. Jim Smith, "Clark, Hogue Face Ex-Teammates," *Newsday*, October 11, 1995, A82.

74. Vukota, telephone interview.

75. Damien Cox, "Leafs Pummel Isles," *Toronto Star*, October 11, 1995, D1; Bob McKenzie, "Huge Hit Returned the Passion to the Leafs," *Toronto Star*, October 11, 1995, D1; Jim Smith, "Utterly Defenseless," *Newsday*, October 11, 1995, A82.

76. Smith, "New Coach Glad to See Kasparaitis."

77. Diamos, "New Top Line Shows Promise for Islanders."

78. Zipay, "No Go on New Logo."

79. Molinet, "New Design Has Young Fans Excited."

80. Zipay, "Switching Styles in Vogue."

81. Jason Molinet, "The Islander Fans Have Spoken: Toss It Back!," *Newsday*, June 30, 1995, A82, A67.

82. Zipay, "No Go on New Logo."

83. "What Do You Think?"

84. Molinet, "Islander Fans Have Spoken."

85. Molinet, "Islander Fans Have Spoken."

86. "Nix the Islanders' Training Camp and New Logo," *Newsday*, July 6, 1995, A39.

87. "A Team Is More than Its Logo," *Newsday*, June 29, 1995, A45.

88. Molinet, "Islander Fans Have Spoken"; Zipay, "No Go on New Logo."

5. DEAD IN THE WATER

1. Mark Herrmann, "Salo to Start Home Opener," *Newsday*, October 12, 1995, A68; Jim Smith, "Lindros on Lindros," *Newsday*, October 14, 1995, A39; Peter Botte, "Kasparaitis Makes Good on Threat to Bolt Isles," *New York Post*, October 14, 1995, 34; Jim Smith, "Isles on Muller: Not Worth $2.5M," *Newsday*, October 13, 1995, A92.

2. Colin Stephenson, "New Rule Has Isles Lost at Sea," *New York Daily News*, October 12, 1995, 72.

3. Hirshon, "Welcome to Nassau Mausoleum."

4. Bruce Bennett, telephone interview with the author, November 16, 2015; Joe Lapointe, "Islanders Have Holes in Locker, and Effort," *New York Times*, November 29, 1993, C2; Bob Halkidis, telephone interview with the author, November 6, 2015; Vukota, telephone interview.

5. Pickett, telephone interview.

6. Jim Smith, "Same Old Story," *Newsday*, October 15, 1995, S7, S26.

7. Mark Herrmann, "Coliseum Facelift Is Being Planned," *Newsday*, July 6, 1995, A78.

8. Mark Herrmann, "Fans Hoping Isles' Image Will Change," *Newsday*, October 15, 1995, S7.

9. Bob Raissman, "Sweater vs. Agent Big-Time Dissdown," *New York Daily News*, October 15, 1995, 60.

10. Herrmann, "Fans Hoping Isles' Image Will Change."

11. "Attack of the Fishsticks!," YouTube video, from the New York Islanders–Philadelphia Flyers game televised by SportsChannel New York on October 14, 1995, posted by "jsmilla," April 23, 2012, http://www.youtube.com/watch?v=hyspS2O05Oc.

12. Mitchell Freedman, "Montauk Point Lighthouse Named a Landmark," *Newsday*, March 6, 2012; Linda Saslow, "Jones Beach Tower Set for Restoration," *New York Times*, May 18, 2008, L15; "Attack of the Fishsticks!"

13. "Attack of the Fishsticks!"

14. Jim Smith, "Isles Give Kasparaitis 4 Years, $4M," *Newsday*, October 15, 1995, S7; Herrmann, "Fans Hoping Isles' Image Will Change."

15. Jason Diamos, "Isles Have Kasparaitis, but No Victories," *New York Times*, October 15, 1995, S10; Smith, "Same Old Story"; "News at 10," WPIX, October 14, 1995, WPIX Archives.

16. Di Fiore, telephone interview.

17. Jason Molinet, "Isles Look Better, but It's Still a Loss," *Newsday*, Octo-

ber 16, 1995, A55; Colin Stephenson, "Islanders Still Feelin' under the Weather," *New York Daily News*, October 16, 1995, S62.

18. Smith, "Isles Need Milbury"; Jim Smith, "Isles Still Lagging in All Areas," *Newsday*, October 17, 1995, A65.

19. Jim Smith, "Ground Zero," *Newsday*, October 18, 1995, A68.

20. Kasparaitis, telephone interview.

21. Smith, "Ground Zero."

22. Peter Botte, "Rangers Rattle Isles," *New York Post*, October 18, 1995, 54.

23. Colin Stephenson, "Curse Is on Milbury, Isles," *New York Daily News*, October 18, 1995, S57.

24. Botte, "Rangers Rattle Isles."

25. Jim Smith, "Isles, Habs in Big Deal of Trouble," *Newsday*, October 20, 1995, A88.

26. Jim Smith, "Victory a First for Isles," *Newsday*, October 21, 1995, A36.

27. Jim Smith, "Sweeney Rescues Islanders in OT," *Newsday*, November 1, 1995, A60.

28. Jim Smith, "Isles' Severyn Is Anxious to Play after Suspension," *Newsday*, November 3, 1995, A91.

29. Jeff Williams, "Lemieux' 3 Goals Overwhelm Isles," *Newsday*, October 27, 1995, A98.

30. Jim Smith, "Milbury Deserves Blame," *Newsday*, November 7, 1995, A64, A59; Jim Smith, "Milbury's Misery," *Newsday*, October 30, 1995, A40; Steve Zipay, "Phil Rates Big Blue's Big Needs," *Newsday*, November 10, 1995, A105.

31. "Long Day for Isles," *Newsday*, November 9, 1995, A92.

32. Jim Smith, "Clark, Muller Out of It," *Newsday*, November 9, 1995, A92; Jeff Williams, "No Cheers Here," *Newsday*, November 5, 1995, S7; *Islander Insider*, November 15, 1995.

33. Jeff Williams, "McLennan Tries to Save Isles," *Newsday*, November 10, 1995, A100.

34. Laura Price, "Reeling Them In," *Newsday*, November 11, 1995, A38.

35. Jason Diamos, "The Rangers Get a Victory and a Touch of Revenge," *New York Times*, November 11, 1995, 31.

36. Kasparaitis, telephone interview; Brent Severyn, telephone interview with the author, November 16, 2015.

37. Joe Gergen, "Fish Stick Follies," *Newsday*, November 12, 1995, S4; Vukota, telephone interview.

38. King, telephone interview; Lance Elder, telephone interview with the author, March 6, 2014.

39. Schneider, telephone interview; Green, telephone interview; Plante, telephone interview; Luongo, telephone interview; Cole, telephone interview.

40. Plante, telephone interview; Chynoweth, telephone interview; Pilon, telephone interview; Jason Holland, telephone interview with the author, September 10, 2015; Charron, telephone interview; Froese, telephone interview.

41. Kasparaitis, telephone interview; Andersson, telephone interview; Chynoweth, telephone interview.

42. Pilon, telephone interview.

43. Calabria, telephone interview.

44. Lenore Skenazy, "He's a Dog and He Loves It," *New York Daily News*, August 28, 1999, New York Weekend, 25.

45. Di Fiore, telephone interview; Jason Diamos, "Kasparaitis Tells Isles He'll Skate by Himself," *New York Times*, October 14, 1995, 32.

46. Di Fiore, telephone interview.

47. Jim Smith, "Bad and Boring," *Newsday*, November 12, 1995, S5.

48. Jim Smith, "His Value Waning, Muller Shown Door," *Newsday*, November 13, 1995, A47.

49. Smith, "His Value Waning, Muller Shown Door."

50. Severyn, telephone interview; Vukota, telephone interview; Kasparaitis, telephone interview.

51. Jim Smith, "Maloney Says Muller May Be Dealt Today," *Newsday*, November 22, 1995, A80.

52. Jeff Williams, "Muller Left Wondering and Waiting for Trade," *Newsday*, November 18, 1995, A40.

53. Jim Smith, "Isles Need an Avalanche of Goals," *Newsday*, November 28, 1995, A69.

54. Chris Taylor, telephone interview with the author, November 6, 2015; Adrian Dater, "Horror Show the Daily Diet for Islanders," *Denver Post*, November 28, 1995, 1D–2D; Jim Smith, "A Lackluster Effort," *Newsday*, November 29, 1995, A73.

55. Jason Diamos, "Islanders Heard the Chanting, Now Don Maloney Is Gone," *New York Times*, December 3, 1995, S8.

56. Greg Logan, "Ax Falls on Maloney," *Newsday*, December 3, 1995, S3–S4.

57. Joe Haberstroh, "Fans Don't Miss Maloney," *Newsday*, December 3, 1995, S5.

58. Logan, "Ax Falls on Maloney."

59. Mark Herrmann, "Regier Ready If Called Upon," *Newsday*, December 4, 1995, A40; Logan, "Ax Falls on Maloney."

60. Jeff Williams, "Potvin Wants In," *Newsday*, December 5, 1995, A66.

61. Williams, "Potvin Wants In."

62. *Islander Insider*, December 15, 1995, 1; Jeff Williams, "Another Hat," *Newsday*, December 12, 1995, A82–A81.

63. Jim Kelley, "Bowness Named Associate Coach," *Newsday*, January 1, 1996, A32.

64. "N.H.L. Standings," *New York Times*, January 1, 1996, 44.

65. Jim Smith, "Schneider Contented with Isles," *Newsday*, December 23, 1995, A47.

66. Joe Lapointe, "East, and Puck, Glow in the All-Star Game," *New York Times*, January 21, 1996, S8; Joe Lapointe, "New York Could Field Full Team in All-Stars," *New York Times*, January 19, 1996, B12.

67. Di Fiore, telephone interview.

68. Jim Smith, "Rookie Spark," *Newsday*, January 31, 1995, A60.

69. "Mathieu Schneider OT Goal vs. Sabres," YouTube video, from the New York Islanders–Buffalo Sabres game televised by Empire Sports Network on January 30, 1996, posted by "Disengage," September 3, 2008, http://www.youtube.com/watch?v=tveMaXFvFe8. The goal horn is isolated in "New York Islanders, 1995–1996 Goal Horn," YouTube video, posted by "GoalHornMaster," http://www.youtube.com/watch?v=I9EZYANJrl8.

70. Jason Diamos, "Lemieux Struts Stuff against Islanders," *New York Times*, December 6, 1995, B21.

71. Jason Herter, telephone interview with the author, October 21, 2015; Jason Diamos, "Islanders Make a Strong Case for Change," *New York Times*, December 7, 1995, B26; Herter, telephone interview.

72. "In Fine Fashion," *Blade*, January 11–17, 1996, n.p.

73. Jeff Williams, "Muller Dealt," *Newsday*, January 24, 1996, A68.

74. Jim Smith, "Deal Is a Gamble for Isles," *Newsday*, January 24, 1996, A69.

75. Jim Smith, "Lindros' Career Is Imperiled," *Newsday*, January 5, 1996, A73.

76. Williams, "Muller Dealt."

77. Jeff Williams, "Berard Is Labeled 'Franchise Player,'" *Newsday*, January 25, 1996, A85.

78. "American Dream," *Blade*, January 30–February 6, 1996, cover.

79. Ken Belanger, telephone interview with the author, September 3, 2015; Williams, "Muller Dealt"; Belanger, telephone interview.

80. Laura Price, "Unfriendly Rivals," *Newsday*, February 9, 1996, A80.

81. Joe Lapointe, "Fish Isn't Only Thing Hurled at Garden," *New York Times*, February 9, 1996, B9.

82. Jeff Williams, "Milbury Zips Lip on Spit," *Newsday*, February 10, 1996, A40.

83. *NHL Live*, December 2, 2015, NBC Sports Network.

84. Lapointe, "Fish Isn't Only Thing Hurled at Garden"; Schneider, telephone interview; Belanger, telephone interview.

85. Tom Croke, telephone interview with the author, September 30, 2015; Tom Croke, "It's the Same Old Song!," *Islander Insider*, February 15, 1996, 4.

86. "Local Businesspeople and Islander Supporters Meet and Agree to Try to End the Deterioration of the Franchise!," *Islander Insider*, December 15, 1995, 1–2.

87. Pat Calabria, "Parting Shot: Fan/Publishers Should Be Responsible, Too," *Blade*, January 11–17, 1996, 8; "Calabria Blasts the 'Insider,'" *Islander Insider*, January 15, 1996, 2, 4; Art Feeney, "Islanders Vice President Blasts Fan Published Newsletters!," *Islander Insider*, February 15, 1996, 3.

88. "STIC Meeting Poll Results!," *Islander Insider*, March 21, 1996, 4.

89. "Slappers," *Blade*, January 11–17, 1996, 2.

90. "Slappers," *Blade*, January 30–February 6, 1996, 2–3.

91. "Slappers," *Blade*, February 23–27, 1996, 2–3.

92. "Slappers," *Blade*, October 14–20, 1995, 2–3.

93. "Slappers," *Blade*, January 30–February 6, 1996, 2–3.

94. Jim Smith, "Another Disaster," *Newsday*, March 4, 1996, A42; Jim Smith, "Milbury, Islanders Await Fines," *Newsday*, March 3, 1996, S15.

95. Chynoweth, telephone interview.

96. Jim Smith, "One More (La)chance," *Newsday*, January 4, 1996, A74.

97. Chynoweth, telephone interview; Vukota, telephone interview.

98. Smith, "Clark Just Too Brittle for Islanders."

99. Jim Smith, "It's a Futures Trade," *Newsday*, March 14, 1996, A92.

100. Jim Smith, "Panthers Claim Waived Straka," *Newsday*, March 16, 1996, A40.

101. Jim Smith, "Isles Deal Sweeney, Obtain Conacher," *Newsday*, March 21, 1996, A103.

102. Pat Conacher, telephone interview with the author, September 1, 2015.

103. "1996 NHL on FOX—Intro Rangers Islanders Flyers Penguins Stars Sabres Hawks Wings," YouTube video, from the New York Rangers–New York Islanders game televised by Fox on March 31, 1996, posted by "enfreygo," May 13, 2011, https://www.youtube.com/watch?v=S2SH4-K9M6E.

104. Jim Smith, "An In-Your-Face Job," *Newsday*, April 1, 1996, A54.

105. Peter Botte, "Todd Adds Punch to Islander Line," *New York Post*, April 1, 1996, 54; Jeff Williams, "Bertuzzi Gets Even with Ulf," *Newsday*, April 1, 1996, A5.

106. Jim Smith, "Bertuzzi, Churla Hit with Suspensions," *Newsday*, April 2, 1996, A63.

107. Associated Press, "A Bad Identity: Photo Puts a Kink in Swim Career," *Southeast Missourian*, March 24, 1996, 2B.

108. Jim Smith, "Fish Sticks All Gone?," *Newsday*, April 4, 1996, A97.

109. Steve Zipay, "Isles Listen to Fans," *Newsday*, April 5, 1996, A72.

110. Associated Press, "Islanders to Send Their Logo Out to Sea," *New York Post*, April 5, 1996, 74.

111. Zipay, "Isles Listen to Fans."

112. Zipay, "Isles Listen to Fans."

113. "Big Shot."

114. Art Feeney, "Over 300 Turnout for STIC Rally! Isles Announce Logo Reversal!," *Islander Insider*, April 21, 1996, 1.

115. John Valenti, "Isles' Skid Is Dead," *Newsday*, April 7, 1996, B8; Colin Stephenson, "Islanders Get Back on Map with Old Logo," *New York Daily News*, April 7, 1996, 47.

116. McDarby, telephone interview; O'Hara, telephone interview; Pickett, telephone interview.

117. Stephenson, "Islanders Get Back on Map with Old Logo."

118. Fichaud, telephone interview.

119. Jim Smith, "Old Logo Gets Go-Ahead," *Newsday*, April 13, 1996, A43.

120. Valenti, "Isles' Skid Is Dead."

121. Mark Herrmann, "Lost Islanders: Nothing New," *Newsday*, April 13, 1996, A43.

122. Jim Smith, "Rookie McCabe: Islanders' Iron Man," *Newsday*, April 14, 1996, B12.

123. Herrmann, "The Windup."

124. "A Bayman's Fate," *Dan's Papers*, May 3, 1996, 1, 12; "Rejected Islander Logos," *Dan's Papers*, May 3, 1996, 1.

125. Calabria to Leo, May 3, 1996, box 6, folder 135, East Hampton Town Baymen's Association Archive.

126. Leo to Calabria, June 3, 1996, box 6, folder 135, East Hampton Town Baymen's Association Archive.

127. Zipay, "No Go on New Logo."

128. "New Is Out, Old Is In," *The Washington Post*, April 5, 1996, C6.

6. SPANO FOR PRESIDENT

1. "Islanders at Canadiens," SportsChannel, April 13, 1996.

2. Jim Smith, "Isles Fire Doc, Trainers," *Newsday*, May 8, 1996, A75.

3. Jim Smith, "Milbury Thinks Forward," *Newsday*, April 15, 1996, n.p.

4. Jeff Williams, "It's All Over," *Newsday*, May 1, 1996, A78.

5. Joe Schad, "Islanders, Berard Agree on Contract," *Newsday*, June 26, 1996, A61.

6. Smith, "Milbury Thinks Forward."

7. Peter Botte, "Milbury's Newest Title: Salesman," *New York Post*, April 15, 1996, 56.

8. Peter Botte, "Logo Won't Change Fate," *New York Post*, April 8, 1996, 50.

9. Laura Price, "Isles Miss by a Digit, to Pick 3rd," *Newsday*, May 20, 1996, A51.

10. Mark Herrmann, "Isles Ready to Deal for a Top Forward," *Newsday*, May 17, 1996, A99.

11. Laura Price, "Milbury Feeling Pressure of Draft Decision," *Newsday*, June 7, 1996, A103.

12. Jim Smith, "Scouts Are Out after Isles Draft," *Newsday*, June 20, 1996, A71.

13. Jim Smith, "Wary of Russian, GM Taps Winger," *Newsday*, June 23, 1996, B3.

14. Jim Smith, "Palffy's Agent Nixes 'Final' Offer," *Newsday*, June 21, 1996, A90.

15. John Valenti, "Milbury Softens Stance—Somewhat," *Newsday*, September 20, 1996, A88.

16. Anthony McCarron, "Palffy Talks Getting Ugly," *New York Daily News*, October 30, 1998, 93.

17. John Valenti, "No Ziggy, No Green and Still No Progress," *Newsday*, September 11, 1996, A72.

18. Jeff Williams, "Isles, Flatley Part Company," *Newsday*, July 10, 1996, A51.

19. Vukota, telephone interview.

20. Froese, telephone interview.

21. Smith, "Palffy's Agent Nixes 'Final' Offer."

22. Charron, telephone interview.

23. Steve Zipay, "Islanders Interested in Roenick," *Newsday*, July 27, 1996, A36.

24. Jim Smith, "Roenick Deal Near," *Newsday*, August 10, 1996, A31, A26; Jeff Williams, "Islanders Targeting Roenick," *Newsday*, August 8, 1996, A92.

25. Roenick, *J.R.*, 97.

26. Jim Smith, "Refusing Isles' Pay Cut, Rangers' Healy Nixed Deal," *Newsday*, October 22, 1996, A68.

27. Mark Herrmann, "Milbury Gives Palffy, Green Ultimatum," *Newsday*, August 23, 1996, A82.

28. "Not Getting Roenick May Be the Best Deal the Isles Never Made," *7th Man*, September 1996, 2.

29. Jim Smith, "'Serious' Isles Plot Plan for Roenick," *Newsday*, August 9, 1996, A87.

30. Zipay, "Islanders Interested in Roenick."

31. Botta, telephone interview. Botta also described this incident on his blog, "On WFAN's Suzanne Somers: We Mean, of Course, Steve Somers," *IslandersPointBlank* (blog), October 26, 2008, http://islanderspointblank .com/news/on-wfans-suzanne-somerswe-mean-of-course-steve -somers/.

32. Zipay, "Islanders Interested in Roenick."

33. Botta, telephone interview; Mark Herrmann, "Roenick Dealt, but Not to Isles," *Newsday*, August 17, 1996, A35, A33; Somers, telephone interview.

34. "Draft Party," *Newsday*, June 21, 1996, A82.

35. "New Building? Palffy Leaving? Berard the Savior? Isles Being Sold? Draft Party a Success?," *7th Man*, July 1, 1996, 2.

36. "25th Anniversary Season Summer Events," *Newsday*, August 11, 1996, B14.

37. Dan Byrnes, "Sudden Impact," *Blade*, October 12–22, 1996, 8.

38. Letta Tayler, "Making Light in the Dark," *Newsday*, July 11, 1996, B3.

39. Valenti, "No Ziggy, No Green and Still No Progress."

40. Steve Zipay, "Switch to WLIR Excites Islanders," *Newsday*, August 22, 1996, A82.

41. "25th Anniversary Season Summer Events."

42. Celeste Hadrick, "Arena Face-Off," *Newsday*, August 21, 1996, A5, A35-A38.

43. Herrmann, "Milbury Gives Palffy, Green Ultimatum."

44. John Valenti, "Milbury: Green Says 'Trade Me,'" *Newsday*, September 18, 1996, A69.

45. Valenti, "Milbury Softens Stance—Somewhat."

46. John Valenti, "Milbury Working on Several Deals," *Newsday*, September 21, 1996, A33; John Valenti, "Talks Crawl Along," *Newsday*, September 25, 1996, A72.

47. John Valenti, "Milbury, Palffy End Standoff," *Newsday*, September 28, 1996, A97.

48. John Valenti, "Isles Show Some Fight in 1st Loss," *Newsday*, October 6, 1996, B18.

49. Jason Diamos, "Isles Tied. Milbury Fit to Be Tied.," *New York Times*, October 10, 1996, B22; John Valenti, "Untimely Tie Pains Islanders," *Newsday*, October 7, 1996, A48.

50. Jim Smith, "Isles Hurry Green," *Newsday*, October 12, 1996, A39.

51. "Texan Ready to Buy Islanders. His Promise: The Puck Stays Here," *Newsday*, October 11, 1996, A1.

52. John Valenti, "Sale Gives Isles New Hope," *Newsday*, October 11, 1996, A84.

53. Craig Gordon, "Shy Guy with Deep Pockets," *Newsday*, October 11, 1996, A3, A40; John Valenti, "New Money Big Plus," *Newsday*, October 11, 1996, A94.

54. Jason Diamos, "Buyer Says Isles Will Stay," *New York Times*, October 11, 1996, B17; Gordon, "Shy Guy with Deep Pockets"; Craig Gordon et al., "A Team Player," *Newsday*, October 11, 1996, A3, A40.

55. John Valenti, "Fishsticks on Ice for Isles Opener," *Newsday*, October 12, 1996, A39.

56. John Valenti, "Just Like Old Times," *Newsday*, October 13, 1996, B9.

57. Jason Diamos, "Islanders Turn Back the Clock and Flyers," *New York Times*, October 13, 1996, S7.

58. Valenti, "Fishsticks on Ice for Isles Opener."

59. *Never Say Die.*

60. John Valenti, "Reality Check for Isles," *Newsday*, October 18, 1996, A86.

61. Jason Diamos, "The Same Old Islanders Return to the Coliseum," *New York Times*, October 18, 1996, B13.

62. Diamos, "The Same Old Islanders Return to the Coliseum"; Valenti, "Reality Check for Isles."

63. Diamos, "The Same Old Islanders Return to the Coliseum"; Colin Stephenson, "Reality Strikes Isles," *New York Daily News*, October 18, 1996, 96; Valenti, "Reality Check for Isles."

64. Valenti, "Reality Check for Isles."

65. John Valenti, "Milbury Throws Book at Islanders," *Newsday*, October 19, 1996, A38.

66. Valenti, "Milbury Throws Book at Islanders."

67. Vukota, telephone interview.

68. Tommy Söderström, telephone interview with the author, September 7, 2015.

69. John Valenti, "Bertuzzi Benched," *Newsday*, October 20, 1996, B10.

70. John Valenti, "Expanded Vocabulary Doesn't Help Islanders," *Newsday*, October 23, 1996, A70.

71. John Valenti, "Salo Needs a 'W' Very, Very Badly," *Newsday*, October 21, 1996, A44.

72. John Valenti, "Raked by Leafs," *Newsday*, November 1, 1996, A100.

73. John Valenti, "What a Clinic!," *Newsday*, November 3, 1996, B3.

74. John Valenti, "King Revels in New Role," *Newsday*, November 4, 1996, A67.

75. Jim Smith, "Isles Building Confidence behind Palffy-Green-King," *Newsday*, November 6, 1996, A82.

76. John Valenti, "2 Isles Off 'Death Row,'" *Newsday*, November 8, 1996, A94.

77. Pilon, telephone interview.

78. John Valenti, "Isles Deal 'D,' Hope for Offense," *Newsday*, November 18, 1996, A59.

79. Bryan Smolinski, telephone interview with the author, September 17, 2015.

80. Smith, "New Coach Glad to See Kasparaitis."

81. Kasparaitis, telephone interview.

82. Valenti, "Isles Deal 'D,' Hope for Offense."

83. Vukota, telephone interview; Smolinski, telephone interview.

84. John Valenti, "Smolinski Helps Isles Earn Tie," *Newsday*, November 21, 1996, A91.

85. "N.H.L. Standings," *New York Times*, December 12, 1996, B26.

86. John Valenti, "Break Up the Isles!," *Newsday*, December 11, 1996, A81.

87. John Valenti, "Splendid Salo Stones Rangers," *Newsday*, December 12, 1996, A103.

88. John Valenti, "Claude Power," *Newsday*, December 8, 1996, B3, B28.

89. Valenti, "Claude Power."

90. Ken Moritsugu, "Spano's Promise," *Newsday*, November 27, 1996, A3.

91. Steve Jacobson, "Let's Build Again, but Do It Better," *Newsday*, November 27, 1996, A89.

92. "HEY! STANLEY!!! YOU CAN COME HOME! PICKETT'S GONE!!!," *7th Man*, December 15, 1996, 1; Islanders advertisement, *Newsday*, November 27, 1996, A81.

93. "STIC MEETS WITH JOHN SPANO!," *7th Man*, December 15, 1996, 4.

94. Moritsugu, "Spano's Promise."

95. Valenti, "Break Up the Isles!"

96. "Done Deals," *Newsday*, November 27, 1996, 1; Colin Stephenson, "New Era Begins for Isles," *New York Daily News*, November 27, 1996, 65; Dave Anderson, "Sports of the Times: Some 1996 Thank-You Notes," *New York Times*, November 28, 1996, B23; Jacobson, "Let's Build Again, but Do It Better"; Joe Lapointe, "High Ambitions for New Isles Owner," *New York Times*, November 27, 1996, B11; Moritsugu, "Spano's Promise"; Jeff Williams, "Wow! An Owner," *Newsday*, November 27, 1996, A88.

97. "Special Holiday Celebration," *Newsday*, November 27, 1996, A78; "You Can Feel It!," *Newsday*, December 11, 1996, A77; "Join Us for a Night to Remember," *Newsday*, December 18, 1996, A81.

98. Green, telephone interview.

99. John Kreiser, "Enchanting Isle," *Rinkside*, February 1997, 50–55.

100. Jason Diamos, "The Americanization of an Offbeat Player," *New York Times*, December 10, 1996, B15.

101. Söderström, telephone interview.

102. "Islander of the Year: Zigmund Palffy," *Blade*, April 6–12, 1996, 7; Pickett, telephone interview; Charron, telephone interview; "This Is Brett Lindros"; "This Is Matt Schneider"; "Weekend Family Fun Continues This Sunday," *Newsday*, February 28, 1996, A59; "He Who Hesitates . . . ," *Newsday*, October 4, 1996, A78.

103. Dan Byrnes, "Ziggymania," *Blade*, November 27–December 3, 1996, 7.

104. Kreiser, "Enchanting Isle"; Diamos, "The Americanization of an Offbeat Player."

105. John Valenti, "Bertuzzi Has Major Lesson in the Minors," *Newsday*, December 14, 1996, A43.

106. John Valenti, "Milbury's Outburst Gets Isles Talking," *Newsday*, December 16, 1996, A47.

107. Jim Smith, "Detroit Demolition," *Newsday*, December 29, 1996, B13; Jim Smith, "Regier Out as Isles' Assistant GM," *Newsday*, December 27, 1996, A92.

108. Jeff Williams, "Palffy Joins Eastern All-Stars," *Newsday*, January 4, 1997, A35.

109. Jim Smith, "Palffy to Miss All-Star Game," *Newsday*, January 15, 1997, A62.

110. "25 Years of Hockey . . . One Magical Weekend," *Newsday*, February 14, 1997, A82.

111. *Never Say Die*; Fischler and Botta, *Pride and Passion*, 234.

112. Smith, "Palffy to Miss All-Star Game."

113. Di Fiore, telephone interview.

114. Paul Kruse, telephone interview with the author, September 11, 2015.

115. Di Fiore, telephone interview.

116. Beach, telephone interview.

117. Ray Weiss, "It's No Laughing Matter," *Gannett Suburban*, January 1997. A clipping, provided by Di Fiore, does not include the exact date or page number.

118. Di Fiore, telephone interview.

119. John Valenti, "Former Isles Doctor to Sue for Unpaid Fees," *Newsday*, October 31, 1996, A81; Valenti, "Raked by Leafs."

120. John Valenti, "Isles Not Making a Case for Playoffs," *Newsday*, January 12, 1997, B11.

121. John Valenti, "An Icy Reception," *Newsday*, January 21, 1997, A61.

122. Kruse, telephone interview.

123. Valenti, "An Icy Reception."

124. John Valenti, "No Time for Waffling," *Newsday*, January 24, 1997, A72.

125. John Valenti, "Milbury Gives One Job Back," *Newsday*, January 25, 1997, A38.

126. Jeff Williams, "Resignation a Big Bonus for Bowness," *Newsday*, January 25, 1997, A39, A37.

127. Plante, telephone interview.

128. John Valenti, "King's 3 Makes Bowness a Winner," *Newsday*, January 25, 1997, A39.

129. Jason Diamos, "Isles Look Defenseless against Amonte," *New York Times*, March 17, 1997, C10.

130. John Valenti, "Doug Pitches In," *Newsday*, February 27, 1997, A82.

131. Green, telephone interview; "Wacky Goal Celebration: Ziggy Palffy Plants a Kiss," YouTube video, from the New Jersey Devils–New York Islanders game televised by SportsChannel on February 26, 1997, posted by "NHL," October 7, 2013, https://www.youtube.com/watch?v=DZLOGhlrOI4; Chris Stevenson, "Puck-er Up for Palffy and Green," *Ottawa Sun*, February 28, 1997, http://jesgolbez.blogspot.com/2006/02/kiss-is-just-kiss-right.html.

132. Jeff Williams, "Isles Deal Veterans King and McInnis," *Newsday*, March 19, 1997, A72.

133. Chris Botta, "One on One with Robert Reichel," *Blade*, April 5–11, 1997, 5–7.

134. John Valenti, "Welcome Addition," *Newsday*, March 20, 1997, A96.

135. Robert Reichel, telephone interview with the author, September 20, 2015; Jeff Williams, "Isles Are Closing In," *Newsday*, March 30, 1997, B7.

136. Smolinski, telephone interview; Jason Diamos, "Islanders Are Making a Serious Playoff Run," *New York Times*, March 30, 1997, S13.

137. Jim Smith, "It's Over Time," *Newsday*, April 10, 1997, A96.

138. Jim Smith, "Low-Pressure Eruption," *Newsday*, April 12, 1997, A34.

139. John Valenti, "Palffy Doesn't Score 50," *Newsday*, April 13, 1997, B8.

140. "Islanders Team Store Super Sale," *Newsday*, May 9, 1997, A64.

141. John Valenti, "Honored Defense," *Newsday*, June 20, 1997, A84.

142. Valenti, "Palffy Doesn't Score 50."

7. FROM SAVIOR TO DEVIL

1. Jim Smith, "Sale of Isles to Spano Approved," *Newsday*, February 25, 1997, A78; Jim Smith, "Spano Intends to Keep Milbury," *Newsday*, May 17, 1997, A38.

2. Joseph Demma, John Valenti, and John Riley, "Artless Dodger," *Newsday*, July 3, 1997, A3, A88.

3. Croke, telephone interview.

4. Croke, telephone interview.

5. "Big Shot."

6. Croke, telephone interview.

7. Fichaud, telephone interview.

8. John Valenti, "Owning Isles Is Not a Lark," *Newsday*, June 15, 1997, B14.

9. Alexander Wolff, "Busted," *Sports Illustrated*, August 4, 1997, 44–49.

10. Croke, telephone interview.

11. "Big Shot."

12. Frank Litsky, "Spano Accepts Guilty Plea Agreement," *New York Times*, October 8, 1997, C2.

13. Ford Fessenden et al., "They Knew Him Back When," *Newsday*, July 13, 1997.

14. Fessenden et al., "They Knew Him Back When."

15. Steve Zipay, "Process to Take Months," *Newsday*, September 13, 1997, A41.

16. John Valenti, "Spano Returns Islanders to Pickett," *Newsday*, July 12, 1997, A5, A15.

17. Wolff, "Busted."

18. John Valenti, "Hogue's Goal Drops Islanders," *Newsday*, April 4, 1997, A81.

19. Wolff, "Busted."

20. Smolinski, telephone interview.

21. Demma, Valenti, and Riley, "Artless Dodger."

22. "Big Shot."

23. Demma, Valenti, and Riley, "Artless Dodger."

24. Demma, Valenti, and Riley, "Artless Dodger."

25. Fischler, interview.

26. "Ownership of Islanders in Dispute," *Newsday*, June 30, 1997, A4, A30.

27. Demma, Valenti, and Riley, "Artless Dodger"; Joe Gergen, "Isles Left in Dark," *Newsday*, July 8, 1997, A53.

28. Valenti, "Spano Returns Islanders to Pickett."

29. Wolff, "Busted."

30. Richard Sandomir, "Fraud in Spano's Isles Deal, Prosecutors Say," *New York Times*, July 24, 1997, B9.

31. Wolff, "Busted."

32. Richard Sandomir, "Spano Draws Prison Term for Fraud in Islanders Deal," *New York Times*, January 29, 2000, D6.

33. "Big Shot."

34. Gergen, "Isles Left in Dark."

35. Wolff, "Busted."

36. Joe Gergen, "Back to the Future," *Newsday*, July 13, 1997, B8; "Spano's Scheme Collapses, So the Ogre Returns!," *7th Man*, September 1997, 1.

37. Chris Botta, "Parting Shot: Mitch, Louis, Arthur and the Original 365," *Blade*, April 5–11, 1997, 16; "Islander Fans Come Home!," *7th Man*, June 1, 1997, 7.

38. "Diary of an Islander Fan!," *7th Man*, April 15, 1997, 6.

39. "Big Shot."

40. "Spano's Scheme Collapses, So the Ogre Returns!"

41. Beach, telephone interview; "Big Shot"; Richard Sandomir, "After Prison, Regret from Man Who Sold a Hoax to Try to Buy the Islanders," *New York Times*, October 19, 2013, D6.

42. Steve Zipay, "Been There Before," *Newsday*, July 24, 1997, A75.

43. "Dancing Decimals," *Sports Illustrated*, July 28, 1997, 24, 26.

44. John Valenti, "Pickett's Promise," *Newsday*, July 13, 1997, A7, A39.

45. Steve Zipay, "High-Powered Trio with an Eye to Buy," *Newsday*, July 12, 1997, A4.

46. Jim Smith, "George on Ice?," *Newsday*, August 27, 1997, A83.

47. John Valenti et al., "A Winner This Time?," *Newsday*, September 12, 1997, A5, A48.

48. Ford Fessenden et al., "The Art of the Deal," *Newsday*, September 12, 1997, A5, A48.

49. Steve Zipay, "Deal Done on Solid Ground," *Newsday*, September 13, 1997, A42.

50. Steve Gluckstern, telephone interview with the author, September 14, 2015.

51. Valenti et al., "A Winner This Time?"

52. Pickett, telephone interview.

53. Faye S. Wolfe, "Growing Up Gluckstern," Fall 2006, http://www .umassmag.com/2006/Fall06/FoundationNews/Gluckstern.html.

54. Craig Gordon, "Success Formula for Phoenix," *Newsday*, September 14, 1997, A4, A23.

55. John Valenti, "On Thicker Ice," *Newsday*, September 14, 1997, A5, A23; Gluckstern, telephone interview.

56. Ken Moritsugu, "Islanders Sold, Period," *Newsday*, February 26, 1998, A3, A60.

57. "We Are Pleased to Announce Our Acquisition of the New York Islanders," *New York Times*, March 2, 1998, A8; "Islanders Fan," *Newsday*, February 27, 1998, B17.

58. "Coming Soon," *Newsday*, March 1, 1998, C34; Gluckstern, telephone interview.

59. Jim Smith, "Trading Frenzy," *Newsday*, February 7, 1998, A40.

60. Beach, telephone interview.

61. Jim Smith, "Owners' Grand Stand," *Newsday*, March 4, 1998, A76.

62. Jim Smith, "Appearance's Sake," *Newsday*, March 3, 1998, A61.

63. John Valenti, "Isles Flashback: Beating Flyers," *Newsday*, March 4, 1998, A76.

64. Smith, "Owners' Grand Stand."

65. Dyan LeBourdais, "Tales of the Jersey," June 28, 2010, http://islanders .nhl.com/club/news.htm?id=533047.

66. Croke, telephone interview; McDarby, telephone interview.

67. Tarik El-Bashir, "Islanders Keep Shooting and Find Hasek's Seam," *New York Times*, March 7, 1998, C3.

68. Jim Smith, "Daigneault Always Player on the Move," *Newsday*, March 9, 1998, A40.

69. Gluckstern, telephone interview; Pickett, telephone interview; Rose, telephone interview.

70. Jenny Kellner, "Act II: Milbury Again behind Islanders' Bench," *New York Times*, March 12, 1998, C1, C4.

71. "Diary of an Islander Fan!," *7th Man*, March 25, 1998, 6.

72. Tarik El-Bashir, "New Coach Will Try to Sell Isles on a Trapping Defense," *New York Times*, January 23, 1999, D2.

73. Chynoweth, telephone interview; "Islanders Dismiss Assistant Coaches Chynoweth, Allen," *Calgary Herald*, April 17, 2012, E2; Chynoweth, telephone interview.

74. Taylor, telephone interview.

75. Luongo, telephone interview.

76. Sherry Ross, "Jonsson's Injury Has Isles Irked," *New York Daily News*, December 20, 1998, 116.

77. Green, telephone interview.

78. Gluckstern, telephone interview; Erin St. John Kelly, "Mascots R Them," *New York Times*, February 15, 1998, CY4; "It's a Special Family Fun Matinee!!!," *Blade*, March 4–8, 1997, insert; Allan Kreda, "A Mascot with a Fuzzy Future," *New York Times*, April 6, 2015, D9.

79. Di Fiore, telephone interview.

80. Valenti, "Isles Flashback: Beating Flyers."

81. Ken Moritsugu, "5-Year Wait for Arena," *Newsday*, September 14, 1997, A4.

82. John T. McQuiston, "Talks on Arena for Islanders Resume," *New York Times*, December 13, 1998, 58.

83. Rose, telephone interview.

84. John T. McQuiston, "Nassau Coliseum's Biggest Brawl Ever Is Off the Ice," *New York Times*, October 4, 1998, L11.

85. Rose, telephone interview.

86. Pilon, telephone interview.

EPILOGUE

1. David Israelson, "First, the Electronic Puck; Now, It's 'Fur' Team Jerseys," *Toronto Star*, January 24, 1996, B8.

2. Scalera, telephone interview.

3. Terry Pluto, "Cleveland Indians Owner Paul Dolan Says Team Is Keeping Chief Wahoo, but Not as Main Logo," *Cleveland Plain Dealer*, April 1, 2016, http://www.cleveland.com/pluto/index.ssf/2016/04/cleveland _indians_owner_paul_d_7.html.

4. Mike Boone, "How Well Do You Know Your Habs?," *Montreal Gazette*, October 11, 2011, B7; Iain Macintyre, "A History from Hideous to Splendour," *Vancouver Sun*, February 13, 2016, C3.

5. Frank Brown, "New-Look Third Jerseys Are No Put-On," *New York Daily News*, January 28, 1996, S69; Chris Peters, "Manchester Monarchs to Honor LA Kings' Infamous 'Burger King' Jerseys," August 15, 2013, http://www.cbssports.com/nhl/eye-on-hockey/23165939/manchester -monarchs-to-honor-la-kings-infamous-burger-king-jerseys.

6. Barry Petchesky, "15 Seasons Later, the Blues' Would-Be Third Jerseys Are Still the Worst Ever," September 23, 2011, http://deadspin.com /5843301/15-seasons-later-the-blues-would-be-third-jerseys-are-still -the-worst-ever.

7. "Former NHL Scam Artist Back in Trouble," *New Brunswick Telegraph-Journal*, June 20, 2015, D9.

8. Erik Larson, "71-Year-Old Money Manager Loses Appeal, Must Serve 20 Years," *Chicago Daily Herald*, April 27, 2016, 2.

9. Patricia Hurtado, "Hedge Fund Manager Gets Prison, but No Teddy Bears," *Toronto Star*, December 4, 2014, S10.

10. Patricia Hurtado, "Ex-CEO's Greed in $2.2-Billion Fraud Lands Him 12 Years in U.S. Prison," *Vancouver Sun*, November 3, 2006, H8.

11. Croke, telephone interview.

12. CamWest News Service, "Milbury Steps Down as Isles' Senior VP," *Ottawa Citizen*, May 30, 2007, B8; David Picker, "Nolan and Smith Are on Board and Aim to Turn Islanders Around," *New York Times*, June 9, 2006, D7.

13. Dave Gross, "Milbury Is King of GM Blunders," *Montreal Gazette*, February 10, 2008, B24.

14. "Starting Lineup 1995 Edition Kirk Muller Islanders," http://www.amazon.com/Starting-Lineup-1995-Muller-Islanders/dp/B0042LFC9C.

15. Richard Sandomir, "Isles' New Ownership Hopes to Reinvent the Team," *New York Times*, April 27, 2000, D5.

16. Rob McGregor, "Check Out Jaroslav Halak's Alternate Islanders Mask," *In Goal Magazine*, November 2015, http://ingoalmag.com/masks/check-out-jaroslav-halaks-alternative-islanders-mask/; Arthur Staple, "Isles Finished from the Start as Halak Is Pulled after First Period," *Newsday*, November 21, 2015, A32.

17. Anthony Perrotti, Twitter post, November 20, 2015, 8:04 p.m., "Halak might want to take his new mask off cuz it's clearly affecting his vision #Isles," https://twitter.com/nutz4hky/status/667871156519763968.

18. Dan Martin, "Halak Struggles as Isles Routed at Home," *New York Post*, December 16, 2015, 53.

19. New York Islanders, Instagram post, March 7, 2016, "The first 10,000 fans at tomorrow's #Isles vs. Penguins game will take home a Jaroslav Halak mini helmet! There's still time to get one. (Link in profile)," https://www.instagram.com/p/BCq2qYREwOK/.

20. Arthur Staple, "Halak Hurt in Islanders' Victory over Penguins," *Newsday*, March 9, 2016, 50.

21. Arthur Staple, "Jaroslav Halak to Miss 6 to 8 Weeks with Groin Injury," *Newsday*, March 10, 2016, 52.

22. Will Palaszczuk, Twitter post, March 9, 2016, 4:57 p.m., "There's a special kind of bad karma to get a long term injury on a night tied to a promotion, Halak injured on his mask night," https://twitter.com/YSRWillP/status/707686834889838592.

23. Eric Hornick, telephone interview with the author, March 18, 2014.

24. Schneider, telephone interview; Plante, telephone interview; Taylor, telephone interview; Kasparaitis, telephone interview; Halkidis, telephone interview.

25. Kruse, telephone interview; "Wendel Clark New York Islanders 'Fisherman' 1995 Authentic CCM Jersey New 48," http://www.ebay.com/itm/WENDEL-CLARK-NEW-YORK-ISLANDERS-FISHERMAN

-1995-AUTHENTIC-CCM-JERSEY-NEW-48-/272171745394?hash=
item3f5eb34072:g:15gAAOSwr7ZW6CaP;Herter, telephone interview.

26. Smolinski, telephone interview.

27. Severyn, telephone interview; Reichel, telephone interview; Söderström,
telephone interview; Green, telephone interview; Andersson, telephone
interview; Pilon, telephone interview.

28. O'Hara, telephone interview. Contrary to O'Hara's quote, Babe Ruth
actually struck out 1,330 times. See "Babe Ruth," Sports Reference,
http://www.baseball-reference.com/players/r/ruthba01.shtml.

29. Calabria, telephone interview.

30. Beach, telephone interview.

Aaker, David A. *Managing Brand Equity*. New York: Free Press, 1981.

Andreff, Wladimir, and Stefan Szymanski, eds. *Handbook on the Economics of Sport*. Northampton: Edward Elgar, 2006.

Batchelor, Bob, and Melanie Formentin. "Re-branding the NHL: Building the League through the 'My NHL' Integrated Marketing Campaign." *Public Relations Review* 34, no. 2 (2008): 156–160.

Bauer, Hans H., Nicola E. Stokburger-Sauer, and Stefanie Exler. "Brand Image and Fan Loyalty in Professional Team Sport: A Refined Model and Empirical Assessment." *Journal of Sport Management* 22, no. 2 (2008): 205–226.

Botta, Chris, Eric Mirlis, and Ginger Killian Serby, eds. *New York Islanders: 1995-96 Media Guide & Yearbook*. New York: New York Islanders, 1995.

Botte, Peter, and Alan Hahn. *Fish Sticks: The Fall and Rise of the New York Islanders*. New York: Sports Publishing, 2002.

Campbell, W. Joseph. *1995: The Year the Future Began*. Oakland: University of California Press, 2015.

East Hampton Town Baymen's Association Archive. Long Island Collection, East Hampton Library, East Hampton NY.

Fischler, Stan, and Chris Botta. *Pride and Passion: 25 Years of the New York Islanders*. Marceline MO: Walsworth, 1996.

Gladden, Jay. "Brand Equity: Management and Measurement in Sport." In *Leveraging Brands in Sport Business*, edited by Mark P. Pritchard and Jeffrey L. Stinson, 3–20. New York: Routledge, 2014.

Hirshon, Nicholas. *Images of America: Nassau Veterans Memorial Coliseum*. Charleston SC: Arcadia, 2010.

———. "Welcome to Nassau Mausoleum: A Case Study of Hockey Telecasts from ESPN's Worst 'Stadium Experience.'" *International Journal of Sport Communication* 8 (2015): 477–499.

Keller, Kevin Lane. "Conceptualizing, Measuring, and Managing Customer-Based Brand Equity." *Journal of Marketing* 57, no. 1 (1993): 1–22.

Kochman, Ladd Michael. "Major League Baseball: What Really Puts Fans in the Stands?" *Sports Marketing Quarterly* 4, no. 1 (1995): 9–11.

Matthiessen, Peter. *Men's Lives*. New York: Random House, 1986.

Miller, Bob. *Tales from the Los Angeles Kings Locker Room: A Collection of the Greatest Kings Stories Ever Told*. New York: Sports Publishing, 2013.

Miloch, Kimberly S. "Introduction to Branding." In *Branded: Branding in Sport Business*, edited by Jason W. Lee, 3–12. Durham NC: Carolina Academic Press, 2010.

Mullin, Bernard J., Stephen Hardy, and William A. Sutton. *Sport Marketing*. 3rd ed. Champaign IL: Human Kinetics, 2007.

Pember, Don R., and Clay Calvert. *Mass Media Law*. 19th ed. New York: McGraw-Hill, 2015.

Pitts, Brenda G., and David K. Stotlar. *Fundamentals of Sport Marketing*. Morgantown WV: Fitness Information Technology, 1996.

Roenick, Jeremy. *J.R.* Chicago: Triumph Books, 2012.

Schaaf, Phil. *Sports Marketing: It's Not Just a Game Anymore*. New York: Prometheus Books, 1995.

Smith, Susan Moloney. "Meltdown in Marketing Professional Ice Hockey: A Survey Exploring Geographical Differences in Strategy." *Sports Marketing Quarterly* 4, no. 3 (1995): 17–23.

Stevens, Robert E., David L. Loudon, and C. William McConkey. "Sport Marketing among Colleges and Universities." *Sports Marketing Quarterly* 4, no. 1 (1995): 41–47.